HOUGHTON MIFFLIN

WORLD REGIONAL STUDIES

Unless we know about the traditions and ways of life of people in other nations, we cannot develop an adequate understanding of the present-day world. The goal of the World Regional Studies series is to provide a well-rounded picture of human experience in six major areas of the world:

The Middle East

Africa

China

India

Japan

Russia

Using history as the organizing principle, the books in this series incorporate concepts and skills from the social sciences and from the humanities. Political and economic systems, geography, social organization and human values, the fine arts, and religion are all discussed in depth.

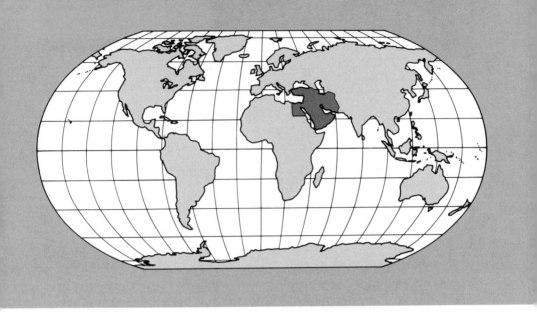

WORLD REGIONAL STUDIES

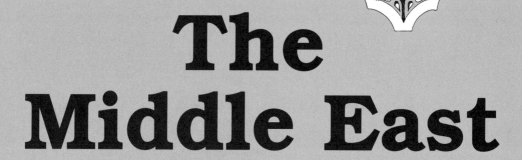

The Middle East

Revised Edition

Don Peretz

Michael Kublin, General Editor

HOUGHTON MIFFLIN COMPANY / Boston

Atlanta / Dallas / Geneva, Illinois / Palo Alto / Princeton / Toronto

Don Peretz

Professor of political science at the State University of New York in Binghamton, Mr. Peretz is the author of numerous articles and books on the Middle East. He has worked in the Middle East with the United Nations and has carried on research programs there under grants from the Ford and Rockefeller foundations. Mr. Peretz served for five years with the Education Department's New York State Center for International Programs and Services and has taught Middle Eastern studies at Williams, Vassar, Hunter, and Long Island University.

Michael Kublin

Dr. Kublin received his Ph.D. in History from New York University. He also has an MBA from Pace University. He is currently Assistant Professor of International Business at the University of New Haven and previously taught history at Kingsborough Community College in Brooklyn, New York.

Howard R. Anderson

Dr. Anderson, consulting editor, taught social studies in Michigan, Iowa, and New York. He also taught at the University of Iowa and at Cornell University, and served as President of the National Council for the Social Studies

For valuable advice and assistance a special thanks to Kenneth Perkins, Professor of History at the University of South Carolina.

Cover Photo: The Dome of the Rock in Jerusalem, Israel

The chapter opener on the first page of every chapter depicts an ornament from the Mosque of Kalaoon in Cairo, Egypt.

Please see page 291 for acknowledgments of permissions to reprint copyrighted material.

Copyright ©1990 by Houghton Mifflin Company. All rights reserved.

Printed in the U.S.A.

ISBN: 0-395-47081-1

BCDEFGHIJK-M-9987654321

CONTENTS

MAPS

CHARTS, GRAPHS, AND TABLES

PHOTO ESSAYS

INTRODUCTION

Many people are aware that the Middle East was a "cradle of civilization" and the setting for the cultural achievements of the ancient Babylonians and Egyptians. A flood of news reports emphasizes the fact that the modern Middle East is a major trouble spot in the world today. Few people, however, have a clear idea of Middle Eastern history from ancient times to the present. Only a handful of Westerners know the principal languages of the region—Arabic, Turkish, and Persian—and not many more understand present conditions of Middle Eastern countries or the hopes of their peoples.

The Roots of European History and Culture

Both in the ancient period and in the later Islamic era, the people of the Middle East made important contributions to the material and intellectual development of the West. Ancient peoples such as the Sumerians, Phoenicians, and Hebrews, as well as the Babylonians and the Egyptians, developed techniques and ideas that influenced the cultures of Greece and Rome. As first the Greeks and then the Romans moved eastward from their Mediterranean homelands, a fusion between Greek and Roman ways and those of the Middle East took place.

After the collapse of the Roman Empire, much of the culture of earlier times was kept alive by the developing Arab civilization. The Arab–Muslim culture that evolved after the appearance of the Prophet Mohammed in the seventh century reached from the Atlantic coast to the borders of India, from southern Russia to the Indian Ocean. Islam, the faith of Mohammed, blended the religious and philosophical ideas of Judaism, Christianity, the Greek world, and Western Asia into a new religion with wide appeal.

As Islam spread and took root, the Middle East transmitted religious and philosophical ideas as well as Arab science and literature to medieval Europe. In addition, the Crusades established cultural links between Western Europe and the Middle East. Although Christian knights fiercely fought the Arabs during the eleventh, twelfth, and thirteenth centuries, these same warriors brought back to Europe Muslim ideas that helped prepare the way for the Renaissance.

Mongol Destruction

In the thirteenth century, the Middle East was overrun by invaders from Central Asia. Similar to tribes earlier known in Europe as Huns, these warriors, called variously Mongols, Tartars, and Turks, destroyed the great centers of civilization created by the Arabs and the peoples converted to Islam by them. When the savage conquerors finally withdrew eastward, great irrigation systems, palaces, and universities were in ruins.

The Ottoman Empire

Out of the wreckage left by the Mongols a new Muslim empire arose. From the sixteenth century to the end of World War I, the Ottoman Turks ruled most of the Middle East as well as parts of southeastern Europe. They established a degree of stability in the Middle East and introduced an administrative order that, in some ways, still prevails in the area. On the other hand, some lands under Turkish jurisdiction, such as Egypt and Lebanon, in time paid only token allegiance to the sultan in Istanbul, the Ottoman capital.

Because of their military might, the Turks were feared by most Western nations until internal decay in the late 1600's seriously weakened their empire. Then the sultan's tottering realm aroused the greed of the European powers. Their goal was either to carve up the empire or to establish bases in it for their own economic gain and from which to spread their religious and cultural influences.

Conflict over Territory

During the nineteenth century the Middle East had high priority in the diplomatic maneuvering of the great powers. Russia sought to take control of the Bosporus and the Dardanelles. First France and then Britain controlled the Suez Canal. To ensure the security of the canal, the latter country made Egypt a British protectorate. To provide a shorter route to India than via Suez, Germany negotiated with the sultan the right to build a railroad from Istanbul to Baghdad and from there southward to the Persian Gulf. By the outbreak of World War I in 1914, the acquisition of parts of the Middle East and the Balkan provinces of the Ottoman Empire in Eastern Europe was a major objective of the chief adversaries in the conflict.

After the war most of the Middle East, including the former Arab provinces of the Ottoman Empire, became British or French spheres of influence or mandates. Little attention was paid to the wishes of the local inhabitants during the period between the two world wars. When the Soviet Union emerged as a superpower following World War II, that country tried to reassert its long-standing claim to influence in the Middle East. Soviet competition with the United States for influence in developing nations has added to the tensions in this part of the world.

Nationalism in the Middle East

The first glimmer of modern nationalism began to flicker among the peoples of the Middle East during the nineteenth century. But it was not until after World War I that nationalist movements gathered momentum. In Turkey the followers of Kemal Atatürk responded to the call of Turkish nationalism. Since the 1960's the Palestinians have been struggling for independence similar to that achieved by other Arab countries after World War II. A chief aim of nationalists throughout the Middle East has been to free their respective countries from the foreign domination or intervention that has long plagued the region since the 1700's. Other goals have been to develop their own cultures, institute the use of native languages, and begin the development of modern economies. Above all, they have striven to gain recognition and respect for their countries as independent political entities.

No Easy Solutions

Despite the wealth that oil brings to some countries of the area, great poverty still haunts the Middle East. Few natural resources other than oil exist. Scanty rainfall and inhospitable soil discourage agricultural expansion. Water resources are scarce, a fact that accounts for the emphasis on projects such as the Aswan High Dam.

Because of meager amounts of natural resources, a low standard of living, a low literacy rate, and the volatile nature of some of its people, the Middle East has experienced political upheaval since World War I. Factional strife has torn some countries, and intervention by one or more neighboring states in support of a faction has further complicated matters. Since World War II constant friction and several wars between Israel and the Arab states have disturbed the region. Recent evidences of Middle East turmoil are the Iran–Iraq war and the Palestinian uprising.

In this day of instant communication people are better informed than ever about worldwide developments. But perhaps we do not give enough attention to seeking causes, to finding out why things are as they are. To facilitate your thinking in greater depth, this volume provides the historical background to twentieth-century problems of the Middle East.

1

Where Continents Meet

The Middle East is the region where people first developed those arts and sciences we call **civilization.** It was for thousands of years the center of the civilized world. It is the birthplace of three great religions—Christianity, Judaism, and Islam. Today it is an area of international concern, largely for three related reasons—**strategic location,** oil, and political instability.

Since the Middle East is a land bridge linking three continents—Asia, Africa, and Europe—it has always attracted traders and conquerors. In recent times, this strategic location has made it a focus for competition between the Soviet bloc nations and the countries of the non-Communist West. Another reason for the interest of the great powers is oil. Since the beginning of the century, petroleum resources in the Middle East have been exploited largely by foreign companies operating under agreements with the countries concerned.

A third factor that has brought the Middle East into world view is the Arab–Israeli conflict and the Iran–Iraq War. These Middle Eastern conflicts have been complicated by other nations, which have supplied one side or the other with arms, funds, and political support. As a result of these conflicts, oil refineries and pipelines have been shut down and tankers moving through the principal shipping routes of the Persian Gulf and the Suez Canal have been attacked. The closing of the Suez Canal for a time and attacks on Persian Gulf shipping demonstrate the impact of Middle Eastern instability on the well-being of the entire world.

1. A Land of Deserts, Mountains, and Rivers

In studying the Middle East, we are not dealing with a single country with clearly defined boundaries, or even with a culture area such as Latin America whose limits are generally agreed upon. Perhaps it has already occurred to you to ask, Exactly what is the Middle East? Is it the same as the Near East?

There is no general agreement on what makes up the Near or Middle East. The term *Near East* came into fashion in the late 1700's when European statesmen wanted to distinguish those parts of Asia closer at hand, especially the provinces of the Ottoman Empire—what are generally today Greece, Eastern Europe, and Turkey—from those most distant from Europe: China and Japan. The term *Middle East* came into use in the late 1800's, in the writings of an American naval expert, Captain Alfred Thayer Mahan. His term became widely used during World War II and has since become the generally used term.

Most definitions of the region include the eastern Mediterranean area from Turkey south through the Arabian Peninsula and the west-east band of countries from Egypt through Iran. Some people extend the boundaries to cover all the lands of North Africa as far west as the Atlantic Ocean and all the territory extending as far as India in the east. In this book the Middle East will be considered as the area containing the following countries: Egypt, Iran (ih-RAN), Iraq (ih-RAC), Israel, Jordan, Lebanon, Saudi (SOWD-ee) Arabia, Syria, and Turkey; and the small states of the Arabian Peninsula: Bahrain (bah-RAYN), Kuwait (kuh-WAYT), Qatar (KAH-tuhr), the United Arab Emirates, Oman, the People's Republic of Yemen (YEHM-uhn), and the Yemen Arab Republic.

These countries form a rough quadrilateral containing about three million square miles and a total population of over 200 million. In area the Middle East is somewhat smaller than the continental United States. Its population may be less than one would expect in view of the publicity given to the high birth rate in the region. It must be kept in mind, however, that much of the Middle East is totally uninhabitable and that 90 percent of the land is not suited to farming. Some parts of the region have a very high population density. In some areas of Egypt's fertile Nile Valley, there are over 2,500 persons per square mile.

Mountainous Zones

The Middle East has three bands of mountains. The northernmost band is part of the mountainous zone that extends from

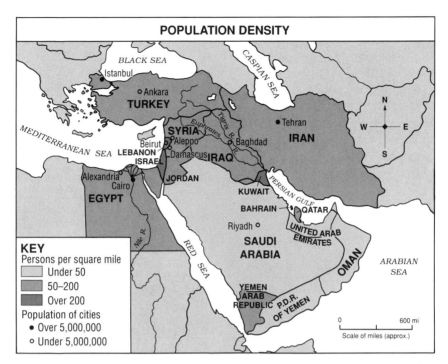

POPULATION DENSITY

KEY
Persons per square mile
- Under 50
- 50–200
- Over 200

Population of cities
- • Over 5,000,000
- ○ Under 5,000,000

PLACE: POPULATION DENSITY. Since much of the Middle East is arid, its population is concentrated wherever water is available: in northern areas with enough rainfall to grow crops, in irrigated river valleys, and in desert oases.

the Alps in Western Europe to the Himalayas in South Asia. In this zone are found the towering peaks of the Taurus Mountains in Turkey and the Zagros (ZAG-ruhs) and the Elburz (uhl-BOORZ) in Iran. Demavend, the highest peak in Iran, soars to over 18,000 feet. Mount Ararat in Turkey, known as the final resting place of Noah's Ark, is 17,000 feet high.

Below the northern band lies a region extending from the Sinai (SY-ny) Peninsula around the northern Arabian Peninsula, into the Tigris–Euphrates River Valley, and onto the shores of the Persian Gulf. (See map, pages 4-5.) Running north-south on the western edge are the Lebanon, Anti–Lebanon, and Hermon ranges. East of the mountains lies the great, oil-rich downslope, which was once, ages ago, covered by the waters of the Persian Gulf.

The third band, widest of all, reaches from northern and eastern Africa eastward across the Arabian Peninsula. Known as the African–Arabian Shield, it is composed largely of great horizontal rock masses and contains sedimentary rock deposits from an ancient sea that account for the presence of oil in the North African desert.

3

THE MIDDLE EAST

KEY

- Fertile Crescent
- - - - Disputed boundary
- ▲ Mountain peak

0 — 500
Scale of miles (approx.)

REGION: THE MIDDLE EAST. The Middle East is a land bridge linking
Europe, Africa, and Asia. Major areas suited to farming are the Nile Valley and
the Fertile Crescent. Seas and rivers cut through the region creating major inter-
sections. Its strategic location and major oil resources make the Middle East

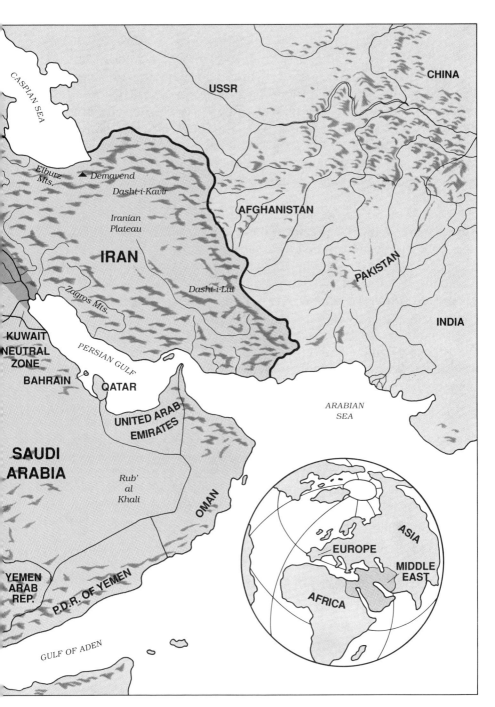

important to world powers thousands of miles away. Disputed boundaries exist in several areas of the Middle East, most notably between Israel and its Arab neighbors. The boundary problems on the Arabian Peninsula are the result of trying to define accurate boundaries in the desert.

Desert Areas

Deserts are the predominant land feature in the Middle East. Deserts have limited vegetation, producing nothing to sustain life—animal or human. Although many people think of deserts as sand dunes, there are many kinds. A desert may be stony or sandy, waterless or dotted with salt marshes, flat or hilly. The Rub' al Khali (ROOB-uhl KAH-lee) at one million square miles is one of the largest sand dune deserts in the world. Known as the "Empty Quarter," it fills most of the southern Arabian Peninsula.

There are no settlements in the Empty Quarter, and only nomads cross it. This region is a continuation of the Sahara and part of the desert belt that extends through Asia. Among other deserts in the Middle East are the Sahara in Egypt, the Nafud (nuh-FOOD) in northern Saudi Arabia and Dasht-i-Kavir (DASHT-eh-kuh-VEER) and Dasht-i-Lut (DASHT-eh-LOOT) in central Iran.

In contrast to the desert, some grasses and trees grow in the steppes, which extend through the Tigris-Euphrates area, across southern Turkey and Iraq, Syria, Jordan, and Iran. There nomads wander with their grazing herds of sheep, goats, and camels.

In both steppe and desert zones, oases are much prized. An oasis generally has a permanent water supply, some cultivated land, often date gardens, and shelter for desert dwellers and travelers. Real pasture land is found largely on the watered slopes of the mountain ranges. There grasses and terraced groves flourish on the lower rises and scrub or forest growth covers the higher elevations.

Climate

The Middle East is probably the driest place on earth. For thousands of years coping with scanty or nonexistent rainfall has been its biggest economic problem. The Arabian Peninsula and Egypt get almost no rain, while Iraq and Iran receive a meager six to fourteen inches a year, most of it in winter or spring. Only do parts of Turkey and the lands bordering the eastern shore of the Mediterranean Sea, particularly Syria, Israel, and Lebanon receive a generous 30 inches of rainfall a year. Snow is common in the mountains, and not unknown in the rest of the area except for Egypt and the far south. Summer everywhere is hot, with average daily maximums between 82° and 92° Fahrenheit. In southern Iran and in the Arabian Peninsula the mercury

THE ENVIRONMENT. Top left, snow-laden evergreens on a mountainside in Bursa, a province in northwest Turkey, contrast sharply with the typical desert scene at the bottom of the page. Camel herds like these still plod the Arabian Peninsula, four fifths of which is desert. The aerial photo of the oasis at Hofuf, Saudi Arabia, (center) shows how vegetation holds back moving dunes. Without such plantings, the desert could encroach as much as 40 feet a year. Rivers are precious for irrigation and transportation. Upper right, a felucca sails the Nile.

bubbles up to a sizzling 130°. Winters are generally cool and very chilly in these parts of Iran and Turkey where below-zero temperatures are common.

River Systems

The best places for agriculture in the Middle East have long been the valleys watered by the Nile and the Tigris–Euphrates rivers. These areas are known as the first centers of civilization in the region.

The Nile, one of the longest waterways in the world, flows more than 4,000 miles from its source near Lake Tanganyika (tan-guhn-YEE-kuh) in Central Africa to the Mediterranean. For centuries the Nile has overflowed its banks each year depositing soil rich in minerals across the neighboring land. Where the river flows into the Mediterranean, these deposits formed a rough triangle of land called the Nile Delta. With the construction of the Aswan High Dam in the 1960's by the Egyptian government with the aid of the Soviet Union, this ended. (See page 192.) The purpose of the dam was twofold: to provide hydroelectric power that would help in the **industrialization** and other development in Egypt and to increase the amount of land that could be irrigated, thus increasing agricultural production. This occurred in part of Egypt but by limiting the flow of the Nile, salt water has backed up around the Delta and the quality of the soil for farming has been damaged.

The Tigris River (1,150 miles) and the Euphrates (1,460 miles) flow south from the highlands of Turkey through the plains of Syria and Iraq and join just above the port of Basra to form the Shatt–al–Arab, a broad waterway into the Persian Gulf. These rivers have long been controlled by an elaborate system of dams and irrigation works. The area watered by these rivers is the site of the earliest civilization for which written records exist. The ancient Greeks called the area Mesopotamia, meaning "land between the rivers."

Smaller river systems are of critical importance in a region so handicapped by a lack of rainfall. The waters of the Jordan River system, shared by Lebanon, Syria, Jordan, and Israel, have long been a source of bitter quarrels. The Jordanian government has brought more land under irrigation by means of the East Ghor Canal Project, using the waters of the Yarmuk River in the Jordan River Valley. The Syrians have built irrigation projects on the Orontes River as well as a large dam on the Euphrates.

The waters and banks of the many seas of the Middle East have long provided food. Fishing and coastal sailing are possible on the Black, Caspian, Aegean, Mediterranean, Red, and Arabian seas and on the Persian Gulf. Despite the aridity of the Middle East, all of its countries have at least limited access to the sea, and, as a result, in some places tidal irrigation is used.

Check Your Understanding

1. What is the difference between the terms *Near East* and *Middle East?*
2. Describe the three bands of mountains in the Middle East.
3. How do people make use of the different kinds of land in the Middle East?
4. How has technology affected the use of the Nile River?
5. *Thinking Critically:* How do the deserts and mountains affect the prosperity of the Middle East?

2. The Middle East's Wealth

Although much of the Middle East is mountainous and desert, parts of it enjoy warm climate, fertile soil, and water for irrigation. Along the Black, Caspian, and Mediterranean seas a variety of agricultural products is raised. Both the climate and the crops grown in these regions resemble those of southern California. Next to the Nile Delta, the most productive area is the Fertile Crescent, an arc of land that begins along the Mediterranean coast of Israel and sweeps northward through Lebanon, across northern Syria and southern Turkey, through the Tigris-Euphrates Valley into Iraq, and southward to the Persian Gulf. (See map on pages 4–5.)

Agricultural Products

It was probably in the river valleys of the Middle East that people first cultivated wild grain. Today wheat and barley are the chief crops grown in the region. Other grains cultivated are corn, rye, and rice, a staple of the Middle Eastern diet as it is throughout Asia. Still, the peoples of the Middle East do not always grow enough food for their needs and in some areas must import large amounts of grain. Several Middle Eastern countries still receive wheat and other foodstuffs from the United States as part of its foreign aid program.

Turkey, Syria, and Lebanon are the chief producers of olives. Olive oil is important in the diet of Middle Eastern peoples and is also a major item for export. The oranges of Turkey and especially of the eastern Mediterranean and Aegean coasts are world famous. Israel's citrus fruits, one of its largest export items, are sold in many Western European countries. Dates are another leading crop with most of the world's imports coming from Iraq. The date is far more than a basic food in the Middle East. Ground-up date pits serve as animal fodder. The fibers of the date palm are used to make rope, and the wood of the trunk is used for fuel and timber.

Among other fruits of the region are the peaches, pears, and apples of the highlands of Lebanon, the apricots and melons of Iran, and the figs of Turkey. Grapes for the production of wine and raisins are grown throughout the area. Since most of the population is Muslim and prohibited from drinking alcoholic beverages, much of the wine, as well as the grapes for wine production, are exported. Almonds, walnuts, pistachios, and hazelnuts are also valuable exports for the area.

Coffee, once an important Middle Eastern product, is no longer a major crop. The famous mocha coffee got its name from the ancient South Arabian coffee-exporting city of Mocha (MOH-kuh), in Yemen. Tobacco is also grown in small quantities, and some Turkish tobacco is used in American cigarettes.

Cotton is the leading industrial crop in the region. Egyptian long-staple cotton is a superior variety, which is used for the production of fine cloth. Cotton ranks among Egypt's important exports, and a poor crop causes the country to suffer a severe economic setback. Other Middle Eastern countries, such as Turkey, Syria, Iraq, Iran, and Israel, have been raising cotton in recent years. They now grow enough to produce their own raw material for textile manufacture, an important industry in **developing nations.**

Livestock

Camels, sheep, and goats are raised by both nomads and settled farmers. The camel is perhaps the most distinctive animal of the Middle East. Although the truck is rapidly displacing the "ship of the desert," the camel is still important to the desert nomads, and is frequently used as a work animal in Arab countries. In Egypt the camel may turn the waterwheel that irrigates the fields, and even pull the plow. Camel milk and meat provide food, camel hair is used for tents and clothing, and the dung is burned for fuel. Nomads still tend to measure wealth by the number of camels owned.

Sheep and goats also provide meat and milk for food, hair for cloth, and skins for leather. White cheese made from goat's milk is a staple of the diet, and lamb dishes are very popular. In the Middle East goats are the scourge of the countryside. By nibbling grass down to the roots, they have turned many once fertile areas into wastelands.

Oil Reserves

The Middle East produces about one-fifth of the world's oil, and the region's known oil reserves amount to more than half the world total. Oil fields are usually found in what geologists call structural basins. One very large area of this type in the Middle East is the Mesopotamian–Persian Gulf basin, circled by the Taurus Mountains in the north; the mountains of Lebanon, Syria, and the Arabian Peninsula in the west; and the ranges of Iran and Muscat and Oman in the east. Another rich oil deposit lies in a basin in Iran south of the capital, Tehran. Since the end of World War II, oil from these two regions has become the chief source of income for Iran, Iraq, Saudi Arabia, Kuwait, Qatar, and the other small principalities of the Arabian Peninsula. Smaller oil fields also exist in Israel's Negev (NEH-gehv) Desert, Egypt's Sinai Peninsula, and Syria.

Oil as a New Factor in the Economy

An Australian prospector, William Knox D'Arcy, was the first person to discover oil for commercial use in the region. By the outbreak of World War I in 1914, the British-owned Anglo–Persian Oil Company was producing enough fuel in Iran to meet the needs of the British navy. After the war, Britain acquired the petroleum fields of Mosul in Iraq, and gave French companies shares in the Iraq Petroleum Company (IPC) to compensate for British control of the country. Because American companies had the most advanced oil field technology, they too were given shares in the IPC to help develop the fields.

American countries subsequently obtained the largest concessions, or rights to extract and market oil, in Saudi Arabia. Kuwait, Bahrain, Qatar, Abu Dhabi, and other Persian Gulf principalities later became big oil-producing states, with British and American companies holding the lion's share of the concessions.

(Continued on page 14.)

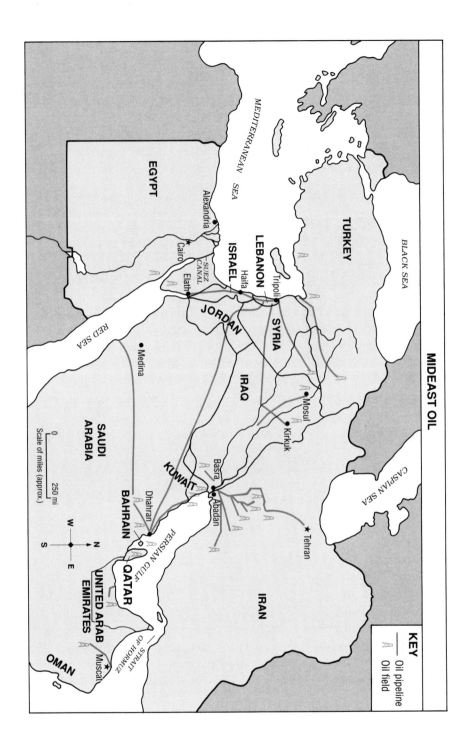

MIDEAST OIL

KEY
—— Oil pipeline
⚐ Oil field

MEDITERRANEAN SEA

BLACK SEA

CASPIAN SEA

RED SEA

PERSIAN GULF

STRAIT OF HORMUZ

SUEZ CANAL

TURKEY

EGYPT

LEBANON

ISRAEL

SYRIA

JORDAN

IRAQ

SAUDI ARABIA

KUWAIT

BAHRAIN

QATAR

UNITED ARAB EMIRATES

OMAN

IRAN

Alexandria

Cairo

Elath

Haifa

Tripoli

Mosul

Kirkuk

Medina

Basra

Abadan

Dhahran

Muscat

★ Tehran

Scale of miles (approx.)
0   250 mi

N
W   E
S

12

BURIED TREASURE

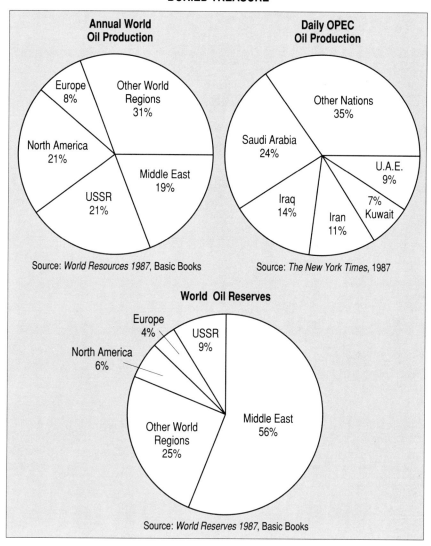

Annual World Oil Production

- Europe 8%
- Other World Regions 31%
- North America 21%
- Middle East 19%
- USSR 21%

Source: *World Resources 1987*, Basic Books

Daily OPEC Oil Production

- Other Nations 35%
- Saudi Arabia 24%
- U.A.E. 9%
- Iraq 14%
- 7% Kuwait
- Iran 11%

Source: *The New York Times*, 1987

World Oil Reserves

- Europe 4%
- USSR 9%
- North America 6%
- Other World Regions 25%
- Middle East 56%

Source: *World Reserves 1987*, Basic Books

OIL: BURIED TREASURE. The Middle East's major resource is oil as the three circle graphs on this page show. The Middle East is the world's leading producer of petroleum (top left). Five Middle East nations (top right) are the biggest OPEC oil producers. Overall, the Middle East holds the largest share of the world's oil reserves. Pipelines carry the oil from oil fields to ports (map, opposite page), where most of the oil is shipped to foreign markets.

THE OIL INDUSTRY. Drilling, refining, and shipping are basic to the production of oil. Top left, a drilling crew inspects the bit on a rig. Below left is a refinery at Ras Tanura in Saudi Arabia. Below right, a tanker in Kuwait harbor takes on oil directly from the oil field by way of one of the pipelines that crisscross that tiny country. Once Kuwait lived on a trade in skins, wool, and pearls. Now oil royalties give its people one of the highest per capita incomes in the world.

The investment of United States firms in the Middle East was the largest of any American holdings abroad. By the 1980's, most foreign concessions had been taken over by local governments, although American and British companies still provided technicians to run the oil fields.

Oil is now providing billions of dollars in income to the countries of the Middle East. Until the 1970's, much of the profit was invested abroad or spent on luxuries for the very small ruling families. In the past few years, however, greater use has been made of oil income for local development projects and for the health and welfare of the people, as you will see in later chapters.

Check Your Understanding

1. **a.** List two major export crops for the Middle East.
   b. List two major crops that Middle Easterners use themselves.
2. Where are the chief oil deposits in the Middle East?
3. How has control of these oil fields changed over time?
4. *Thinking Critically:* Do you think technology will ever completely replace the camel in Middle Eastern life? Why or why not?

3. An Agricultural Way of Life

In a region where geography and climate combine to make more than 90 percent of the land uncultivable, it may seem strange that most people make their living by farming. Much of the Middle East is desert, marsh, or mountains. It is besieged by drought and agricultural pests such as locusts. Its farmers have been locked in a system that has kept them poor, uneducated, and passive for centuries. Yet with farming the number-one occupation and the population increasing, Middle Eastern governments must give priority to agriculture.

The Land–Tenure System

Unlike farmers in Western countries, most of the farmers in the Middle East do not live on or own their land. Their houses are in villages within walking distance of the fields. Some of the land is owned by landlords, who give peasants a share of the crop in return for their labor. The share is often so small that the peasant family can barely exist on it. Since they are often too poor to purchase seed and work animals, they must also turn over a share of the crop for these necessities, or borrow the money to buy them. Until the land reform measures of the 1960's and 1970's, the system of **land tenure** prevalent in some Middle East countries accounted for more than agricultural inefficiency. It was also responsible for the feeling of hopelessness that darkened life for so many Middle Easterners.

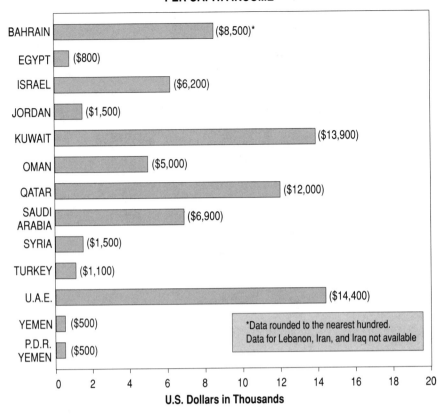

PER CAPITA INCOME

Country	Per Capita Income
BAHRAIN	($8,500)*
EGYPT	($800)
ISRAEL	($6,200)
JORDAN	($1,500)
KUWAIT	($13,900)
OMAN	($5,000)
QATAR	($12,000)
SAUDI ARABIA	($6,900)
SYRIA	($1,500)
TURKEY	($1,100)
U.A.E.	($14,400)
YEMEN	($500)
P.D.R. YEMEN	($500)

*Data rounded to the nearest hundred.
Data for Lebanon, Iran, and Iraq not available

U.S. Dollars in Thousands

Source: World Population Date Sheet, 1988

PER CAPITA INCOME. The annual average income per person for each country is arrived at by dividing its gross national product by its population. The average for the world is $3,000, while developed nations average about $10,700. How do you account for the wide differences among Middle Eastern nations?

Living Conditions

Much like the houses of centuries past, peasant houses are built of mud and straw or of sun-dried brick. Most families of seven, eight, or more live in a single, sparsely furnished room. Few of these dwellings have windows. Almost all have earthen floors. The peasants usually sleep on mats that are rolled up in the morning to make room for the day's activities. In recent years some governments have begun village improvement programs to raise living conditions among farmers. In the Middle East today, one sees an increasing number of village schools, medical centers, agricultural cooperatives, and rural development projects.

But life is still hard for the Middle Eastern peasant. Families, including boys and girls as young as five or six, work from

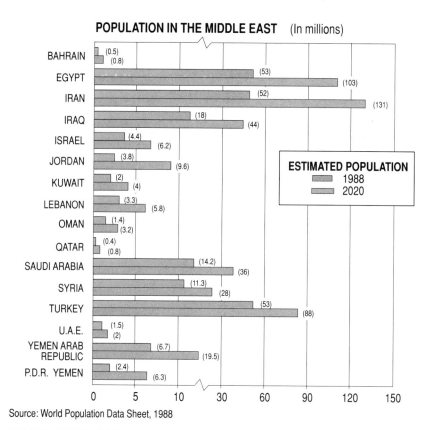

POPULATION IN THE MIDDLE EAST (In millions)

Country	1988	2020
BAHRAIN	(0.5)	(0.8)
EGYPT	(53)	(103)
IRAN	(52)	(131)
IRAQ	(18)	(44)
ISRAEL	(4.4)	(6.2)
JORDAN	(3.8)	(9.6)
KUWAIT	(2)	(4)
LEBANON	(3.3)	(5.8)
OMAN	(1.4)	(3.2)
QATAR	(0.4)	(0.8)
SAUDI ARABIA	(14.2)	(36)
SYRIA	(11.3)	(28)
TURKEY	(53)	(88)
U.A.E.	(1.5)	(2)
YEMEN ARAB REPUBLIC	(6.7)	(19.5)
P.D.R. YEMEN	(2.4)	(6.3)

ESTIMATED POPULATION
1988
2020

Source: World Population Data Sheet, 1988

POPULATION SPIRAL. One result of improved health conditions in the Middle East has been a population explosion. But the rapidly spiraling increase threatens the region's stability and economic progress. Which nation has the largest population?

sunrise until evening before returning to their overcrowded huts. Their food is a monotonous diet of bread, rice or other grain, and a few locally grown vegetables. Meat is a luxury enjoyed only a few times a year on holidays. Because of unsanitary living conditions, poor diet, and the lack of proper medical facilities, the death rate has been very high and life expectancy relatively short. In recent years rural health programs have helped to improve conditions and to reduce infant mortality rates.

Land Reform

Since the 1952 revolution that ended the monarchy in Egypt and the subsequent militant reform movements in Syria, Iraq, Turkey, and Iran, conditions have begun to improve in some regions. The size of the large estates, many held by absentee landlords, has been reduced by legal intervention, and their holdings parceled out to individuals. The breaking up of big

17

estates does not solve all problems, but it was a much needed first step to help farmers in the Middle East have some hope for a better future.

Check Your Understanding

1. Describe the traditional landholding system in the Middle East.
2. What are living conditions like for Middle Eastern peasants?
3. What land reforms have been introduced?
4. *Thinking Critically:* How have rural health care programs had both good and bad effects on the growth of Middle Eastern nations?

4. Urban Life

Life in Middle Eastern cities is rich in variety. The greatest extremes of poverty and wealth and the largest number of minorities can be found in urban areas. Many Middle Eastern cities were once ancient centers of glory. Alexandria, Damascus, Istanbul (formerly Constantinople), and Jerusalem are examples of ancient cities that have evolved into vibrant, modern, urban centers. Alexandria, named after Alexander the Great, was founded by the ancient Greeks and was once a world center of learning. Damascus is believed to be one of the world's oldest cities, and Constantinople, named after the Roman emperor Constantine, was the proud capital of the Byzantine emperors.

Walled Cities of Old

Many of the older cities were enclosed by stone walls built for protection against enemies. Within the walls residents of different religions, ethnic origins, and professions dwelt in separate parts of the city. In old Jerusalem, for example, there were special sections or streets for shoemakers, tailors, money changers, metalworkers, cloth merchants, and other occupations.

A characteristic of many old Middle Eastern cities is their covered bazaars. Streets often wind for miles beneath the "roofs" built of elaborately ornamented masonry or wooden beams inlaid with colorful tiles. Private homes are built around courtyards, and high outside walls prevent passersby from seeing into the

URBAN LIFE. Cities provide political and social dynamism. Top left, a crowded market street in Cairo. Top right, replacing slum housing with modern housing, above right in Kuwait and below in Istanbul, is a high priority of many Middle Eastern governments.

interiors. Thus it is often difficult from outside to distinguish between the homes of the rich and those of the poor. Within the winding alleyways and covered streets, one is able to find beautifully furnished modern homes in the midst of crowded slums.

Modern Cities

Modern cities have grown up outside the old walled towns. The newer section of many ancient cities often greatly exceeds the area enclosed within the original walls. Modern steel and glass office buildings and high-rise apartment houses now overshadow the ancient walls.

Not all the recent growth has meant progress, however. In many cities new slums have been created as one of the by-products of **modernization**, and new problems have emerged. One is overcrowding, as thousands of peasants have migrated to the cities. On the average, however, urban workers are not much better off than their rural cousins. Most city dwellers eke out a living as artisans, shopkeepers, and workers in the growing industrial sector or in the service industries concentrated in the urban centers. Middle Eastern cities face many of the difficulties of large cities elsewhere—juvenile delinquency, pollution, overcrowded public transportation, traffic jams, water shortages, and too few schools.

Financial and Cultural Centers

Traditionally, the large cities have been centers of Middle Eastern life because they have been the capitals of empires, kingdoms, and modern states. Equally important, the powerful and influential classes have usually resided there. Even the owners of large rural estates often made their homes in the cities. Today the cities are centers of political and economic activity and the seats of culture and learning.

Most of the Middle Eastern cities are now in the throes of the economic and social revolution sweeping across the region. When you read about individual countries in the following chapters, you will examine in detail how urban life has been affected by the impact of the late twentieth century. You will also read about the ways in which Middle Eastern governments have responded to changing conditions. In addition, you will learn about the programs these governments have undertaken to help bring their people, both urban and rural, into the mainstream of twentieth-century life.

Check Your Understanding

1. List two characteristics of the older cities of the Middle East.
2. What problems has urban expansion created for these cities?
3. What are two functions Middle Eastern cities have traditionally filled for their societies?
4. *Thinking Critically:* What steps do you think Middle Eastern governments may have to take to ease some of the problems of their cities? List three.

5. The Muslim World

Long ago the people who settled in Mesopotamia and the eastern Mediterranean were largely Semitic desert tribes, related racially and linguistically to the people of Egypt. The terms *Semite* and *Semitic* properly refer to a family of languages including Hebrew and Arabic but are also used to denote ethnic groups speaking these languages. Over centuries of migration and invasion, other ethnic groups, such as the Persians speaking an Indo-European language and the Turks speaking a Ural-Altaic language, were added to the cultural mosaic of the Middle East. A large number of these people now call themselves Arabs and claim membership in an ethnic-linguistic grouping that cuts across national boundaries. Non-Arab groups in the Middle East are the Turks, Persians (Iranians), Armenians, and Kurds. This latter group, scattered throughout Turkey, Iran, and Iraq, has a deep-rooted national consciousness and has for years been fighting a bitter war for **autonomy** against the governments of Iraq, Turkey, and Iran. (See Sidelight to History, page 22.)

Contrary to popular belief, the word *Arab* does not designate a member of a particular religious group. It is applied to Muslims, Christians, or Jews who speak Arabic and identify themselves with the Arab way of life. Originally the Arabs were just one among the many Semitic peoples living in the Middle East. By the end of the sixth century A.D., most of the inhabitants of the Arabian Peninsula and the inner part of the Fertile Crescent were members of Arabic-speaking **tribes** with similar patterns of family life, social organization, food, and other culture traits.

S IDELIGHT TO HISTORY

The Kurds

The present-day descendants of the ancient Medes live in Kurdistan, a mountainous region where Iran, Iraq, Turkey, and Syria meet. They number several million and form a sizable minority in the four countries. Defeated by Alexander the Great in the 300's B.C. and later conquered and converted to Islam by the Arabs, the Kurds have maintained their tribal culture and nomadic ways until recently.

Modern states have attempted to destroy the Kurdish culture, but each time they have only added to the fires of Kurdish **nationalism**. In 1920 an Allied promise of an independent Kurdistan, broken by a later treaty, further increased the Kurds' frustrations. Since then many rebellions have been suppressed by national governments. Yet the Kurds continue to fight. To these descendants of Saladin (1137–1193), guerrilla warfare is a way of life.

Kurdish life is changing. Most Kurds have abandoned the nomadic life. Some have become laborers for the oil companies. Political parties are taking over tribal loyalties. Today the Kurds are seeking political and cultural autonomy *within* existing states. In 1966 the government of Iraq granted many of the rights demanded by the Kurds. However, disagreements continued between Iraqi and Kurdish leaders over the extent of these rights. Fighting resumed periodically between the Iraqi army and Kurdish guerrillas, at times reaching the proportions of a major civil war.

The Turkish government has refused to grant autonomy to its Kurdish citizens, even denying that they are a distinct people. In Turkey, Kurds are called "mountain Turks," and the government prohibits use of the Kurdish language. Relations between the Iranian government and Kurds have varied. The government has encouraged Kurds living in Iraq to rebel against the Iraqi government while suppressing its own Kurdish population. However, the Iraqi Kurds identified primarily as Iraqis and generally opposed Iranian efforts to turn them against Iraq.

Bedouin Influence on Middle Eastern Culture

It was the nomadic Arabs living outside the cities who gave Middle Eastern society many of its distinctive qualities. Called **Bedouin** (BED-oo-in), meaning "desert dwellers," these wandering herders even today roam the desert to find grazing land for their flocks. They have few possessions. Their homes are goatskin or sheepskin tents; their clothing and their food are provided by the camels, sheep, and goats of their herds.

In earlier times the Bedouin gained some of their livelihood from raids on merchants' caravans crossing the desert and on the settled communities of the Arabian Peninsula. Sometimes town merchants would try to buy off the Bedouin. At other times they fought them. Several governments have turned the Bedouin into settled farmers as part of development projects to improve their living conditions. The oil industry especially has changed the Bedouin way of life, as former nomads have settled down to work as skilled mechanics, oil drillers, and technicians.

Many Bedouin still live under a tribal system based on blood kinship. Probably this system developed out of a need for mutual protection against the perils of desert life. The tribes consist of clans headed by **sheikhs** (SHEEKS) or sayyids (SEYE-ids). In the early days there were no formal laws. The ancient principle of "an eye for an eye, and a tooth for a tooth" prevailed. Under it the tribe exacted vengeance from the wrongdoer or relatives. Even today many settled Arabs trace their ancestry to Bedouin tribes of the A.D. 500's, and many Bedouin customs still exist among urban Arabs, often in some modified form.

Once the Bedouin worshipped many deities thought to inhabit particular places such as rocks or trees and believed in a higher God, Allah. Much of the Bedouin religious feeling was expressed in oral poetry, which grew to be a very important part of their culture. A poetic dialect, understood by all tribes, in the sixth century developed into the classical Arabic language. The medium of a common language encouraged the spread of the Muslim religion.

The Influence of Islam

Late in the sixth century an Arab named Mohammed, meaning "praise-worthy," was born in the town of Mecca 40 miles inland from the Red Sea. He grew up to be a successful merchant. While meditating one night on a mountain, Mohammed believed that he heard a message from God or Allah calling him to be

(Continued on page 26.)

The Arabic Language

If you were to learn the 28 symbols of the Arabic alphabet pictured above, you would still be unable to read a sentence. The reason? Vowel sounds have no separate symbols but are indicated by marks placed above or below the letters they follow. For example, to write a *b* sound, an Arab would make the symbol ٮ . To write *ba*, he or she would form the letter ڊ . Another symbol used to show pronunciation is the *hamza*, which indicates a sort of "catch" in breathing. It is something like the push of a breath that comes when an English sentence begins with a vowel, such as "Is he here yet?" or the pause in a word like "cooperate." Hamzas usually appear above or below a letter, but there are many exceptions. One hamza looks like this: ء . Another complication in learning Arabic is the fact that most letters have separate forms when they begin a word, come in the middle, and at the end. As we have seen, *b* alone is ٮ, but in the middle of the word it looks like this: ـبـ .

A DIVERSITY OF PEOPLE. Kurdish women (top left) in vivid dresses and gold and silver jewelry offer a striking contrast to modern working women (top right). Left, an Israeli boy celebrates his bar-mizvah, or religious coming-of-age. Below, Bedouin enjoy a light moment together. How do these photos exemplify diversity in the Middle East?

25

a prophet. He preached his revelation in Mecca and won a small following, but had to move to Medina (meh-DEE-nuh) because of disagreements with merchants in his home city. Within 10 years Mohammed had united many of the tribes of the Arabian Peninsula into a religious group called *Muslims*, meaning "those who submit to the will of God." The religion was called Islam (ISS-lahm), the word for its central belief, "surrender or submission to the will of God." Islam provided the Arabs with a strong belief in one God, or **monotheism**, and an idea of community based on a higher law than blood kinship. Beyond the Arabian Peninsula, the faith was spread by conquering Arab armies. Islam will be treated fully in Chapter 3.

Despite the fact that Islam won and held the regions that are today Turkey and Iran and that 90 percent of the Turks and Iranians are Muslim, they do not speak Arabic. They have their own distinctive customs, traditions, and national identity, and at times their national interests clash with those of the Arab states.

Minority Religious Groups

Not all Arabs are Muslims. In the Middle East there are several groups of Christian Arabs, including several million Copts in Egypt, and more than a million followers of various sects in Syria, Iraq, Jordan, Israel, and Lebanon. Some of the Christians are followers of the Roman Catholic and Greek Orthodox faiths. Others belong to Eastern **sects** that are remnants of ancient Christian groups. There once were several hundred thousand Jewish Arabs—Jews who lived in Arab countries, spoke Arabic, and practiced many Arabic customs. As a result of the wars between Israel and the Arab states, most of these Jews have left their homelands to settle in Israel or elsewhere.

Muslim Culture as the Unifier

The spread of Islam in the second half of the A.D. 600's was carried out by military, social, and political means. As a result, many converts to Islam acquired not only a new religion but also the language and culture of their new rulers. Many embraced Islam because it did not make great demands on them. Unlike Christianity, it had no elaborate rituals. It also did not persecute nonbelievers. Others became Muslims because it was the religion of their conquerors.

As you will see in later chapters, the influence of Islam is reflected in present-day attitudes toward the state and toward life in general. In everyday life this influence is evident in dress, food, family organization, and social practices. For example, in Middle Eastern countries women from conservative family backgrounds often wear plain, dark-colored clothing when they appear in public. Family ties are very close. Indeed, the relations between cousins and even second cousins are often more closely knit than those between brothers and sisters in some Western countries. Great respect is paid to parents and elderly people, and guests are received with elaborate hospitality. These all reflect the value Islam places on the family.

Check Your Understanding

1. What grouping does the term *Arab* describe?
2. How have the Bedouin influenced modern Arab life?
3. What religion most strongly influenced Arab development?
4. **Thinking Critically:** Give examples from your reading to explain the following: All Muslims are not Arabs; all Arabs are not Muslims.

CHAPTER REVIEW

■ Chapter Summary

Section 1. The Middle East is a land bridge linking Asia, Africa, and Europe. Its strategic location, oil resources, and conflict between Arabs and Israelis have long made it a center of international conflicts.

Geographically the region is one of great variety. Climate ranges from tropical to temperate, and agricultural products vary similarly. In areas where most of the population lives, the land and the environment resemble southern California or the southwestern parts of the United States. Other areas have snow-capped mountains or vast uninhabited deserts.

Section 2. Most of the people of the region live in the great river valleys of the Nile and the Tigris–Euphrates and along the Fertile Crescent. In these areas, most of the population are farmers and their chief crops are wheat, barley, and other grains. Fruits and vegetables similar to those raised in California are also grown. Most farmers also raise sheep and goats. In the more arid semidesert, nomads, called Bedouin, move from place to place with their herds.

Section 3. For thousands of years peasant farmers have eked out a living working for landlords and making little for themselves from their toil. Under the land-tenure system, large landholders received most of the income from the crops their tenants planted. Since the 1960's the governments of Egypt, Iran, Iraq, Turkey, and Syria have established reforms to redistribute land among the peasants.

Section 4. Urban life in the Middle East dates back to ancient times. Many of the older walled cities still exist, but within the protective shadows of skyscrapers and apartment buildings. Modern cities have grown up around these older ones, and with them have come modern problems—overcrowding, pollution, and traffic jams among others.

Section 5. The Middle East is a region of many peoples, most of whom practice Islam. Not all Muslims, however, are Arabs. Turks, Persians, and Kurds are non-Arab Muslims. Arab culture has had many influences working to shape it. Among these have been the Bedouin people and Islam.

■ Vocabulary Review

Define: civilization, strategic location, industrialization, developing nation, land tenure, modernization, autonomy, tribe, Bedouin, nationalism, shiek, monotheism, sect

■ Places to Locate

Locate: Nile River, Tigris River, Euphrates River, Empty Quarter, Fertile Crescent, Arabian Peninsula, Mecca, Medina

■ People to Know

Identify: Semite, Mohammed

■ Thinking Critically

1. Why is it difficult to fix the boundaries of the Middle East? What do you think should be considered in defining a world region? Consider geography, language, customs, religion.

2. In recent years the number of Bedouin tribes has decreased and many former nomads have taken jobs in the oil fields. What conclusions might you draw from this about the effects of modern technology on people living by ancient

tradition? Use examples from other cultures to support your conclusions.

3. Contrast life in the cities with life in the villages of the Middle East. Why have thousands of peasants migrated to the cities in recent years? Has this kind of migration occurred in nations outside the Middle East? What do these nations have in common with those in the Middle East?

Extending and Applying Your Knowledge

1. Although grain is one of the most important crops of the Middle East, some nations have to import grain. Research and prepare an oral report explaining such factors as climate, farming methods, and population growth. Find out which countries import the most grain and from where. Use graphs in your presentation.

2. Research and write a brief report on why oil did not bring immediate prosperity to the nations of the Middle East. Find out who owned the oil fields, how they got them, and what the Middle Eastern nations received in return. Also indicate how the nations finally took ownership.

2

The Ancient Middle East

The earliest people in the Sahara region of North Africa and on the Arabian Peninsula were hunters who ranged across a rich savanna watered by many rivers and populated by large numbers of animals. About 9000 B.C. when the glaciers of the last Ice Age melted, the rainbearing winds changed direction and deserted these hunting lands, eventually leaving them barren wastelands. The inhabitants were forced to migrate northward and eastward to the shores of the Persian Gulf, to the southern highlands, or to the Anatolian-Iranian Plateau.

Archaeologists believe that the earliest agricultural centers developed on this plateau and in the region now composed of Syria, Lebanon, and Israel. With its mild Mediterranean climate, well-watered soil, and variety of food plants, the area provided an environment favorable for human life. There, probably about 6500 B.C., people began to sow and harvest wild grain and to domesticate animals such as sheep, goats, pigs, cows, and fowl. In one of the most significant shifts in the world's history, they became food *producers* rather than food *gatherers.*

By being able to grow their own food rather than hunt for it, these people were assured of food. They also had free time, that is, time they did not have to devote to finding food. As a result, they began to develop metalworking, pottery making, handicrafts, and building techniques. Their religious ceremonies came to center on the all-important steps of planting, growing, and harvesting crops. Thus the change to agriculture established the basis for the growth of civilization.

1. The First Centers of Civilization

The story of Western civilization begins in the Tigris–Euphrates Valley. There the earliest forms of government developed, and people first formed themselves into complex societies. The first systems of writing were invented, and many scientific and technological advances were made.

Settling the Tigris–Euphrates Valley

As you have read, the Tigris and Euphrates rivers flow from the Taurus and Zagros mountains to empty into the Persian Gulf. Between them lies the plain of Mesopotamia, "the land between the rivers," which is the eastern arm of the Fertile Crescent. (See map, pages 4–5.) It was here, along the riverbanks, that farming peoples from the hills to the north and east began to settle some 6,000 years ago. The land was very different from what they had known. Here there was little rainfall, but the flooding of the two rivers left behind rich soil and a maze of swamps and marshes.

The newcomers, however, had to tame the floods and channel the waters to prevent their crops from being washed away in the rainy season and withered during the hot, dry months. In the hills each farmer had worked independently. In the valley everyone had to cooperate in digging the canals, building the dikes, clearing the ditches, and sharing the water. Since the bed of the Tigris is lower than the surrounding plain and the bed of the Euphrates is higher, distribution of the water to the fields called for technical skill. Drainage in such flat land was yet another problem to be solved. Thus valley agriculture called for human cooperation as much as for control of the rivers.

By using these methods, the farmers were able to increase their food supply many times. With a steady food supply, the population increased. This abundant food supply also meant that some people were freed from the necessity of farming. In time a class of craftsworkers, merchants, and traders grew up in addition to those administrators, priests, and military leaders needed to supervise the irrigation system and the community. Over time, some villages grew into large urban centers.

Sumerian City–States

The shift from simple village life to a complex urban society first took place in communities located on the southern reaches of the Tigris–Euphrates rivers. The first inhabitants of the region were a people still unidentified, who belonged to a different eth-

TIMETABLE

The Ancient Middle East

6500–6000* B.C.	Settled communities in Syria and Palestine
4000–3000 B.C.	Sumerian cities Cuneiform writing
2700–2200 B.C.	Old Kingdom of Egypt
2450–2270 B.C.	Akkadian Empire
2100–1788 B.C.	Middle Kingdom of Egypt
1900–1600 B.C.	First Babylonian Empire
1750 B.C.	Hammurabi's code of laws
1750–1200 B.C.	Hittite Kingdom
1580–1090 B.C.	New Kingdom of Egypt
1292–1225 B.C.	Rameses II
1200 B.C.	The Hebrews' Journey out of Egypt
1013–586 B.C.	Kingdoms of Israel and Judah
625–538 B.C.	New Babylonian Empire
550–330 B.C.	Persian Empire
333–323 B.C.	Alexander's Empire
322–90 B.C.	Hellenistic period
146 B.C.	Destruction of Carthage
31 B.C.	Roman control of the Mediterranean world
A.D. 73	Masada
117	Roman Empire at its height
135	Diaspora
395	Roman Empire divided
476	End of Roman Empire in the West
527–565	Eastern Roman (Byzantine) Empire at its height

*Dates for the early period of history may vary from source to source because different systems of calculation are used.

ARTIFACTS OF SUMER. Two remarkable objects discovered in the Royal Cemetery at Ur in Sumeria are shown here. At left is a bull's head of gold and lapis lazuli atop a lyre, a musical instrument. Below is the oldest game board in the world (c. 2500 B.C.), made of wood inlaid with shells and lapis lazuli and accompanied by dice. No one is sure about the rules of the game. What might artifacts such as these tell us about early peoples?

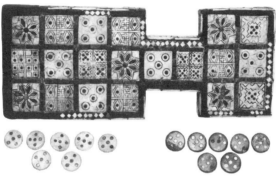

nic group and spoke a language other than the Semitic tongues of the peoples farther north. Although definite dates are impossible to establish, it is generally believed that sometime around 4000 B.C., these first settlers were joined by a group of Semitic people from the east. The fusion of the two laid the foundation of the world's first civilization. It is the mixture of these people that has come to be called Sumerians (soo-MEHR-ee-unz).

The early villages of Mesopotamia each had their own set of gods and goddesses whose worship was the center of the community's life. For example, a village might have a river god, a goddess of love, and a goddess of death. The people looked on themselves as "tenants" farmed the land for their local deity. The priests served the local deity, who was believed to control rivers and land. The priests also administered the cultivation of the land. Because their position combined their religious functions with the control of agriculture, the priests were the most powerful people in the city. They allotted each farmer a

SIDELIGHT TO HISTORY

Insight into the Past

In the hills and plains of the eastern Mediterranean lies buried the history of Western civilization's ancient past. In recent years archaeologists have brought to light fragments of evidence revealing the development of human culture. From their discoveries made at various excavations, scholars have traced the appearance of permanent settlements and the beginnings of farming, pottery making, metallurgy, and a variety of other crafts. These discoveries indicate that people began to live in permanent communal groups and to raise crops more than 8,000 years ago.

One such example is Beidha in Jordan, a village of the New Stone Age (roughly 5,000 to 12,000 years ago). Beidha is important to archaeologists because it provides one of the best examples of early Neolithic life yet discovered. Archaeologists working at the site have exposed four main types of architecture at six different levels, all semi-subterranean. The top level has been almost completely destroyed because of later farming, but the second and third levels revealed a large house with plaster floors and walls.

Attached to the house were enclosures and pens. Near the large house was a series of rectangular buildings. Since no hearths or fireplaces have been discovered in the smaller buildings, archaeologists think that the large house was the community meeting and eating place and that the others were workshops. In one were stone, bone, and shell beads—many of them ground and polished, ready to be used in ornaments. In another room, the bones, hammers, and choppers indicate that it was a butcher shop.

By level six there appeared some of the earliest neolithic houses known. These were constructed in clusters, and their design hinted at the mud and grass huts that must have preceded them. In these houses were found lifelike figurines and crude clay bowls. From seeds that were still preserved in their baskets, scholars know that these people raised barley and wheat similar to the grains that grew wild in the valley. Probably, too, these people had begun to domesticate animals.

share of land to farm. Besides this personal land, everyone also had fields to farm for the deity and owed taxes and services to the temple.

The priests ruled from ziggurats (ZIG-uh-rahts), the name for Sumerian temples. Later Babylonians and Assyrians also used this design for their temples. It was a pyramid-like structure built with layers of brick on a rectangular or circular base. The number of bricks per layer decreased as the ziggurat rose in height. There were usually from two to seven tiers. At the top, reached by a series of ramps, was a shrine to one of the local gods or goddesses. Today in southern Iraq there are remnants of ziggurats that resemble similar structures built by the ancient Mayans in Central America.

In addition to controlling agriculture, the priests also managed the **economy** of the city. Grain produced from the fields had to be stored and sold, supplies had to be bought for the temple, and luxury items such as gold and jewels imported to adorn it. The priests supervised the workers required to operate the temple bakery, workshops, and kilns that baked the pottery, and directed a staff of artists and craftsworkers. As the Sumerian city-states prospered, their economy expanded. Foreign trade extended as far as India and Egypt, to which Sumeria sold fine weapons, textiles, and jewelry. As the economy developed, a new and powerful merchant class arose.

The merchants as well as the priests needed some means of keeping business records and accounts. Two inventions answered this need: writing and arithmetic. The system of writing that the Sumerians devised was based on pictures of objects, supplemented by symbols representing sounds. These characters were impressed on soft clay tablets with a wedge-shaped tool called a stylus, in order to produce writing called **cuneiform** (kyoo-NEE-uh-form, from *cuneus*, Latin for "wedge").

For counting, the Sumerians developed an arithmetic system that is the origin for our 60-second minute, 60-minute hour, 24-hour day, and 360-degree circle. The priests also developed simple geometry and astronomy. Both were important in calculating seasonal changes and in religious ceremonies.

The Rise of Empires in Mesopotamia

Each city of the Sumerian plain was a separate unit, feeling no bond with the other cities. With one city often at war with another, the problem of defense eventually led to a change in political organization. Leaders who could guarantee protection to their cities were able to assume power and dominate the

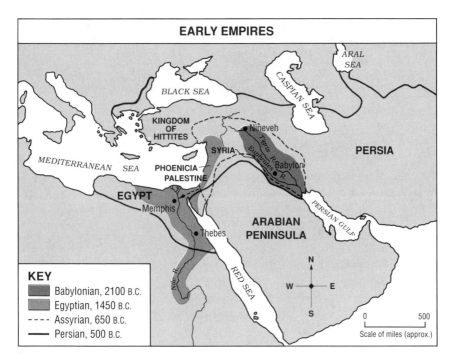

EARLY EMPIRES

ARAL SEA

BLACK SEA

CASPIAN SEA

KINGDOM OF HITTITES

Nineveh

SYRIA

MEDITERRANEAN SEA

PHOENICIA
PALESTINE

Tigris R.

Euphrates R.

Babylon

PERSIA

EGYPT

Memphis

Thebes

ARABIAN PENINSULA

PERSIAN GULF

Nile R.

RED SEA

N
W — E
S

KEY
- Babylonian, 2100 B.C.
- Egyptian, 1450 B.C.
- - - - Assyrian, 650 B.C.
- —— Persian, 500 B.C.

0   500
Scale of miles (approx.)

MOVEMENT: EARLY EMPIRES. The influence of Egypt and Babylon spread outward from the first centers of civilization in the valleys of the Nile River and of Mesopotamia. Invaders from the north and east, such as the Hittites, Assyrians, and Persians, in turn became great empire-builders. Why were no empires created on the Arabian Peninsula?

government of the city-state. Inevitably, an ambitious leader would seek to extend control beyond his own city-state to create an **empire.**

The city-states of Sumeria remained independent until about 2450 B.C. when the state of Akkad (AK-ahd) in the northern part conquered and united the region for a brief period. The Akkadians had borrowed freely from the civilization developed around Sumer and had even adopted cuneiform for their own written language. Under their leader Sargon, they swept through the valley subduing the other cities. Sargon declared himself ruler of them all and created the first Mesopotamian empire. It extended beyond the Sumerian plain from the Persian Gulf to the Mediterranean, and included Akkad, Sumer, Elam, Assyria, and northern Syria. Trade flourished throughout the Akkadian Empire, enriching the cities of Sumeria.

Sargon's success was short-lived. Hardly more than a century after his conquests, his empire had fallen. The cities of the plain reverted to another period of struggle, this time between the older centers and challengers from the less-developed re-

LEGACY OF SUMER. The statue at the right is often identified as the head of King Hammurabi. At left is the top of the 8-foot-high stele, or slab, on which his code of laws is inscribed. It shows Hammurabi receiving the royal insignia from a god (seated). What is the significance of Hammurabi's code?

gions on the fringes of the area. Internal conflict drained away much of Sumer's strength. When the cities finally were reunited, unification came from outside.

Babylonia

For generations people had been filtering into the Mesopotamian valley. About 1900 B.C. the Amorites from the northwest were strong enough to win control over a wide area and create an empire with the city of Babylon as its capital. The Amorites did not destroy Sumerian culture. Instead they absorbed its art, religion, and science into their own.

At its height, about 1750 B.C., the Babylonian Empire was ruled by the great Hammurabi (ham-uh-RAHB-ee), its sixth king. He introduced a legal code that applied to all the peoples of the empire and replaced the codes of the individual city-states. Harsh in its provisions and punishments, the code of Hammurabi is nevertheless of great historical importance because it is based on the idea that the state, rather than the individual, is responsible for justice and punishment.

Like its predecessors, the Babylonian Empire had a short history. Following its fall, Mesopotamian civilization suffered a decline for several centuries. Trade diminished, and contacts with the outside world dwindled. Surrounding the region on every side were new kingdoms of warrior peoples. It was a thousand years before Mesopotamia was again united under a single ruler.

Check Your Understanding

1. What problems did the early settlers in the Tigris–Euphrates Valley confront?
2. Why did the life of the Sumerian city-states center around the temple?
3. What did the Akkadians borrow from Sumer?
4. Why is Hammurabi's law code considered important?
5. *Thinking Critically:* Why is the change from food gathering to food producing considered of major importance in the development of civilization?

2. The Growth of Egyptian Civilization

The climate changes that affected northern Africa after the melting of the glacier influenced the Nile Valley. Gradually people from North and East Africa began to settle on and farm the land beyond the banks built up by the annual flooding. Eventually they ventured onto the banks themselves.

Besides being extremely fertile, the Nile Valley had two other important advantages for the development of civilization. Bounded by desert on either side and meeting the Mediterranean Sea at the mouth of the river, it was protected from land invasion. On the other hand, the Nile, being easily navigable, united the communities along its banks and made it possible for them to be kept under a central authority, which could impose order and uniformity. (See map, page 36.)

Egypt United

While Sumerian culture centered around its city-states, the organization of the Nile Valley remained one of small farming villages. Early in the history of the valley these villages waged constant warfare, which meant that most of their attention was given to defense.

About 2900 B.C. there appeared a leader strong enough to subdue the other villages and unite the settlements of the Upper and Lower Nile Valley. "Lower" refers to the Delta region. Egyptian legend calls this leader Menes (MEE-neez) and tells of his building a capital at Memphis in the Delta. He took the title **pharaoh** (FAIR-oh), meaning "great or royal house." Menes's reign began Egypt's first period of greatness. During the next 400 years while the First and Second Dynasties ruled, Egypt enjoyed a period of tranquillity. Peace continued during the next 500 years, known as the Old Kingdom. During this time art and learning flourished, massive pyramids were built, and a strong government ruled through a trained **bureaucracy.**

The Pharaoh

Just as religion had been a dominant force in the lives of the people of Mesopotamia, so was it central to the Egyptians. Like the Mesopotamians, the Egyptians practiced **polytheism** in which their many gods and goddesses represented the forces of nature. The sun, symbolized by a disk with hawk's wings, was a central object of worship. The hawk represented the god Horus, the son of the king who ruled the region of the dead. The pharaoh was considered to be the incarnation of Horus. According to later belief, the pharaoh was descended from Amon-Re, king of the gods and goddesses and himself god of sun and air.

Egypt was ruled by a series of **dynasties**. Pharaohs usually married within their families because they believed that if gods and goddesses married humans, their children would be human and not divine. During the period of the New Kingdom (1580–1090 B.C.), women as well as men ruled. Hatshepsut (hat-SHEP-soot), whom you will read about later, ruled in the 1400's B.C. and was the first great woman ruler of history.

The pharaoh was the sole proprietor of the land and all the wealth that came from it. In order to rule, the pharaoh needed a large staff to oversee planting and harvesting and to collect taxes. The pharaoh appointed officials from each locality, called monarchs, to supervise agriculture and tax collection. Other officials in the central government kept the pharaoh's accounts, handed out justice, and supervised the affairs of the royal court. Even merchants were considered semi-officials because trade was a **monopoly** of the pharaoh.

The Middle Kingdom

For centuries after the reign of Menes, Egyptian pharaohs were strong, vigorous rulers who personally supervised the complex government, required strict loyalty, and put down any threat to

(Continued on page 42.)

The Hall of Double Right and Truth

Although the ancient Egyptians believed in a life after death, they did not consider it easy to achieve. The spirits of the dead were believed to face many tests before they were welcomed into the company of the immortals. The most important of these tests took place in the presence of the deities, seated in the Hall of Double Right and Truth. Here the heart, or conscience, of the dead person was weighed against a feather, the symbol of truth and righteousness. If the balance were to tilt in his or her favor, the deceased had to recite, truthfully, the following confession:

> Verily I have come unto thee, and I bring before thee Right and Truth. For thy sake I have rejected wickedness. I have done no hurt unto [a person], nor have I wrought harm unto beasts. I have committed no crime in the place of Right and Truth. I have had no knowledge of evil; nor have I acted wickedly. Each day have I labored more than was required of me. . . . I have not despised God. I have not caused misery; nor have I worked affliction. I have done not that which God doth abominate. I have caused no wrong to be done to the servant by his master. I have caused none to feel pain. I have made [no one] to weep. I have not committed murder; nor have I ever bidden any [one] to slay on my behalf. I have not wronged the people. . . . I have not stolen from the orchards; nor have I trampled down the fields. I have not added to the weight of the balance; nor have I made light the weight in the scales. . . . I have not driven the cattle from their pastures. . . . I have not turned back water at its springtide. I have not broken the channel of running water. . . . I have not disregarded the seasons for the offerings which are appointed; I have not turned away the cattle set apart for sacrifice. . . . I am pure. I am pure. I am pure. I am pure.
>
> [From The Egyptian Book of the Dead, translated and introduced by E. A. Wallis Budge.]

ARTIFACTS OF EGYPT. Above is part of a wall painting showing farming in ancient Egypt. Found in the tomb of the scribe Menna, this detail depicts officials recording the amount of grain harvested. Below is a detail from a papyrus of *The Book of the Dead*, quoted on page 40. The heart of a dead person is being weighed by the dog-headed god Anubis.

their absolute power. But when weaker pharaohs began to succeed each other on the Egyptian throne, wealthy nobles, who had accumulated large estates by serving the pharaoh, grew powerful enough to challenge the royal family.

Finally civil war broke out with noble family fighting noble family and the central government at the mercy of the warring factions. Only after more than a century of disorder and chaos was Egypt reunited, this time under the leadership of the city of Thebes (THEEBZ). The new pharaoh established the capital of the Middle Kingdom about 2100 B.C. Its life was to prove brief. Powerful families again troubled the peace of the country, and, worse, invasion followed civil war.

Around 1800 B.C. the Hyksos (HIK-sohs), a Semitic people from the region of Syria and Lebanon, invaded Egypt with war chariots and weapons superior to anything possessed by the Egyptians. The land of the Nile passed into the hands of foreigners for 150 years.

The New Kingdom

Once again Thebes came to the rescue of Egypt. Another powerful leader, Ahmose I (AH-mohs-suh), appeared who drove out the foreign rulers while adopting their techniques of warfare. In a brilliant period of conquest in the 1400's B.C., Thutmose II (thoot-MOH-suh) sent his troops into Syria and Palestine to carve out an empire that he added to his Egyptian kingdom. Egyptian power spread southward too as Egypt extended its economic and cultural dominance into Africa. This period is known as the New Kingdom.

After Thutmose's death, his wife Hatshepsut seized power. During her 20-year rule she sent trading expeditions to other lands and increased Egypt's power through influence rather than military conquest. Her son Thutmose III expanded Egypt's control through conquests along the Euphrates.

In the 1300's B.C. Amenhotep IV, known also as Akhenaton (ah-kuh-NAH-tuhn) ruled. He is famous in history as a religious thinker who first introduced the concept of monotheism into Egyptian religion. His subjects, but especially the powerful priest class, resisted the idea of one god and Akhenaton's attempt to change the basis of their religion—and power. After his death, the nine-year-old Tutankhamen (too-tangh-KAH-muhn) came to the throne, and the priests restored the old nature worship.

Although the period of empire-building was marked by great luxury at the court at Thebes and among the upper class, the events of the preceding centuries had their ill effects on Egyptian culture. Life for the farmer and small craftsworker grew more rigid and oppressive. The demands for taxes and forced labor became increasingly great. The old sense of confidence and security had faded with the invasion of the Hyksos. The Egyptian empire, like one of its pyramids, endured for centuries more, but added little to the growth of its civilization.

Rameses II (RAM-uh-seez) who ruled from 1292 to 1225 B.C. tried to restore Egypt's empire in Asia and built great temples and palaces in the Delta region, but the days of Egypt's true glory were past. Around 925 B.C. the Libyans, a western desert people, seized the throne and ruled for about 200 years. There followed a period of internal strife and invasions by Nubians, Assyrians, and Persians. In 525 B.C. Persia conquered and ruled Egypt for 80 years. The Egyptians regained control but lost it to the armies of Alexander the Great in 332 B.C., ending native Egyptian rule.

Advances in Learning

The elaborate bureaucracy of the pharaohs required well-trained officials, and temples needed priests to perform religious ceremonies and carry out the many activities related to religion in Egypt. In temple schools young men were taught numbers and writing to prepare them for the priesthood or for the bureaucracy. Important among the latter were the scribes, who were trained to keep records.

Egyptians wrote using hieroglyphics (heye-ruh-GLIF-iks), a form of writing that uses pictures for objects and ideas. In the Egyptian system, each symbol came to stand for a sound composed of consonant and vowel. In time, some 24 such symbols were combined in a kind of alphabet. Rather than inscribing these characters on clay tablets as the Sumerians had, the Egyptians used sheets and rolls of papyrus (puh-PEYE-ruhs). This paper was made from tall reeds that grew along the Nile.

It was not until the 1800's that Egyptian hieroglyphics were understood. French soldiers with Napoleon in Egypt in 1799 discovered a stone with three inscriptions—Greek, hieroglyphics, and a later form of Egyptian. By comparing the three inscriptions, a French scholar unlocked the Rosetta Stone's message and with it much of ancient Egypt's history.

The murals on the Egyptian pyramids from the Old Kingdom and from later temples also tell us much about Egyptian life. From these and the papyrus manuscripts, we know that Egypt had a large bureaucracy with the pharaoh at the top followed by priests, nobles, and government officials. Next came scribes, merchants, craftsworkers, farmers, and, at the bottom, slaves.

During the Old Kingdom period, Egyptians entombed their pharaohs in massive stone pyramids. Except for passageways and chambers in the center for the mummified body of the pharaohs and their companions, the pyramids were sheer stone. Besides being buried with servants to take care of them in the afterlife, the pharaohs were buried with such goods as they might need—food, jewelry, and clothing. One of the pyramids at Giza near Cairo containing over two million blocks of stone is the largest ever built. During later periods Egyptians built stone temples to their pharaohs and also sphinxes, half-lion and half-human creatures symbolizing their strength.

In order to build these massive monuments, the Egyptians had to master certain engineering principles. They were the first, for example, to use columns and pillars as roof supports. The ancient Egyptians also devised a calendar of 365 days, developed a system of weights and measures, and discovered various principles of geometry.

Check Your Understanding

1. How did the Nile River help the development of Egyptian civilization?
2. Describe the role of the pharaoh.
3. Identify the importance of each of the following:
   a. Menes. **b.** the Hyksos. **c.** Thutmose II.
   d. Hatshepsut. **e.** Akhenaton.
4. What ended native rule in Egypt?
5. *Thinking Critically:* What internal problems can you trace through each period in Egyptian history that so weakened it that foreign forces could conquer Egypt?

3. The Rise of Other Middle Eastern States

For centuries, outsiders, attracted by the abundant harvests and wealthy towns, had periodically invaded the Tigris–Euphrates Valley to plunder and raid. The civilization of Mesopotamia, however, was never completely destroyed by these pillagers, who often carried home with them certain elements of the older cultures, particularly language and writing. About 2000 B.C. invaders from as far away as the steppes of eastern Europe began to penetrate the area.

The Hittites

The Hittites were a people from the north and east who had settled in Asia Minor between the Black and Mediterranean seas in what is present-day Turkey. (See map, page 36.) They raised horses and used them to draw war chariots. They also discovered the secret of smelting iron ore to produce a metal that was harder than bronze. Other peoples in the Middle East were still using bronze to make weapons, so that in battle the Hittites' iron weapons proved far superior and deadly.

For many centuries the Hittites lived on the fringes of Mesopotamia borrowing writing and learning from these more highly developed states. But with the discovery of iron, they were ready to move. About 1900 B.C. they rode across Asia Minor, challenged Egypt in Syria and Palestine, and conquered the central part of the Fertile Crescent. The Hittites held their conquests only a few centuries. However, through **cultural diffusion**, they spread Mesopotamian culture northward into Asia Minor.

Smaller Kingdoms

Syria, Lebanon, and Palestine had been settled for the most part by wandering Semitic peoples from the Arabian Desert. They formed small farming or herding communities and were not part of the great civilizations to the south and west. The trade of the Sumerians, the conquests of the Egyptians, and the invasions of the Hittites, however, opened up a wider world to these peoples. Like the Hittites, they borrowed much from the civilization of Mesopotamia to add to a desert culture similar to the Bedouin's, and for a brief period their societies flourished. (See page 36.)

After the fall of the Hittites, the little kingdom of Lydia in northern Asia Minor expanded into an empire. Its significance, however, lies in the fact that Lydians introduced the use of coins around the 6th century B.C. Until this time all trade had been in the form of barter in which people exchanged goods for goods. Coins made trade much easier because people no longer had to search out someone who wanted exactly what they had to barter and in return would give exactly what they wanted. The use of coins soon spread throughout the Mediterranean.

A second significant group were the Arameans who had come from the Arabian Desert about 2000 B.C. to settle in Syria. By the beginning of the 600's B.C., their language, which was closely related to Arabic and Hebrew, had spread through the eastern Mediterranean, including Palestine. The Jews spoke Aramaic in their daily business and used Hebrew for religious purposes. Eventually Aramaic was displaced by Arabic after the Muslim conquests of the A.D. 600's.

The Phoenicians

One of the most important coastal peoples in the Middle East at this time was the Phoenicians (fih-NISH-uhnz). They were a trading people with city-states along the eastern Mediterranean. (See map, page 36.) Building fine ships from the tall cedars of Lebanon, they sailed throughout the Mediterranean Sea. They traded in the Aegean region, Malta, Sicily, and Sardinia, and even ventured past Gibraltar to England, where they exchanged their products for tin. A few great cities carried on most of Phoenicia's trade. Tyre, Sidon (SEYE-duhn), and Byblos imported raw materials from other countries and turned them into finished products for resale in distant ports. The most famous Phoenician product was a purple cloth, which was valued by rulers in the Middle East and the Mediterranean. The Phoenicians also made fine weapons, jewelry of gold and silver, and excellent glassware.

Like any people who depend on trade, the Phoenicians needed means of keeping accounts and communicating with their merchants abroad. They, too, devised a method of writing, probably based on Egyptian hieroglyphics. It eventually contained 22 symbols representing the sounds of consonants or consonants combined with vowels. Some of the Phoenician signs were used by the Greeks in creating the first phonetic alphabet, forerunner of the one we use today.

The Phoenicians were colonizers as well as traders. One of their colonies is today the Spanish city of Cadiz (KAH-deeth). Another was Carthage, near the present-day city of Tunis on the North African coast. After Phoenicia had fallen to invaders and its major cities had come under the control of one or another foreign power, Carthage became the great naval and commercial power of the Mediterranean region. Eventually Carthage was challenged by the rising Roman Republic. Following the third fierce war between these two powers, in 146 B.C., the Romans destroyed the city and forced its citizens to accept humiliating conditions of peace.

EARLY JEWISH SITES. This crudely scratched version of the "Star of David," below, symbol of the modern Jewish state, was found at the site of ancient Megiddo. Pictured at left is a sanctuary believed to have existed in the 9th century B.C., part of royal buildings in Arad.

The Kingdoms of Israel and Judah

Compared to the Phoenicians, the Israelites were a poor agrarian people. They lived in the region of Palestine, which lay south of Phoenicia on the coastal plain between the Mediterranean and the Jordan River. (See map, page 36.) For many centuries Palestine was under the rule of Egypt. During this period some Israelites migrated to Egypt where, after several generations, they were made slaves of the pharaoh. About 1200 B.C. during the rule of Rameses II, they rebelled against their harsh masters and escaped from bondage under the leadership of Moses, an Israelite who had been an official of the pharaoh's government. The departure from Egypt is described in the Book of Exodus in the Bible and is commemorated each year by the Jewish feast of the Passover. It is called Passover because the Angel of Death passed over the homes of the departing Hebrews, sparing their sons but killing the firstborn son of every Egyptian household.

According to the Bible, the Israelites wandered in the desert of what is now the Sinai Peninsula for 40 years before reaching the Promised Land. This is roughly the area of the modern state of Israel. During their wanderings in the desert, God gave Moses

47

the Ten Commandments, the basis for Judaeo-Christian moral teachings and the foundation of Jewish law.

When the Hebrews reached the Promised Land, they found it inhabited by other Semitic groups including the Canaanites (KAY-nuh-nytes) and the Philistines (fih-LIS-teenz) with whom the Hebrews fought for many years. At first the twelve Hebrew tribes, led by a group of wise men known as Judges, were loosely joined in a confederation. About 1000 B.C. they chose a king, Saul, and became the Kingdom of Israel.

The new Kingdom of Israel was able to subdue its enemies and to expand its frontiers beyond Palestine. David, Israel's second king, made Jerusalem Israel's capital. Under his son, Solomon, the kingdom reached the height of its glory. It was Solomon who built the first Temple in Jerusalem, thus making the city the spiritual center of Hebrew life.

Solomon's heavy taxes and lavish way of life caused unrest among the Israelites, and after his death the kingdom divided into two parts—Israel in the north and Judah in the south. Constant quarreling and hostility weakened the two kingdoms and made them easy victims for their more powerful neighbors.

In 722 B.C. Israel was conquered by Assyria, and the Hebrews there were exiled across the Middle East. The Kingdom of Israel disappeared, and no one knows what happened to the exiled Israelites, often called the ten lost tribes. In 586 B.C. the Babylonians of the new Babylonian Empire conquered Judah, destroying Solomon's Temple and exiling the Jews. Many were taken to Babylon, beginning a period in Jewish history known as the Babylonian Exile.

In 539 B.C. when Cyrus the Great conquered Babylon, he permitted the Jews to return. They soon rebuilt the Temple. Although the Jews were not independent, they were allowed a measure of self-rule under Persian and later Greek, Syrian, and Roman rule. They were able to choose their own religious leaders, to develop their own culture, and to maintain their own social organizations.

In the second century B.C., the Jews revolted against the Seleucid, who ruled this part of Alexander the Great's empire. They were led by members of the Maccabee family who restored the Temple, which had been occupied by non-Jewish priests. The revolt of the Maccabees and the rededication of the Temple is commemorated in the Jewish holy day of Hanukkah (HAHN-uh-kuh).

The period of semi-independence under the Maccabee dynasty ended in 63 B.C. when the Romans intervened. A series of rebellions resulted. In 70 B.C. Rome crushed one of the more violent ones by exiling the Jews again and destroying the Temple. For a short period, resistance continued under Bar Kochba. The last stronghold of the Jews against the Romans was the Judean desert fort of Masada. When the Roman army captured it in A.D. 73, the remaining Jews—men, women, and children—killed themselves rather than be taken by the Romans.

The final revolt occurred in A.D. 135. As punishment, the Romans once again expelled most of the Jews in what is known as the **Diaspora** (deye-AS-puh-ruh). Unlike earlier times, it would be 1,800 years before the Jews could return.

Jewish Contribution to Religious Thought

Although their nation was short-lived, the Israelites made important contributions to human thought, mainly in the sphere of religious and moral teaching. They were among the first people to adopt monotheism. Like other Semitic-speaking tribes, the Israelites had at first worshiped many gods. Sometime before they settled in Palestine, they had come to worship a single deity, **Yahweh** (YAH-weh) or Jehovah. Although they believed that other gods existed, the Israelites were convinced that they were the special people of Jehovah and that He was the only God of Israel. When the Babylonians brought an end to the kingdom of Judah in 586 B.C., Israelite belief in one god was transformed by their prophets, or holy men, into belief in one God who ruled the entire universe. The prophets taught that the people of Israel were being punished by exile for having sinned against Him.

Check Your Understanding

1. Why are the Hittites important in the history of the Middle East?
2. What major contribution did the Lydians make to civilization?
3. What was the basis of the Phoenician economy?
4. How did the religious beliefs of the Israelites differ from those of the Egyptians?
5. *Thinking Critically:* Cultural diffusion is the process by which traits or characteristics of one culture are spread through contact with another. What examples of this process can you find in this section?

4. Later Empires

The peoples, city-states, kingdoms, and empires of the Middle East jostled with one another for territory, power, and wealth for centuries. One kingdom rose while another fell into decline. One group invaded another and took away with it not only wealth but learning. However, these empires were never forced to come to terms with a totally different but equally well-defined civilization until the 300's B.C. Then for a thousand years, beginning with the conquests of the Macedonian leader Alexander the Great, the Middle East came under the influence of the Mediterranean civilizations of Greece and Rome.

Assyrian Conquerors

The Assyrian people from the upper Tigris area were one of several societies on the borders of the Mesopotamian world. When the Hittites began their drive into the Middle East, the Assyrians acted as a **buffer state**. Hard-pressed by both Hittites and Egyptians, the Assyrians built a well-trained army equipped with war chariots and iron weapons. Armed with these, they in turn after 900 B.C. began a period of invasion and pillage. Egypt, Syria, Israel, and Mesopotamia fell before the Assyrian army, and even cities as strong as Tyre and Sidon paid **tribute** to protect their trade routes.

At first the goal of the Assyrians was to plunder the conquered states and to use this wealth in building the magnificent city of Nineveh (NIN-uh-vuh). Eventually they tried to rule the captive states, sending governors to oversee the provinces and troops to put down revolts. Roads were built to speed messengers and armies throughout the empire.

The cruelty of the Assyrians led to a long series of revolts. Time after time cities rose against them until at last the allied forces of the Chaldeans (kal-DEE-unz) and the Medes, a people from northwestern Persia, were strong enough to overthrow an empire already weakened by years of almost constant warfare.

The New Babylonian Empire

The most famous ruler of the new Babylonian, or Chaldean, Empire was Nebuchadnezzar II (neb-yoo-kud-NEZ-er), who ruled from 605 to 561. He brought the coastal cities into submission, invaded Judah, and destroyed Jerusalem. In Babylon Nebuchadnezzar gathered around him scholars from all over the Middle East and maintained a library filled with Sumerian treasures. Perhaps the new Babylonian Empire's most original contribution

ANCIENT PERSIAN ARTIFACTS. The gold coin (left) with an archer on its face was issued by Darius I of Persia. The symbol of the Persian god Ahura Mazda (right), the god of goodness, decorates a doorway to the Tripylon at Persepolis, ancient capital of Persia.

to learning was in the field of astronomy. Believing that the stars and planets that ruled human fate were divine powers, Chaldean scholars charted the relationship of the planets and predicted eclipses of the sun by studying the heavens.

Persian System of Governing

Like other Middle Eastern empires before it, the new Babylonian Empire was short-lived. In less than a century it had fallen to an enemy from the east, the Persians, whose homeland lay east of the Arabian Peninsula and south of the Caspian Sea. During years of fighting off invading Assyrian armies, the Persians had adopted their enemy's military techniques and weapons. What they lacked was unity and leadership. They found their leader in Cyrus (SEYE-rus). Advancing through Lydia and Babylonia, Cyrus conquered Asia Minor and Mesopotamia, then turned west to Egypt, which was finally taken by his son, Cambyses (kem-BY-seez). In the east other Persian armies seized parts of India. By 500 B.C. the Persian empire encompassed well over two million square miles and stretched from the Mediterranean to the Indus River, from the Caucasus Mountains to the Indian Ocean.

To rule this far-flung empire, the conquerors needed skillful administrators. Darius (duh-RY-uhs), one of the successors of Cyrus, divided the empire into 20 **satrapies** (SAY-truh-peez), or provinces, each ruled by a governor to collect taxes and a general to keep order. The Persians built a vast network of roads, established a postal service, and introduced one system of coinage for the whole empire. In Egypt they built a canal linking the Nile with the Red Sea. All these innovations helped to tie together peoples of different beliefs and customs. At the same time, part of the success of the Persians was due to their policy of allowing conquered peoples a measure of self-government, and permitting them to worship their own deities and follow their own customs. As long as they paid taxes to the central government and recognized the Persian emperor as their supreme ruler, the provinces enjoyed a large degree of freedom.

The Persians, in turn, learned much from the people they conquered. From Mesopotamia, Egypt, and Asia Minor they borrowed cuneiform writing, architectural styles, and scientific knowledge. In religious matters the Persians followed their own teacher Zoroaster (zawr-oh-AS-tuhr), who taught that there was one supreme being, Ahura-Mazda (AH-hoo-ruh-MAZ-duh), creator of all life and the god of light and truth.

Despite superior organization, the Persian Empire grew weak. Officials became corrupt, and the empire was ripe for defeat when it was invaded by a new enemy from the West—the Greeks.

Greek Conquests and Hellenism

During the 400's B.C. the Persian Empire and the Greek city-states had gone to war many times over the Greek colonies in Asia Minor. Final defeat for the Persians came at the hands of Alexander the Great, the son of the Macedonian king who had conquered and united the Greek city-states in 338 B.C. Not content with freeing the Greek cities in Asia Minor, Alexander swept down through Syria, Palestine, and Egypt, retraced his steps through the Middle East, and pushed eastward as far as India.

. Alexander had begun his conquests at 21. On his death at 32 the enormous territory his armies had conquered was divided among his generals into three kingdoms. Ptolemy (TAHL-uh-mee) began a dynasty in Egypt and the Seleucids (sih-LOO-sidz) ruled Syria and much of Asia Minor.

The culture, learning, and experiences of the Greek city-states were brought to the Middle East by Greek soldiers and promoted by the policies of Alexander. The conqueror wanted a Mediterranean world united in an ideal community. To achieve his aim, he planted groups of Greek soldiers, government officials, merchants, and craftsworkers in cities throughout his empire. Of course, they also increased the wealth of Greece.

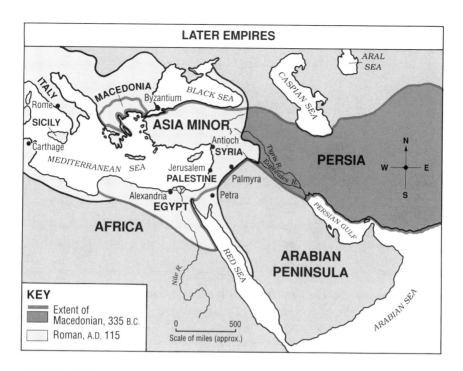

LATER EMPIRES

ARAL SEA

ITALY
Rome
SICILY
Carthage
MACEDONIA
Byzantium
BLACK SEA
CASPIAN SEA
ASIA MINOR
MEDITERRANEAN SEA
Antioch
SYRIA
Jerusalem
PALESTINE
Palmyra
Alexandria
Petra
EGYPT
AFRICA
Nile R.
RED SEA
Tigris R.
Euphrates R.
PERSIA
PERSIAN GULF
ARABIAN PENINSULA
ARABIAN SEA

N
W E
S

KEY
Extent of
Macedonian, 335 B.C.
Roman, A.D. 115

0   500
Scale of miles (approx.)

MOVEMENT: LATER EMPIRES. Led by Alexander the Great, the Greeks of Macedonia marched east and took over the whole Persian Empire. Alexander's new empire broke up when he died, but Syria and Egypt remained under the rule of Greek dynasties until they became part of the Roman Empire. Below, a mosaic from a house in Pompeii, Italy (first century A.D.), shows Alexander galloping toward Darius I of Persia, whom he routed on the Plain of Issus in Asia Minor in 333 B.C.

This coin shows Alexander the Great with the "horn of Ammon" in his hair. Ammon, or Amen, was the ram-headed deity the Greeks identified with Jupiter, their "ruler of the gods."

This policy was continued by his successors. Some of the most distinguished cities of the Middle East were the result—Antioch (AN-tih-ahk), founded in Syria by Seleucus I, and Alexandria in Egypt. Under Ptolemy, Alexandria grew into one of the most brilliant cultural and commercial centers of the ancient world.

This process of spreading Greek culture and blending it with native cultures is called **Hellenism**. As a result of this process, Greek became the language of government and learning throughout the Middle East. Greek ideas and learning spread throughout the Mediterranean. Greek culture also gained as the learning of the Middle East was transmitted to Europe. For example, Euclid working in Alexandria used earlier Greek and Middle Eastern learning to develop the basic principles of geometry. For the most part Hellenism was a product of the urban communities. The country people remained untouched by it and continued to follow their traditional customs, worship their local deities, and speak their native languages. This rural isolation was to be an important factor in the later success of Islam.

The Roman Empire in the Middle East

By the first century B.C. the Seleucid Empire had lost its eastern possessions and had shrunk to a small state in northern Syria. The Roman general Pompey had little trouble conquering it. Syria, Lebanon, and Palestine were governed by a proconsul, or governor, but states outside the immediate vicinity of Antioch were permitted to keep their native rulers as long as they paid allegiance to Rome. By 30 B.C. Egypt, too, had become part of the Roman Empire.

The peace resulting from Roman rule strengthened the unity and Hellenization that had begun with Alexander's conquests. Rome provided good roads, common law, and the protection of its legions. These factors stimulated commerce and travel. Cities

Surviving from Roman rule in what is now Lebanon, the ruins of the Temple of Jupiter overlook the village of Baalbek. Once identified with the worship of the sun-god Baal and called Heliopolis, "City of the Sun," by the Greeks, the area was torn by conflict between Syrian troops and Lebanese militia in the 1980's.

like Antioch and Jerusalem became more and more important as centers of Hellenistic culture. Others, like the caravan cities of Petra, in what is modern Jordan, and Palmyra in Syria, grew into important centers of international trade.

Today there are many remains of the Roman Empire in the Middle East. They include temples, amphitheaters, and aqueducts. Many Roman concepts of law and government, including the practice of permitting conquered peoples to maintain their own cultures and social organizations, were followed by later empires. This approach allowed both the Romans and their successors to rule diverse peoples and cultures effectively.

The unity of the Roman Empire was important for the growth of one of the world's great religions, Christianity. Christianity had its origin in Palestine and was at first a reform movement within the Jewish community. It made converts, however, outside Palestine. The most important of the new believers was Paul, a Hellenized Jew from Asia Minor, who turned Christianity into an international religion through his widespread missionary work. As it became an organized faith with a body of doctrine, it absorbed many of the ideas current in the Hellenistic world, particularly those of the philosopher Plato, who taught that the way to the highest good was through love. Despite severe persecution by the Roman emperors, Christianity spread throughout the empire, penetrating Asia Minor, Syria, and North Africa.

Byzantium

Despite its wealth and strength, the Roman Empire was not invincible. By A.D. 200 Visigoths, Huns, Vandals, and other German peoples had begun to threaten the northern borders of the empire. More and more of Rome's resources were drained off for military defense, and the army, as the strongest body in the state, made and broke its emperors at will.

Diocletian (deye-uh-KLEE-shun), who ruled from 284 to 305, and Constantine who ruled from 324 to 337, halted the inroads and restored stable government for a brief period. Diocletian divided the empire into western and eastern halves, and Constantine actually moved the capital from Rome to Constantinople, the new city he was building on the Bosporus. This change marked an important shift in the center of power. The eastern half of the empire had always been the wealthier, both in trade and in agriculture. It was also the area least threatened by invasion. When the Western Roman Empire fell in 476, the eastern provinces of Asia Minor, Syria, and Egypt were left to prosper as the Eastern Roman, or Byzantine, Empire.

Check Your Understanding

1. How did the Assyrians and the Persians differ in their method of governing conquered peoples?
2. How was Greek culture spread throughout the Middle East?
3. What policies did the Roman Empire follow in order to unify the peoples it conquered?
4. Why was the Byzantine Empire able to endure long after the fall of the Roman Empire in the West?
5. *Thinking Critically:* Why do you think that the Persians were more successful in holding their empire together than the Assyrians were? What do you think the Romans might have learned from the Persians?

CHAPTER REVIEW

■ Chapter Summary

Section 1. About 6,500 years ago, the first agricultural settlements developed in the Middle East. People moved from hunting and gathering to settled agriculture. With this shift came increased population, government, social organizations, and the specialization of labor that resulted in the growth of arts and crafts and trade. The civilizations that emerged in the Tigris–Euphrates Valley in ancient Mesopotamia are the first examples of these developments.

From simple village life, urban city-states evolved, populated by Semitic-speaking peoples who established complex religious and political systems and devised the cuneiform writing system. Strife among these Sumerian city-states led to the rise of the Akkadian and Babylonian empires, which conquered large parts of the Middle East. One of the great leaders of the Babylonians, Hammurabi, introduced a legal code that unified the legal systems of the region.

Section 2. Egypt also developed an ancient civilization, based in the Nile Valley and Delta regions. A series of dynasties founded by pharaohs, who were considered to be divine, ruled over the area for almost 3,000 years. The Egyptians mastered many engineering techniques, as evidenced by their massive pyramids and temples, developed a system of hieroglyphics for writing, and devised a calendar of 365 days.

Section 3. Other states rose and fell in the Middle East during this period. The Hittites brought their war chariots and iron weapons against Egypt and Mesopotamia. The Phoenicians built a trading empire that spread throughout the Mediterranean world. The history of the Hebrews is wrapped up with the major empires that swept across the Middle East. From prisoners of the Egyptians to subjects of Rome, the Hebrews developed a religion that is today one of the world's major religions.

Section 4. The small, independent states were followed by a succession of empires—the Assyrian, the Persian, the Greek, and the Roman. Of these empires, the Greeks contributed the process of Hellenization to the region. Perhaps the Romans who defeated the Greeks contributed the most. The unity that was imposed by the Roman Empire led to an exchange of ideas and cultures that made the Mediterranean a single region—the Roman lake. Rome's heritage was passed on to the Byzantine Empire, which ruled part of the Middle East until the rise of Islam.

■ Vocabulary Review

Define: economy, cuneiform, empire, pharaoh, bureaucracy, polytheism, dynasty, monopoly, cultural diffusion, Diaspora, Yahweh, buffer state, tribute, satrapy, Hellenism

■ Places to Locate

Locate: Mesopotamia, Sumeria, Akkad, Babylon, Memphis, Thebes, Palestine, Alexandria, Macedonia, Byzantium

■ People to Know

Identify: Hammurabi, Hatshepsut, Thutmose III, Akhenaton, Moses, the Maccabees, Cyrus, Darius, Alexander the Great

■ Thinking Critically

1. Why did people in early civilizations develop religions based on nature?
2. Often less-advanced societies adopt the innovations of more developed civilizations, even where the less advanced peoples come as conquerors. What examples of this do you find among the ancient civilizations of the Middle East? What kinds of things were most often and most completely adopted? Why, do you think, was this so?
3. Why did cities become increasingly important over time in the Middle East?

■ Extending and Applying Your Knowledge

1. Research and write a brief report on archaeological findings in the Middle East in the last 20 years. Choose an area such as Israel or Egypt and determine who conducted the dig, where, what was found, and the significance of the find.
2. Imagine you are a Phoenician merchant planning a trading voyage to Britain. Do research to determine your route. List what your ports-of-call would be, what you would pick up at each, what sorts of ships would carry your cargo, and what the dangers might be that you would face.

3. The prophet Jeremiah prophesied and was present at the fall of Jerusalem to the Babylonians. Read the "Book of Jeremiah" and the "Lamentations of Jeremiah" for his version of events. Use this information along with histories to prepare and deliver an oral or written report on the fall of Jerusalem.

3

The Rise of Islam

At the time of Islam's rise, the Middle East was a battleground between two opposing empires. The Christian Byzantine (BIZ-uhn-teen) Empire had holdings that stretched eastward along the North African coast, northward along the lands bordering the Eastern Mediterranean coast and into Asia Minor, and westward into the Balkan Peninsula. The Sassanian Empire of the Persians reached from the borders of Byzantium (bih-ZAN-shum) to India.

Weakened by constant warfare, both empires suffered from depleted treasuries and a lack of loyalty among their subjects. Neither controlled the Arabian Peninsula, a vast desert inhabited by herders and their flocks. Merchants, however, flourished in cities and towns along the peninsula's southern coast and in oasis communities throughout the peninsula.

The merchants had developed a wealthy trade with India and China in ivory, silk, spices, and gold. The merchants then carried these goods by caravan to the great cities of Mesopotamia and the Mediterranean world. One of the caravan routes paralleled the coastline of the Red Sea. Situated along this route was Mecca, an ancient town taken over by the Quraysh (kuh-RYSH), an Arab merchant tribe.

Every year hundreds of Arabs visited Mecca to worship at the Kaaba (KAY-uh-buh), a holy place. Mohammed, the founder of Islam, was born in or around Mecca, about A.D. 570.

1. The Founding of Islam

Islam is one of the world's largest religions. In Arabic, *Islam* means "submission." People who follow Islam are called Muslims. They submit their will to God, who in Arabic is called Allah. After its founding by Mohammed, sometime about 610, Islam became a dynamic spiritual and political force that swept across the Arabian Peninsula, westward into North Africa, and eastward toward Mesopotamia, Persia, and India.

Mohammed's Early Life

Mohammed came from a trading family related to the rulers of Mecca, the Quraysh. His father died before he was born, and he was raised by his grandfather. The deprivations of his early life seemed to have made Mohammed especially sensitive to the needs of the poor and the helpless. When Mohammed was about 25, he married a wealthy Meccan widow and managed her business affairs so astutely that he soon won high esteem in his hometown. But despite his success, Mohammed often withdrew from the city to meditate in the surrounding hills, a practice that was often followed by other Arabs.

One night, probably around 610, Mohammed fell asleep in a cave near the city when, according to his biographer, an angel suddenly appeared carrying a woven scroll on which there was writing. "Read!" the angel ordered. "What shall I read?" asked Mohammed, who is thought to have been illiterate. But again the angel commanded: "Read!"

> Read in the name of your Lord who created,
> Who created man from a clot of blood.
> Read! Your Lord is the most beneficent,
> Who teaches by the Pen,
> Teaches man that which he knows not.
>
> [*The Koran*, Sura xcvi. Note that the Koran uses masculine terms when referring to all of humanity.]

Mohammed awoke. Looking up he saw the figure of a man standing astride the horizon who said: "O Mohammed, you are the apostle of God and I am the Archangel Gabriel."

Mohammed remained filled with doubt. After a time, the angel reappeared, giving him more messages from God and ordering him to begin his work. These messages were later collected, forming the Koran (kuh-RAN), or "Recitations," Islam's holy book.

Islamic Expansion

A.D.

570	Mohammed's birth.
622	Hegira.
630	Mohammed's return to Mecca.
632–661	Arab conquest of the Middle East.
632	Mohammed's death.
661–750	Umayyad dynasty.
711–715	Arab conquest of Spain.
750	Rise of the Abbasid dynasty.

Mohammed as Messenger and Prophet

Mohammed never claimed to be the founder of a new religion, only a messenger of the one true God. Mohammed thought that over the centuries God's original message had been distorted by both Jews and Christians. He saw his role as restoring the faith that God had revealed to Abraham, Moses, and Jesus.

Mohammed preached that Allah was the sole eternal power of the universe. This message was contrary to the traditional Arab belief in polytheism. Mohammed also taught that Muslims were all equal before God and that all should share their wealth with the poor. Because Judgment Day would come for all, death was only the start of a new existence—a glorious life for those who accepted God and Mohammed as God's messenger, and eternal damnation for those who rejected God and Mohammed's message.

Mohammed's preaching contained many themes found in Judaism and Christianity. A number of stories in the Koran are similar to stories in the Bible. The Koran mentions Adam, Noah, Abraham, David, Solomon, and Job from the Old Testament and John the Baptist, Mary, Joseph, and Jesus from the New Testament. As a result of his revelations, Mohammed charged that Christians had perverted the pure faith of Abraham by transforming Jesus from his role as the greatest prophet of God's message into a god. Mohammed considered himself the last in a line of great prophets. For that reason he is referred to as the "seal of the prophets."

MUSLIM ART. Turkish artists of the 16th century did these paintings for a book called *The Progress of the Prophet.* According to Muslim custom, the artists veiled Mohammed and surrounded him with a halo-like flame. This picture shows the Angel Gabriel appearing to the Prophet.

Animosity toward Mohammed in Mecca became so intense that one day some residents stoned him. Abu Bakr wept and pleaded with them to desist. Finally, emissaries from Medina invited Mohammed and his followers to move to their city, some 200 miles away.

When Mohammed was 63, the Angel of Death appeared and offered him two choices. He could either live on earth forever or join Allah in Paradise. Despite the sorrow of his people, the Prophet chose to go to God. Before his departure he distributed his goods to the poor.

Establishing a Community of Believers

At first Mohammed revealed his mission only to a handful of close friends. In 613 he began to preach openly in Mecca. Members of the Quraysh scorned him. His disciples were abused and persecuted by the townspeople, who feared the thrust of Mohammed's message. They thought it threatened their livelihood. If too many people began to believe in one god, they thought the Kaaba would lose its attraction for believers. Life grew so difficult that some of Mohammed's followers fled Mecca with his blessing. Mohammed, however, remained. His family protected him from attack until the death of the family patriarch in 619. Then life became too dangerous for Mohammed.

In 622 Mohammed left for Yathrib, a city about 280 miles northeast of Mecca. For some time the city had been torn apart by feuding Arab factions. Trying to restore peace, the people of the city turned to Mohammed and asked him to mediate between the rival factions.

Mohammed's departure from Mecca is called the **hegira** (hih-JY-ruh), and it marks the beginning of the Islamic era. Before coming to Yathrib Mohammed had been a religious man preaching a religious message. But in Yathrib (which changed its name to Medina al nabi, meaning "city of the prophet") he became a powerful political leader, the governor of an Arab community. This change is reflected in his later revelations, which focus on political and social questions as well as religious matters.

After the move to Medina, the customarily shortened form of the city's name, Mohammed set new patterns for Muslims to follow. How one pattern came about is preserved in a document that Mohammed wrote for Medina. In it he defined relations between the newcomers and the people of Medina and between all Muslims and the Jews in the city. The document recognized the traditional Arab kinship structure and customs, but it also asserted that all disputes formerly settled by blood feud would now be settled by Mohammed. In this way faith rather than kinship became the bond holding together the community of believers, which Mohammed called the Umma. Just as the sheikh had been the final and absolute authority when kinship was most important, so Mohammed the Prophet now became the final and absolute authority when religion was most important.

Initially Mohammed accepted many Jewish religious practices. On coming to Medina, he had hoped that the Jews of the city would offer him a warm reception and accept him as one of their prophets. But the Jews received him coolly and con-

SIDELIGHT TO HISTORY

The Kaaba

The Kaaba is Islam's holiest sanctuary. This small structure is built in the shape of a cube. Many legends surround the Black Stone and the Kaaba.

According to one Muslim legend, when Adam challenged the will of God and was driven from paradise, God placed him on a lofty mountaintop in India. The angels were moved by Adam's sorrow and asked God to have mercy on him. Responding to their request, God gave Adam the task of seeking the Divine Throne on earth.

Then Adam began his long search. It took him from India to the Hejaz, a region of the Arabian Peninsula of which Mecca became the chief city. There he found a basin ringed by huge, black mountains. He recognized this as the navel of the earth, the axis of God's throne. In the middle of the basin stood a canopy supported by four emerald columns and roofed with a giant ruby. Under it lay a luminous white stone. Adam made this place God's temple, and when he died, one of his sons buried the stone with him.

Another legend tells a story that is similar to the Biblical story of Abraham and Isaac, his son. In the Biblical story God, testing Abraham's obedience, asked him to sacrifice his son. Obedient to God's will, Abraham began his preparations to sacrifice Isaac. Just as Abraham was about to kill his son, God withdrew his request. But the Muslim legend holds that Abraham was actually sacrificing Ismail, Isaac's stepbrother, and the sacred Black Stone was the sacrificial rock on which Abraham had placed Ismail.

Muslims consider Arabs to be the descendants of Ismail. Muslim legend says that Abraham visited Ismail at the Hejaz where he lived, and while he was there, the two decided to build a temple for God. They were directed to build on the former site of Adam's temple. The temple they built was the Kaaba—the one true House of God.

Every year during the month of Haj, or pilgrimage, about 600,000 Muslims representing every race and nearly 60 countries, come to visit the Kaaba.

spired with the Meccans against him. Stung by their rejection and treachery, Mohammed drove the Jews from Medina and turned over their rich agricultural lands to Muslims. He then modified some of the practices he had adopted from the Jews.

Beginning in 624, Mohammed instructed all Muslims to worship facing Mecca rather than facing Jerusalem. Ramadan (RAM-uh-duhn), the Muslim month of daytime fasting, replaced fasting on the Jewish Day of Atonement.

Expansion

By the end of 627, Mohammed had established Medina as a united community bound together by one religion. Although Medina was mainly an agricultural community, his followers were not farmers. They needed to earn a livelihood. They also felt they had a right to avenge the injustices suffered at the hands of the Meccans. In 624 the Muslims, led by Mohammed, surprised and plundered a rich Meccan caravan. Interpreting their success as a sign of Allah's approval, they adopted militancy as an important means of spreading Islam.

Under the impetus of this new militancy, Muslims fought Meccans back and forth across the desert. Once when the Meccan army was approaching Medina, Mohammed ordered a great ditch to be dug on the less protected sides of the city. After a two weeks' siege the Meccans withdrew, claiming that the trench was a dishonorable means of waging war. The Battle of the Ditch subsequently became celebrated throughout Islam. By 630 Mohammed was strong enough to enter Mecca without opposition and demand that all the idols in the Kaaba be destroyed. Mohammed then demanded that the Kaaba be rededicated to the one true God.

After Mohammed's victory over the Meccans, many more Arabs swore allegiance to Islam. Devotion to the new faith replaced the traditional ties of blood and kinship. Thus the core of Muslim believers developed into a confederation, a kind of political union made up of many independent units. But it was loyalty and allegiance to the Prophet's ideas, not loyalty and allegiance to an organized body of officials, police, or soldiers, that bound together the converts to Islam.

Death of the Prophet

The Prophet lived until his early sixties. His favorite wife Aisha (AH-ee-shah) survived him by many years, playing an important behind-the-scenes role in the struggle for leadership that followed Mohammed's death in 632. Mohammed made no provision for a successor and left his followers uncertain about the choice of a successor. Mohammed's closest friend, Abu Bakr (uh-BOO BAHK-ur), a prominent merchant from Mecca and the father of Aisha, succeeded the Prophet. It was Abu Bakr who announced the Prophet's death to the people of Medina with these words: "Whoever of you worships Mohammed know that Mohammed is dead. But whoever of you worships God know that God is alive and does not die. Mohammed is only a Prophet; there have been prophets before him. . . ."

Check Your Understanding

1. What is Islam?
2. How did Mohammed become the prophet of Islam?
3. What messages and beliefs did Mohammed preach as the last of the great prophets?
4. How did Mohammed go about establishing a united community of believers?
5. *Thinking Critically:* Why does the hegira mark the beginning of the Islamic era?

2. Islam's Basic Beliefs and Duties

The basis of Muslim belief is the Koran and the teachings of Mohammed gathered by his followers after his death. The major part of the Koran is concerned with the nature of the one true God, his powers, and his relationship to men. The duties required of Muslims are the famed "five pillars of Islam," the religious actions that express the individual's recognition of the omnipotence of God.

The Koran

This holy book containing revelations received by Mohammed is to the Muslims what the Torah is to Jews and the Old and New Testaments are to Christians. During the 20 years that Mohammed transmitted messages from God, his followers memorized and spread them by word of mouth. Sometimes they wrote them on parchment or carved them on camel bone. Indeed, the word *Koran* means "lecture" or "recitation." According to legend, Abu Bakr, Mohammed's successor, distressed when many "reciters" of the Koran were killed in battle, ordered that the words of the Prophet be written down lest his teachings be lost. The version of the Koran now used by Muslims throughout the world was compiled from several different texts in the 650's under the direction of the caliph Uthman. The Koran's approximately 78,000 words (almost as long as the New Testament) are divided into 114 suras, or chapters. Because there is uncertainty about the order in which Mohammed received the revelations, the suras are arranged according to length, with the longest ones coming first. The only exception is "The Opening," a seven-line eulogy praising God.

The Koran contains the Prophet's views on God, religion, and other matters pertaining to Arab life during the seventh century. Like the Bible, the Koran contains advice on relationships between parents and children and husband and spouses; on the treatment of slaves, health, diet, business, prayer; and on the routine of daily life.

Muslims believe that the Koran was transmitted to Mohammed in the Arabic language. Because translation of the Koran into other languages was not permitted, Arabic became a common tongue among all literate Muslims, non-Arabs as well as Arabs. Not until President Mustafa Kemal Atatürk (keh-MAHL ah-tah-TURK) of Turkey authorized a translation into modern Turkish during the 1920's was the Koran officially available to Muslims in a language other than Arabic. (See page 147.) The Koran is considered the finest example of Arabic writing. Consequently the Koran is used as a model for the study of Arabic by students in Muslim schools from the Philippines to Nigeria and even by non-Muslims.

The Five Pillars of Islam

Mohammed's concept of one God, merciful and compassionate but fiercely jealous and all powerful, remains the basis of Islam today. To become a Muslim one needs only to stand before another Muslim and make a simple profession of faith: "There is no God but Allah and Mohammed is the messenger of Allah." Acceptance of this fundamental doctrine is the first of the five pillars of Islam.

Prayer is the second pillar of Islam. The pious Muslim must perform ritual prayer five times a day. The first prayer is offered shortly after dawn, followed by four other prayers at noon, in the later afternoon, just after sunset, and following nightfall. The ritual prayer is performed in unison in the **mosque**, but individuals may pray wherever they happen to be at the prescribed times.

Devotion to Muslim prayer is practiced faithfully by Muslims at Sunna Mosque in Babeloved, Algeria, as it is by Muslims everywhere. When a mosque is crowded, latecomers say their prayers outside the mosque.

At the appointed hours, the **muezzin** (moo-EZ-in) climbs the mosque **minaret** and summons the faithful to prayer with the following chant, heard throughout the Muslim world.

> God is most great
> I testify there is no god but Allah
> I testify that Mohammed is the messenger of Allah
> Come to prayer;
> Come to salvation;
> God is most great!
> There is no god but Allah.

Before beginning prayers the worshiper must wash face, hands, and arms up to the elbows, feet up to the ankles, and the head. Because of Islam's early desert heritage, sand may be used when water is not available. Worshipers also remove their shoes and cover their heads before entering the mosque. Throughout the ritual the worshiper repeats the phrase *Allah is great!* many times. The ritual concludes with each worshiper facing first to the right, then to the left, saying "Peace be with you and the Mercy of God."

69

Ritual prayer has played an important role in unifying Muslims all over the world, but the practice of ritual prayer in the mosque traditionally excluded women for centuries. Women were expected to perform ritual prayer but in the privacy of their own homes. Women in most Muslim countries today are segregated from the men when they attend ritual prayer at a mosque. In practice few women attend mosque services.

Almsgiving is the third pillar of Islam. Muslims consider almsgiving a pious act that is recorded in the heavenly book of good deeds. They believe that the giving of a part of their wealth to the poor purifies the rest of their wealth. Originally Mohammed levied a tax (2.5 percent) on the produce and income of Muslims. The Muslims used the tax to finance the expansion of Islam, to assist the needy, to carry out government functions, and to help slaves buy their freedom. Later, when the central authorities were no longer powerful, government ceased to collect the alms in a formal process. For Muslims today the guideline of almsgiving remains, but is less formal than before.

Fasting is the fourth pillar of Islam. From dawn to sunset during Ramadan no food or drink passes the lips of healthy pious Muslims. They also abstain from sexual activity and the use of tobacco. Muslims practice fasting during Ramadan because it was during this month that the Koran was first revealed to Mohammed. He and his followers also achieved their first great victory over the Meccans in this month. In the Muslim calendar, which is based on the cycles of the moon (about $29\frac{1}{2}$ days), Ramadan rotates, sometimes falling in cooler winter weather, sometimes in the hot summer weather.

According to Muslim tradition, Ramadan fasting begins when daylight makes it possible to tell "a white thread from a black one," and continues to sunset. After sunset festive eating and drinking often last throughout the night. At the end of Ramadan there is a joyous feast lasting three days, during which new clothes are worn and special delicacies are served. While the strictness of the Ramadan fast varies from country to country, in Saudi Arabia violators are severely punished.

A pilgrimage to Mecca is the fifth pillar of Islam. At least once in a lifetime able-bodied Muslim men and women are required to visit the holy city. Mohammed adopted this custom and the observances in Mecca and in the hills near the city from ancient Arabian rites. At the Kaaba these acts include kissing the sacred black meteorite that Muslims believe was brought from heaven by Gabriel and received by Abraham. The title of *hajji* (HAJ-ih), or one who has made the pilgrimage, is highly

JOURNEY TO MECCA. As they have for centuries, pious Muslim men and women make the haj, or pilgrimage, to Mecca. Pilgrims circle and kiss the Kaaba (right), sanctuary of the "Black Stone." On the tenth day of the month, the faithful travel to the holy hill of Arafat (below), 25 miles from Mecca, where they hear a lengthy sermon. Halfway between Mecca and Arafat is Mina, where each pilgrim hurls some 70 pebbles at pillars symbolizing the devil, in a rite called "stoning the devil" (below right).

valued in Islam. Hajjis frequently wear some distinctive headgear. Muslims often save throughout their lives to collect enough money to make the arduous journey to Mecca.

Check Your Understanding

1. How does the Koran govern Muslim life?
2. Explain each of the five pillars of Islam.
3. *Thinking Critically:* How have the Koran and the five pillars of Islam helped maintain the unity of the Muslim world?

3. Middle East Conquests

On Mohammed's death, the leadership of the Muslim community passed to Abu Bakr, who received the title of **caliph**. He ruled as caliph for only two years, but he continued the expansion of Islam by solidifying Muslim control of the Arabian Peninsula, making Khalid ibn al-Walid (KAH-lid IB-n al-wuh-LEED) his chief lieutenant. From 634 through 661 a succession of three more caliphs continued the Islamic expansion by moving against the Byzantine and Persian empires, attacking and conquering Syria, Palestine, Egypt, and parts of Persia.

Establishing Muslim Authority

Although Mohammed had converted the nomadic bands of the Hejaz to Islam after the capture of Mecca in 630, he had not succeeded in converting to Islam those bands more distant from the center of Muslim authority. But he had secured political agreements from them. In these agreements the sheikhs recognized the overlordship of Medina and promised not to attack Muslim territory. They also agreed to pay the Muslim religious tax.

When Mohammed died, many of the sheikhs renounced their political agreements with Medina. To re-establish Medinese authority, Abu Bakr turned to Khalid, who then used force to subjugate the entire peninsula.

Between 634 and 642 when Khalid died, the Arabs conquered all of the Middle East. The once-rich cities of the Byzantine and Persian empires—Damascus, Jerusalem, Alexandria, and Herat—were lost as the heavily armored and slow-moving Byzantine and Persian armies proved no match for the Muslim cavalry. (See map, page 73.)

Results of Middle East Expansion

The Koran had made no provision for governing the vast territories the Arabs had won. Without a political system of their own, the Muslims adopted the political systems of the people they had conquered, retaining their officials and institutions. By adopting Byzantine and Persian laws, procedures, coinage, and

MOVEMENT: THE SPREAD OF ISLAM. After Mohammed died in 632, his followers overran Persia and won Syria, Palestine, and Egypt from the Byzantines who halted further northward progress into Europe. The Arabs then swept westward across North Africa and moved north into Spain. Further advances into Europe were stopped at Tours in 732.

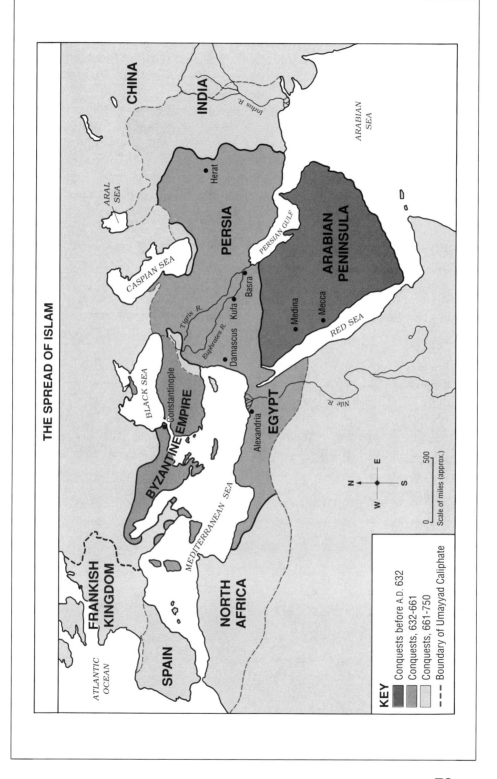

THE SPREAD OF ISLAM

Herat

ARAL
SEA

CHINA

INDIA

Indus R.

PERSIA

ARABIAN
SEA

CASPIAN SEA

PERSIAN GULF

ARABIAN
PENINSULA

Tigris R.

Basra

Kufa

Mecca

Medina

Euphrates R.

Damascus

RED SEA

BLACK SEA

Constantinople

BYZANTINE EMPIRE

EGYPT

Nile R.

Alexandria

MEDITERRANEAN SEA

FRANKISH
KINGDOM

NORTH
AFRICA

SPAIN

ATLANTIC
OCEAN

N
E
W
S

0   500
Scale of miles (approx.)

KEY

Conquests before A.D. 632

Conquests, 632–661

Conquests, 661–750

– – – Boundary of Umayyad Caliphate

73

institutions of government, the Arab conquests allowed life to continue without major interruptions.

The conqueror's religion and language gradually infused the region. When the Muslims took over a country, they set up camps outside conquered cities. The inhabitants of these cities came to the camp to sell produce, pay taxes, and conduct their business. Gradually some of these camps became important cities such as Kufa and Basra in Iraq and al-Fustat (later joined with Cairo) in Egypt. Although Arabs were in the majority in these outposts at first, the conquered peoples blended in and in time outnumbered the Arabs.

As extensive trade and commerce developed between the Muslim warriors and the subject peoples, Arabic began to replace the local tongues. As Arab warriors married local women, cultural barriers between the conquered and the conquerors began to disappear.

Many Arabs seeking to buy confiscated state land migrated to the new territories. The Muslim religion and the Arabic language soon infused the cultures of most conquered areas. Communities in which established religions had many followers, such as Orthodox Christians, the Egyptian Copts, and the Jews, however, retained their faiths and adopted only the Arabic language and customs. On the other hand, whole populations in some of the former territories of the Persian Empire converted to Islam without changing their language to Arabic. Today the majority of people in Afghanistan, Pakistan, and Iran are Muslims. They use Arabic script to write their native language, but they speak their own languages instead of Arabic.

In Syria and Egypt large numbers of Christians held beliefs that differed from those of the established Byzantine church. These people suffered persecution as a result of their differences. Arab success in Egypt and Syria was due in part to the hostility that was created by the religious intolerance of their Byzantine masters. Christians, Jews, and Zoroastrians welcomed the Muslims because they seemed to offer conquered peoples religious toleration. As proof of this spirit of toleration, many Christians and Jews were appointed to high positions by the Muslim leaders.

Only the people who worshiped many gods and spirits in nature were ordered to become Muslim. Once these polytheists accepted Muslim civil authority, they fared better than they had under their former rulers. The only way they were treated differently from Muslims was in the payment of a special tax levied on all non-Muslims.

During the early decades, when Islam was thought of as an Arab religion, non-Arab peoples could convert to Islam by becoming clients of the Arabs. The non-Arab converts who flocked to the Arab encampments outside the conquered towns soon demanded that they be treated as equals with their Arab conquerors. The Arabs started to limit non-Arab converts, however, when the non-Arab Muslims began to outnumber the Arab Muslims. Nevertheless, Islam was on its way to losing its identity with Arab culture and language and would soon become a truly international faith.

Check Your Understanding

1. What role did Abu Bakr play in Arab expansion?
2. Why were the Arab armies able to defeat the Byzantine and Persian armies so easily?
3. *Thinking Critically:* Why did the Arab language and culture spread so rapidly throughout the conquered regions?

4. Umayyad Rule

During the years of rapid expansion, the Muslims changed caliphs frequently, often as the result of violence. Before Abu Bakr died of natural causes in 634, he chose his valued adviser Umar to succeed him. Under Umar's leadership, Islam made its greatest conquests. But Umar was stabbed by a slave as he was about to begin devotions in a mosque. Uthman was chosen to succeed Umar as caliph.

Conflicts over the Caliphate

Uthman was a member of the powerful Umayyad (oo-MAY-yad) family of Mecca, most of whom converted to Islam after its successes. Uthman ruled for 12 years before he was murdered. The next caliph was Ali, son-in-law of Mohammed and husband of Fatimah (FAT-ih-muh). Ali's succession to the caliphate was fervently opposed by the party of Aisha, Mohammed's widow. When Ali failed to produce the killers of Uthman, Muawiyah (muh-AH-wih-yah), the Umayyad governor of Syria, challenged Ali. But Ali was barely able to maintain himself in power, and Muawiyah continued to rule Syria. When Ali was stabbed to death in 661, Muawiyah took over as caliph and established the new Muslim capital at Damascus.

The Alhambra Court of Lions in Granada, Spain, is an outstanding example of Muslim architecture. The vaulted arches rest on 124 white marble columns. Traditional Muslim patterns executed in fine detail can be seen. Granada was the last Moorish stronghold, falling to Spain in 1492.

A Split in Islam

Ali's followers claimed that the highest office in Islam was hereditary and belonged to the descendants of Ali and Fatimah. They disputed the method of selection that brought Ali's successor to power. For more than two centuries Ali's followers tried to unseat the Umayyads. Frustrated at failing to regain power, Ali's followers formed a separate group called **Shi'a** to rival the majority of the Muslim community called **Sunnis**. (For more information on the Shi'a, as the members of this group are called, see the Sidelight to History on page 78.)

Military Achievements

After conquering North Africa and Spain, the Umayyad armies crossed the Pyrenees into France. There in 732 the warriors of Islam were halted at the Battle of Tours by Charles Martel, ruler of the Franks. But the Muslims, having established a base in North Africa, preyed on European shipping in the western Mediterranean and made sporadic attacks on the coasts of France and Italy for several centuries.

To the east the Umayyads drove the Byzantines across the Bosporus and in 717 laid siege to Constantinople. But the Byzantines withstood the siege and regained their lost territory from the Umayyads. Other Muslim forces swept eastward, carrying Islam into central Asia to the borders of the T'ang Empire in China. By 750, the Muslim Empire reached beyond the Indus River to India, where the people in the northwest corner became Muslim.

Umayyad Society

As the Arabs and the native inhabitants intermarried, four main classes developed in Umayyad society. Warriors from the Arabian Peninsula who could trace their ancestry to one of the noble families of Mecca or Medina made up the first class. Umayyad rulers listed all these "pure" Arabs on an imperial registry to ensure that they received payments from the state treasury. These men dominated Umayyad society. Successive caliphs granted them leases over much of the land formerly owned by the Byzantine and Persian empires or abandoned by the great Byzantine landlords. From these holdings many Arabs built up immense fortunes. Together with the caliphs they formed the wealthy class, living in great luxury in the cities.

The second class in Muslim society was made up of the non-Arab Muslim converts. As artisans, shopkeepers, and merchants, they rapidly increased in number to form a large urban class resentful of its inferior position.

The third group included Jews, Christians, and other believers in one god. Also known as "people of the book," they were tolerated and allowed to maintain their churches and synagogues because of the similarity of their religious beliefs with those of Islam. They had their own religious courts, lived within their own communities, and generally practiced their faith unmolested.

Slaves were at the bottom of the social scale, although their lot improved considerably under Islam. Indeed, slaves often rose to high public office, and those who came from socially respectable backgrounds were frequently treated as members of the family.

Growth and Decline

The Umayyads divided their empire into five provinces, each ruled by a governor responsible to the caliph. The provinces of the empire were Iraq and the lands to the east; the Hejaz, the central part of the Arabian Peninsula, and Yemen; the region

Sunnis and Shi'a

The split of Islam into sects stems from Mohammed's insistence that there be no division between religion and politics. Political disagreements have religious overtones. As a result, political disagreements end up with religious consequences. The Shi'a split began with a political dispute over succession to Islam's leadership, but it ended with the formation of a separate branch of Islam that eventually modified Islamic customs and beliefs with Persian customs and beliefs.

Today the followers of mainstream Islam are called Sunnis, from *sunna*, the Arabic word for "custom." Sunnis follow the customs of Islam as they were taught by Mohammed and handed down through the ages by those recognized as his successors. The term *Shi'a* comes from the Arabic phrase *Shiat Ali*, which means "the party of Ali." Today the Shi'a make up about 10 percent of the world's 860 million Muslims. Most of the Shi'a live in Iran and Iraq.

The Shi'a devised their own doctrines, basing them on the theory that Ali had passed on to his descendants a divine inspiration to interpret the Koran. Then as other Shi'a leaders exercised this power, they formed their own Shi'a subgroups. The most familiar of these were the Ismailis, which included the Assassins and the Fatimids. Still another group, the Druse, split from the Fatimids and established their own religious traditions.

The largest Shi'a sect has its center of power today in Iran. Its members led the revolution in 1979 that overthrew the Shah of Iran and re-established a **theocracy**.

The majority of the Shi'a believe in the tradition of 12 **imams**. They believe that the line of imams began with Ali and continued to the twelfth successor who mysteriously disappeared more than 1,000 years ago. They believe that the twelfth imam, whom they call the Mahdi, will reappear before the world's end to save it. Until the Mahdi reappears, Islam is led by Mahdi's agents on earth—scholars who are also called mujtahids. In Iran's Islamic revolutionary government, the Ayatollah Khomeini, until his death in 1989, was recognized as the imam charged with final authority while awaiting the Mahdi.

between Iraq and the Mediterranean Sea, extending from the Black Sea and the straits to the Arabian Peninsula; Egypt; and North Africa and Spain. After local expenses were paid out of tax revenues collected in each province, the remainder was sent to Damascus. Muawiyah staffed his government with the government employees he found in Syria, Iraq, and Egypt. Muslim judges were chosen by the provincial governors to preside over criminal cases involving Muslims. In governmental disputes the caliph's representative dispensed justice.

Internal weakness led to the decline of central authority, as palace life became increasingly luxurious and corrupt. The governors squeezed larger taxes from their subjects and kept a greater share for themselves. Dishonesty and favoritism increased. Intense rivalries among Arab leaders competing for the caliphate weakened the empire, and non-Arab Muslims became increasingly hostile to the Umayyad aristocracy.

Revolt against Damascus was channeled into religious conflict among possible successors to the caliphate. By the middle of the eighth century the various groups supporting the cause of Ali chose Abu al-Abbas, descendant of the Prophet's uncle,

ARCHITECTURAL STYLES. The obelisk-shaped minaret at Agadès, once a caravan station on the south Saharan trade route through Africa, and a prayer meeting at a mosque in Indonesia symbolize the wide geographical spread of Islam. Where else might you see mosques?

to lead them in revolt against Damascus. Within a few months the Umayyads were defeated, and Damascus itself fell in 750. The new Abbasid (AB-uh-suhd) rulers, seeking to destroy the last vestige of Umayyad domination, murdered about 80 of them at a banquet. Later other members of the former ruling family were mercilessly hunted down. Only one Umayyad escaped. He made his way to Spain, where he established a new and independent Umayyad dynasty at Cordoba (KOR-doh-buh).

Check Your Understanding

1. Who was the founder of the Umayyad dynasty?
2. What gave rise to the Shi'a?
3. What were the four main classes of Umayyad society?
4. What led to Umayyad decline?
5. *Thinking Critically:* Why was military conquest so important in the expansion of Islam? How might social and cultural patterns have aided Muslims in making the Middle East a Muslim region?

CHAPTER REVIEW

■ **Chapter Summary**

Section 1. Islam first appeared in the Arabian Peninsula as a religion and a way of life after the Prophet Mohammed began to preach it in the early seventh century. After rejection by the Arabs of Mecca, he migrated to Medina, where he became a powerful leader and turned to military conquests as a means of spreading Islam.

Section 2. Islam emphasizes belief in one god as expressed in the Koran, Islam's holy book, and other teachings of the Prophet. Devout Muslims practice the five pillars of Islam. They are acceptance of the one god and Mohammed as his Prophet, ritual prayer five times daily, almsgiving, fasting during the month of Ramadan, and pilgrimage to Mecca.

Section 3. Driven by a desire for converts, the Muslim armies easily defeated the Byzantine and Persian empires, adopting their political divisions and using many of their methods of administration. At its height, the Muslim empire reached across North Africa into Spain, took in the entire Middle East, and extended eastward into India. As Muslims intermingled with their conquered peoples, a great cultural mixing took place that resulted in Arabic becoming the Middle East's dominant language and Islam its dominant religion.

Section 4. The first major Muslim dynasty was the Umayyad, which came to power after the death of Ali in 661. Umayyad society had four main classes of people within the five provinces of their empire. The Umayyads ruled for almost a century before greed and decay led to their overthrow by the Abbasid dynasty in 750.

■ Vocabulary Review

Define: hegira, mosque, muezzin, minaret, caliph, Shi'a, Sunni, theocracy, imam

■ Places to Locate

Locate: Mecca, Medina, Jerusalem, Damascus, Alexandria, Herat, Tours, Mediterranean Sea, Egypt, Palestine, Syria, Byzantium, Persia

■ People to Know

Identify: Abu Bakr, Khalid ibn al-Walid, Ali, Fatimah, Aisha, Muawiyah, Charles Martel, Abu al-Abbas

■ Thinking Critically

1. Compare Mohammed's teachings to the earlier religious beliefs of the Arabs, mentioning those practices and beliefs that were new, borrowed, or retained.
2. Discuss how each of the five pillars of Islam expresses Islam's central idea, the greatness of Allah.
3. The Muslims did not compel religious groups that worshiped one God to accept Islam. What ideas in Mohammed's teachings or in Arab customs made this tolerance possible?

■ Extending and Applying Your Knowledge

1. Research and prepare a modern political map that shows the spread of Islam at its height. Use symbols or color

to indicate the present-day countries whose lands were once part of this empire.

2. Using the map as a base, research in an almanac or other reference work the population of these nations and the percentage of each that is Muslim. Use the information to create a pie chart.

4

The Muslim Empires

The Muslim Empire entered a new phase when the Abbasid dynasty transferred the capital from Damascus to Baghdad. With the transfer, the officials of the empire were no longer almost exclusively Arab. Officials and administrators were drawn from all peoples of the region. The only two constants were the Arab language and the Muslim religious roots.

The shift of the capital to Baghdad reflected an increase in Eastern influence on the caliphate, on the governing institutions of the empire, and on the cultural and intellectual life of the people. It also reflected the growing importance of trade with Asia for the continued growth of the empire.

During the Abbasid reign, the political power and authority of the central government weakened, and by 945 the Abbasid caliphs ruled only a small part of the Muslim world. The disintegration of Abbasid control had many causes. Among them were inadequate financial resources, the laxity of the caliphate in controlling local rulers, religious dissension and rivalry that often erupted into full-scale rebellion, and attacks from groups outside the empire.

Under the Abbasid Empire, however, Islamic civilization reached its greatest height, experiencing a golden age of achievement that had far-reaching influence on other parts of the world, especially Western Europe. It is the brilliant flowering of its arts and sciences and not its political instability that makes the history of the Abbasid Empire worth studying.

1. The Abbasid Empire

After the founding of Islam, interest in expansion gave the Muslims an image as hard-driving warriors of the desert. But under the Umayyads the image of Muslims as warriors changed to Muslims as rulers, managers, and administrators of a vast territory. Under the Abbasids, the image continued to change, and along with the changing image came new patterns of life.

A New Capital

It took four years and the labors of thousands of workers to build Baghdad, the new capital ordered by Mansur, the second Abbasid caliph. Situated on the Tigris and only 20 miles from the Euphrates, Baghdad was started in 762. It soon became the hub of Muslim commerce and culture and remained the empire's central city for nearly 500 years.

At the very center of the circular city, Mansur placed the mosque and his royal palace of marble and stone, with a green dome rising 120 feet above the main audience hall. The setting suggested the nature of Abbasid rule: elaborate, autocratic, and awesome.

A Changed Caliphate

Two important changes made the caliphate different. First of all the caliphs abandoned the simplicity and closeness to the people

This drawing shows Mansur's elaborate plan for eighth-century Baghdad. It is based on a version by F. Sarre and E. F. Herzfeld.

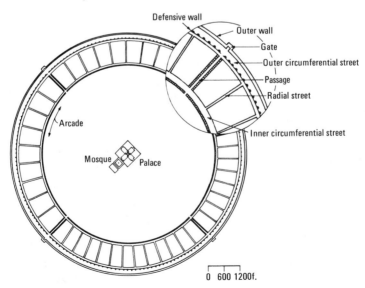

The Muslim Empires

750–1258	Abbasid caliphate
909–1171	Fatimid caliphate
1037–1109	Seljuk Empire
1096–1300	Period of the Crusades
1249–1517	Mamluk rule in Egypt
1258	The destruction of Baghdad by the Mongols

of earlier caliphs. Following Persian customs, the Abbasid caliphs assumed the trappings of powerful rulers. Taking on a status above all other men, they allowed only a privileged few into their presence. Calling themselves the "Shadow of God on Earth," they surrounded themselves with religious attendants and rituals—all symbols of their elevated status. For example, when visitors approached a caliph's throne, they kissed the floor, lowering themselves full length upon it.

The other change that affected the empire was the creation of an elaborate bureaucracy, or levels of organization, with a hierarchy of officials to manage the government. The bureaucracy was organized into **diwans,** or departments. The officials of the diwans were supervised by the **wazir** (wuh-ZEER), who ran the government. As the caliph's highest official, the wazir's position was very powerful, but it was also very dangerous. At any time, the wazir could do something to displease the caliph and lose his office, fortune, and even his life.

A Flourishing Economy

The wealth of the Abbasid Empire rested on improved agriculture and expanded trade. The ancient canal system of the Tigris–Euphrates Valley was operated more efficiently than ever before with the result that wheat, barley, and rice harvests were the largest in the region's history. The textile industry became a mainstay of the economy. Every city and province excelled in some special product, pattern, or technique. Carpets from Bukhara in Turkestan, damask from Damascus, brocades from Shiraz in Iran, and linens from Egypt were especially prized textiles. The art of papermaking was acquired from the Chinese and

Arabic in English

An interesting example of Muslim influence in the Western world is the many kinds of Arabic words that have found their way into English. Most of the words first became a part of medieval Latin. Then they became a part of one of the different European languages that were derived from the Latin. These words relate to aspects of Muslim culture that interested or impressed Westerners. The list that follows shows some of these English words and their Arabic sources and meanings.

English	Arabic source/meaning
admiral	*amir-al-bahr*/commander of the sea
alcohol	*al-kuhul*/powdered antimony
algebra	*al-jabr*/the reduction
almanac	*al-manakh*/list of sun and planet positions
arsenal	*dar-sina'ah*/house of manufacture
candy	*qandi*/sugared
cotton	*qutn*/name of plant
guitar	*qitar*/instrument's name
lemon	*laymun*/name of fruit
lute	*al-'ud*/instrument's name
orange	*naranj*/name of fruit
sherbet	*sharbah*/drink
sugar	*sukkar*/pebble
syrup	*sharab*/fruit juice
tariff	*ta'rif*/notification

paper mills set up in several provinces. The ceramics industry, important in the Middle East since ancient times, produced objects of high quality.

Ships carried these products to ports throughout the known world. Caravans traveled overland and returned laden with silk, ink, peacocks, porcelains, and saddles from China and rubies, silver, sandalwood, coconuts, ebony, and dyes from India. From Africa came slaves and gold. From Byzantium, traders obtained drugs, trinkets, and more slaves. From Russia and Scandinavia came furs, amber, and swords.

The trade with different regions of the world brought Muslims into contact with many different cultures from which they assimilated, or learned, new techniques. By assimilating information from other cultures and adapting it to their own culture, Muslims were instrumental in preserving the best of other cultures. The "good life" that resulted brought the Muslims under the Abbasids to a "golden age" of great literary, intellectual, and scientific achievement.

Check Your Understanding

1. Why is Baghdad often called the "Round City"?
2. What two important changes made the caliphate under the Abbasids different from the caliphate under the Umayyads?
3. *Thinking Critically:* How did trade figure in the making of the new image of Muslims under the Abbasids?

2. The Golden Age of Islam

As Baghdad became known for its great wealth, luxury, and far-flung commerce, it also became known for its great learning. In their writings and discoveries, Muslim scholars drew upon Jewish and Christian concepts, classical Greek thought, Persian traditions, and Indian accomplishments. They then integrated these rich and varied ideas, traditions, and values to create a distinctive Islamic culture and period of cultural flowering that is known as Islam's Golden Age.

Famous Muslim Scholars

Much of Islam's scholarly work was done at the House of Learning in Baghdad. Established in the early ninth century A.D., the House of Learning was a center where the works of Greek, Persian, and Indian philosophers and scientists were translated into Arabic. The Muslim scholar was many-sided, with interests ranging over many fields.

An early scientist who represented the Muslim ideal was al-Razi, or Rhazes (RAY-zeez, 865–925), chief of the Baghdad hospital. He compiled a medical encyclopedia and wrote scores of papers on medicine and surgery, including a pioneer study of smallpox. Even more famous is Ibn Sina (IB-n SEE-nah, 980–1037), known to Europeans by his Latinized name, Avicenna (ah-vih-SEN-ah). This Arabic-speaking Persian, often called the "Prince of Philosophers," was said to have memorized the entire Koran at the age of 10 and in his lifetime wrote 170 books on such subjects as medicine, mathematics, and astronomy. Ibn Sina strongly influenced European thought and passed on to Western scholars the ideas of the Greek philosopher Aristotle. Ibn Sina's five-volume work on medical science, reprinted many times, was used in European universities for more than five centuries.

Another important Muslim scholar was the Spanish doctor Ibn Rushd (ROOSHT, 1126–1198), or Averroes (ah-VEHR-oh-EEZ). Chief physician to the ruler of Spain, he too wrote on a wide variety of subjects including medicine, philosophy, and astronomy. His commentaries on the works of Aristotle were more popular in Christian Europe than they were in the Middle East and had a great impact on later Christian philosophers. The Jewish scholar Maimonides (meye-MON-uh-DEEZ), or Ibn Maymun, also a Spanish-born philosopher-physician, is the author of *Guide for the Perplexed*, a study blending religious thought with the scientific views of Aristotle.

The writings of these scholars encouraged practical advances in medicine. These included innovations in surgery, the use of improved anesthetics, and a whole range of drugs carefully cataloged for the treatment of diseases.

Scientific Advances

Muslim scientists were concerned with many aspects of chemistry. The word *chemistry* derives from alchemy (AL-kuh-mih), *al-kimiya* in Arabic. Alchemy is the medieval science that sought the "philosopher's stone" to turn base metals into gold. In the course of their experiments in alchemy, the Muslims evolved a real science based on the structure of chemical compounds and developed techniques for using some of them industrially (such as manganese dioxide in the manufacture of glass). Rhazes wrote 12 books on alchemy and devised laboratory equipment such as beakers and crystallizing dishes of a type still in use by scientists today.

The Muslims made some important observations in the field of optics, the study of light and vision. Early Greek scientists

SCIENCE AND LEARNING.

All Muslims recognize the Koran with its 114 suras, or chapters, as their holy book. The illustration to the right provides an example of the beautiful calligraphy used in preserving Mohammed's words. Below left is an illustration from a collection of Arabian tales that shows a seminar in a mosque library (Baghdad, 1237). Below right is the constellation Sagittarius (the Archer) in a drawing that dates from the thirteenth century.

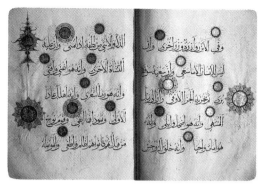

At right is a detail from a painting in a thirteenth-century translation of Dioscorides' **De Materia Medica** A.D. 50). It shows the preparation of a medicine from honey in a pharmacy.

wrongly believed that sight was the result of rays emitted from the eye. In his book *On Optics* the Egyptian Alhazen advanced the idea that vision depends on the impact of light rays on the retina. He also experimented with the movement of light rays and produced another important study called *On Light.*

Contributions to Mathematics and Astronomy

From India the Muslims adopted the so-called "Arabic" numerals, the decimal system, and the concept of zero. The Muslims combined these numerical elements into a system that simplified calculation and that enabled mathematicians to take the square and cube roots of numbers.

The Muslims applied their knowledge of mathematics to such problems as computing the distance of stars from the earth, finding the speed of falling bodies, and investigating various other problems in astronomy and navigation. Arab sailors greatly refined both the techniques of sailing and the instruments mariners used in navigation. By improving the astrolabe, a device for taking the attitude of the sun and stars to determine location at sea, mariners were able to sail far from land without getting lost. Long before Columbus, Muslim scholars, like others of their time, realized that the earth was a sphere and were able to estimate its circumference and diameter. Today many stars and constellations have names given to them by Arab scientists and sailors, and many terms used in astronomy and navigation have come to us from the Arabic language.

Contributions to Geography and History

In their ocean travels Arab sailors acquired a great deal of information, some of which disproved the long-cherished theories of early geographers. Scholars, too, were constantly gathering information about people and places in other countries. One scholarly traveler compiled a 30-volume work. Muslim maps of such places as China, India, and Russia and charts of the seas and skies served as basic sources of information for European merchants and seafarers until the seventeenth century.

Ibn Khaldun (IB-n kahl-DOON), a Muslim geographer who traveled widely throughout the known world, is even better known for his theories of the nature of history. In his *Muqaddima, an Introduction to History,* he set forth his theories and analyzed things that in his opinion strengthened and weakened human societies. With this work, Ibn Khaldun gave history a new dimension and a new direction.

Check Your Understanding

1. **a.** Who were some of Islam's famous scholars?
   b. For what achievement was each known?
2. How did Muslim alchemists help found the science of chemistry?
3. What contributions to mathematics were made by Muslim scholars?
4. *Thinking Critically:* Why is a period of great intellectual and scientific achievement frequently called a Golden Age?

3. Achievements in Arts and Literature

Except for the lyrical poetry of the Bedouin, the pre-Islamic Arabian Peninsula had been barren of artistic expression. But as Islam expanded into Byzantium and Persia, the Muslims acquired a wealth of ideas and techniques which, when integrated with their religious beliefs, flowered into a distinctive and advanced art.

A Rich and Varied Architecture

The house of Mohammed was the first gathering place for the Muslim faithful. Along one side palm trunks covered with leaves were placed. One follower would stand on the roof to call people to hear the Prophet. From this simple beginning came the essentials of mosque architecture. The first mosques were plain buildings of stone or brick, roofed over with palm branches. Often they had courtyards and sometimes narrow walkways on three sides. Early in the eighth century a niche was placed in the wall facing Mecca. At one corner of the building stood the minaret from which the call to prayer was made. In some places the minaret was a square structure. In other places the minaret took its now-familiar pencil shape. As centuries passed, mosque architecture grew vastly more elaborate.

Decorative Arts

Muslim religious tradition forbade the portrayal of the human figure. The prohibition on the representation of human beings is thought to have originated in a religious tradition attributed to Mohammed's young wife Aisha. Mohammed came home one day to find her making a pillow with a picture on it and scolded her, saying, "Don't you know the angels won't come to a house where there are pictures? And on Judgment Day God will ask you to give life to the pictures you have created." The idea behind this is probably that God alone has the right to create living creatures. Mosque interiors were decorated with abstract designs using such motifs as plants, trees, and geometric figures. The most famous Muslim design is the **arabesque,** which consists of a motif such as a flower or a leaf repeated in a variety of intricate patterns. **Calligraphy,** the art of elegant writing, was also a very important art form. Verses of the Koran rendered in beautiful script are considered to be the highest form of art.

Muslims became equally skilled and inventive in painting and decorating. One of their most admired arts was displayed in the illuminated manuscripts, some of which were commissioned by the caliphs. Inspired by Persian motifs and styles, Islamic artists illustrated nonreligious texts with scenes drawn from legend or from court life. When the manuscripts had been copied on parchment and the bright miniatures painted in on gold backgrounds, artisans bound the books in tooled leather.

Other craftsworkers produced ceramics of great beauty. Their most famous product was luster-painted ware, achieved by coating the piece with metal oxides and firing it to a high metallic sheen. Muslim glass and rock crystal were equally renowned. Skillful metalworkers decorated objects of brass and bronze with intricate gold, silver, and copper inlays. Carpets, tapestries, and textiles also reflected the Muslim fascination with color and pattern. Many of the abstract designs used in architectural interiors were adapted for rug weaving to produce some of the most prized carpets and wall hangings ever created.

A Distinctive Literature

Muslim poetry had its origins in Bedouin **oral tradition.** Desert bards developed a rich and flexible vocabulary to proclaim the glories of the nomadic way of life and to praise the bravery and honor of Arab warriors. The Arabic language was itself a vehicle for Bedouin lyrics. As Islam spread from the desert, the range of poetry widened. By the Abbasid period it reflected the prevailing urban way of life. Most of the poets were Persian and scorned the more rural Arab ways. They wrote of the joys and sorrows of love, of wine, of courtly manners and morals, and of the pleasures of the senses. The form in which the poem was written actually became more important than the content—how things were said far outweighed what was said.

Muslim prose also had its origins in the desert, but its genesis was much less remote. It was the Koran that shaped the Arabic language into a vehicle that could be used to translate the works of foreign philosophers, historians, and scientists and ultimately serve for a wide range of Muslim writings. Philosophy, history, and geography were the most popular subjects, and the anthology, usually a collection of anecdotes, a new and favorite literary form.

The best-known Muslim literary work may not be a classic of Arabic prose, but it is one of the most popular books of all time. Almost every reader knows about Aladdin and Sinbad the Sailor. They appear in *Alf Layla wa Layla, A Thousand and One Nights,* also called *The Arabian Nights.* This lively collection of fairy tales, legends, and anecdotes drawn from Arab, Indian, Persian, and Egyptian sources is another example of the Muslim genius for blending diverse elements into a creation distinctly their own. In addition to expressing Islamic values and ideals, *The Arabian Nights* gives a vivid picture of court and city life from the ninth to the sixteenth centuries.

Featured in *The Arabian Nights* is one of the most famous of the Abbasid caliphs, Harun al-Rashid (hah-ROON al-rah-SHEED, 786–809). In real life, Harun had a splendid court where all the dishes were made of gold and the tapestries studded with jewels. Once when a favorite son married, bride and groom were showered with a thousand matched pearls as they sat on a golden mat interlaced with gems.

The tales recorded in *The Arabian Nights* were told to Harun by Shahrazad (shah-RAH-ZAHD). No single author is responsible for the tales, which really are a collection of stories drawn from many cultures. But a kind of unity was imposed on the collection by having Shahrazad as the only narrator.

The framework for the stories is this: Once upon a time a Persian king was betrayed by his wife. To prevent future disloyalty, he decided to marry a different woman every night, then have her executed in the morning. But when he chose Shahrazad, daughter of the Grand Vizier (wazir), as a bride, she thought of a way to outwit him. On their wedding night she told him a fascinating story that reached its most crucial point just at daybreak. So that he could hear the end of the tale, the king decided to spare her life for one more day. The next night Shahrazad finished that story and began another one that was just as exciting. Again the king spared her life in order to hear the end of the story. By the time a thousand and one nights had

(Continued on page 96.)

ISLAMIC ARCHITECTURE.

Mosque structure and decoration reflect the artistic traditions of Muslim culture. The largest mosque in the world, built c. 850 in Samarra, Iraq (top), has a Mesopotamian look. Classical influence is seen in the arches (right) of the former mosque at Cordoba, Spain, begun in 786 and now a Christian church. The seventeenth-century dome and minaret in Isfahan, Iran (below left), show the delicacy of the Persian style. Istanbul's Blue Mosque (below right) resembles the Byzantine Hagia Sophia.

ISLAMIC ART. Some of the distinctive modes of Islamic art are represented on this page. At top left is a detail from one of the earliest surviving "pictorial" works, a landscape mosaic on the walls of the Great Mosque, Damascus, Syria (eighth century). At the top right is a painted bowl made at Nishapur, Iran, in the tenth century. Above is a large bronze incense-burner of the Seljuk period. The detail from a hunting scene shows the magical interweaving of shapes for which Persian miniaturists are famous.

been spent in this fashion, the king decided to reward Shahra-zad's cleverness by letting her live.

Check Your Understanding

1. **a.** What is the most famous Arab design? **b.** When does calligraphy become the highest form of art a Muslim can express?
2. How did Arab poetry change during the Abbasid empire?
3. What is the best-known literary work of the Abbasid period?
4. *Thinking Critically:* How have Muslim religious beliefs influenced Islamic forms of art?

4. Islamic Law

By the time the Abbasid dynasty was founded in A.D. 760, the religious and moral content of the Islamic faith had been in the process of development for almost 200 years. Islam permeated every phase of the life of its followers. As the empire grew, there developed a massive body of beliefs, practices, and rulings that had to be systematized.

Sources of Islamic Law

As Islam spread, new situations that the Prophet could not have anticipated arose. The Prophet's followers then sought authoritative sources of religious and moral guidance to supplement the Koran. The **Hadith** (hah-DEETH), or Traditions, became the most important. The Hadith were sayings, stories, and actions attributed to Mohammed. In the early period the Hadith were simple and straightforward, disclosing the Prophet's opinion on various everyday topics, for example, "God curse the woman who wears false hair and the woman who ties it on." Or: "The best house . . . is the one which contains an orphan who is well treated, the worst, one wherein an orphan is wronged."

Within 200 years after Mohammed's death, some 600,000 Hadith were said to be in circulation. His widow Aisha was the source of several thousand. Some sayings were set down by immediate followers. Others were recorded centuries later. The Hadith became very involved and technical and were the subject of endless debate. Along with the Koran, six collections—each representing different interpretations—form the most important bases of Islamic Law and are called **Sunna** (SUHN-uh). Muslims who abide by the Sunna are called Sunnis or Sunnites. Sometimes students of Islamic law relied on the opinions of legal experts in accepting or rejecting Hadith. At other times they found similar elements in the old and the new situation and based their judgment of the new on past decisions. In this way, the Hadith were supplemented by still more rules and guidelines.

Schools of Sunni Law

Through the centuries various schools of legal thought and interpretation arose. As Islam became worldwide, it was influenced by the beliefs of people in Europe and Asia. The Muslims frequently encountered classical Greek and Roman moral thought. In the East they came in contact with the theories of such religions as Zoroastrianism, Hinduism, and Buddhism. Ultimately four principal schools of Sunni Muslim law, tradition, and custom were recognized. All were based on the Koran, but they gave varying emphasis to other sources of law.

Sharia

The combination of Islamic law forms the **Sharia,** or the straight path of sacred law. Religious courts that administer this law are called Sharia (shuh-REE-uh) courts. Until modern times they were often the only courts in Muslim countries dealing with all legal cases. Sharia laws cover nearly every aspect of Muslim daily life, such as how to divide land and other property among heirs, divorce, criminal penalties, and allocation of water in the desert.

Judges in the Muslim religious courts were called **qadis** (KAH-diz). When particularly difficult cases arose, they consulted **muftis** (MUF-tiz), who were religious authorities learned in law. All learned men dealing with Muslim law were called the **ulema** (OO-leh-MAH) because they possessed *ilm*, or knowledge of the law. As might be expected, the ulema held great power in Muslim society.

Check Your Understanding

1. What are the sources of Islamic law?
2. How is Islamic law administered?
3. *Thinking Critically:* Why did different schools of Sunni Muslim law arise?

5. The Breakup of the Abbasid Empire

Almost as soon as it was founded, the Abbasid Empire came under attack from various dissatisfied groups within its boundaries. The caliphate became a pawn in the hands of its own governors and generals. Local rulers took control, establishing small independent states in the western and eastern provinces. Attacks from European Christians trying to recapture Jerusalem and other places in Palestine connected with the birth of Christianity occupied Muslim armies for two centuries. At the same time, the Turks entered the empire, first as slaves, then as hired warriors, and finally as invaders. The Turks quickly brought Arab and Persian dominance of the Abbasid dynasty to an end.

Breakup in the West

A religious movement in Egypt brought about by a splinter Shi'a group called the Isma'ilis caused the first break in the Abbasid Empire. In the eyes of the Isma'ilis, the only rightful caliphs were those in a direct line from the descendants of Ali and Fatimah. The Isma'ilis referred to a caliph in this line as an imam. In 909 the Isma'ilis enthroned the then current imam as the first Fatimid caliph, ruling over North Africa and Yemen. In 973 the Fatimid capital was moved to Cairo. At its height (1036–1094) the Fatimid Empire included Palestine, Syria, Egypt, all of North Africa, and parts of the Arabian Peninsula.

Losses in the East

As power slipped from the caliph, Persian notables ignored the central authority at Baghdad and established a number of smaller independent states and kingdoms, leaving only Iraq under the rule of the Abbasid caliphate. Then in 945 the Buyids (BOO-yidz), a Persian noble family, invaded Iraq. They seized Baghdad and forced the caliph to recognize their prince, called a **sultan,** as the sovereign of Iraq.

The Turkish Takeover

When the Abbasids were powerful, they had recruited many Turkish converts to Islam as soldiers. They purchased other Turks as slaves and then assigned them to Arab military service. As the Abbasid caliphate grew weaker, the government hired whole armies of Turks. These Turks also embraced Islam and became ardent supporters of the faith.

In 1055 the Seljuks (sel-JOOKS), a group of fierce Turkish warriors from Central Asia, pushed westward into Iran and took over Baghdad. The Abbasid caliph was nothing more than a figurehead because the Turkish commander held the real power throughout the empire, taking over the title of sultan. The Turks eventually extended their power at the expense of the Fatimid caliphs, taking control of Jerusalem in 1071 and Damascus in Syria in 1076.

As central authority weakened, the caliphate lost control of tax collecting and the revenues from it. In the past, the tax collectors appointed by the empire paid only a fixed amount to the government, even though they extracted taxes from the inhabitants of their districts as they saw fit. Now as a first step toward building independent states and local dynasties, local landlords began to collect the taxes, keeping great amounts for themselves. When the Seljuks rose to power, they put landholding (and thus tax collecting) on a military basis. Military service became the means of acquiring grants of land. With the land grant came political rights over the tenants, including the right to collect taxes. In Egypt, the sultan assigned almost half the available land to mercenaries, or hired soldiers. Eventually the landholdings became hereditary, giving the Abbasid Empire under the Turks a system of landholding similar to that of European **feudalism.**

The Impact of the Crusades

In expanding the Abbasid Empire, the Seljuk Turks defeated the Byzantine Empire in a battle fought at Manzikert in 1071. The Byzantine ruler feared further attacks and called on the Pope in Rome to ask Christian monarchs in Europe for help in defeating the Muslim Turks. Christians in Europe responded to the Pope's call in 1096 with the first of a series of four wars called the Crusades.

Reasons for the Crusades are complex. The Pope, like many other Christians, had a deep religious desire to free the Holy Land, the birthplace of Christianity, from Muslim control. He also wanted to distract Christian monarchs from warring against each other. Christian monarchs responded to the Pope's call because it was a chance to gain glory for themselves and their countries. Merchants in the Italian city-states of Venice, Genoa, and Pisa saw the Crusades as an opportunity to develop trade with the Middle East.

Episodes from the Crusades found their way into the religious art of medieval Europe. This picture comes from a window formerly in the Abbey of St. Denis, France, and shows Christian knights (left) meeting Saracens (right), as Europeans called Arabs. The window probably commemorated a battle between the Seljuk sultan Kilij Arslan and Godfrey of Bouillon during the First Crusade (1096–1099).

Christian Europe united against the Muslims at a time when the Muslim states were divided and at odds with one another. When the Christians of the First Crusade captured Jerusalem in 1099, they established four states. But one by one the Muslims recaptured the Christian states, with the last one falling in 1291.

Despite their victories over the Crusaders, the Muslims had to face yet another attack on their authority and rule. This attack came from the Mongols of Asia, who swept into Baghdad in 1258, ending the Abbasid caliphate.

Check Your Understanding

1. **a.** Where did the Fatimid Empire arise? **b.** What led to its establishment?
2. How did the Abbasid Empire lose its eastern provinces?
3. When did the Seljuk Turks become the ruling sultans of the Abbasid Empire?
4. Why was the First Crusade against the Muslims successful?
5. *Thinking Critically:* What part do you think Middle Eastern feudalism played in the breakup of the Abbasid Empire?

The fall of Baghdad to the Mongols was an event of lasting importance in the Middle East. When the warriors of Hulagu laid siege to the city in 1258, they ended an era. The miniature painting (c. 1315) shows Mongols swarming around the walls. Inside a Mongol cavalryman confronts a mounted Arab. The white birds and the garments of the lady suggest the delicacy of all that was under attack by the invaders from the East.

6. The Mongol Onslaught

Early in the thirteenth century the Mongols swept out of Central Asia. Under the leadership of Genghis Khan (JENG-ghis KAHN), the Mongols moved into the Indus Valley and Persia. The heirs of Genghis completed the conquest. Kublai (KOO-bly) Khan subdued the last of the Southern Song rulers to bring all of China within the Mongol Empire. By the middle of the thirteenth century, Hulagu (hoo-LAH-goo) Khan, the grandson of Genghis, had destroyed or terrorized much of the Middle East.

The Sack of Baghdad

In 1258 Hulagu laid siege to Baghdad, which fell after two months. The sack of the city was as terrible as that of Jerusalem by the Crusaders a century and a half earlier. Fifty thousand people were slaughtered, including the caliph and most of his family. The great palace designed by Mansur was burned to the ground.

The assault of Hulagu reached beyond Baghdad into Syria; Antioch was made a Mongol satellite. Throughout the Middle

101

East, millions of people lost their lives. Many of the great cultural achievements of the Muslim Golden Age were lost when libraries, art collections, and religious monuments were destroyed by the invaders. The destruction of Baghdad ended an era. Never again would an Arabic-speaking caliph preside over the Muslim world. Indeed, Muslim lands were so weakened by the Asian conquerors that they were easily overrun by other invaders from Turkey (Anatolia). The Islamic faith, however, was strengthened by Mongol conversions.

Mamluk Rule

Early in the twelfth century the Ayyubid (eye-YOO-bid) regime ruling Egypt faced a growing shortage of soldiers. It then brought in large numbers of Turkish and Russian slaves to serve as bodyguards, soldiers, and officers. In 1249 one of these slave officers rose in the ranks, gained his freedom, and married the widow of the sultan. When he took control of the government, Mamluk (MAM-look) rule, meaning slave rule, began in Egypt, a dynastic system in which one former slave officer succeeded another as sultan. The Mamluks never learned to speak Arabic, keeping aloof from their subjects. Although some were cruel and oppressive tyrants, others worked to enhance commerce and agriculture. The Mamluks remained in power in Egypt until 1517. Even after that date, when the Ottoman Turks took over Egypt, they kept the Mamluks as local rulers because they were able to control the local population.

Baybars (beye-BARS), the fourth Mamluk sultan, then a general, stopped the Mongols at Ayn Jalut in Palestine in 1260. On his way back to Cairo after his victory, Baybars stabbed his sultan-master and took over the sultanate. Baybars not only defeated the Mongols, he attacked and subdued some of the Crusader castles and crushed Antioch, one of the oldest of the Christian states in the Middle East. Succeeding Mamluk leaders leveled Tripoli and Akka, two Crusader strong points.

Baybars reinstituted the caliphate in Cairo by inviting one of the surviving members of the Abbasid family to become caliph in name only. This move gave a kind of legality to the Mamluk regime. The Mamluk dynasty reached the height of its power

ENVIRONMENT: THE MIDDLE EAST IN 1294. The Turks, followed by the Mongols, pushed into the Middle East from Central Asia, crowding both the Arabs and the rival Byzantine Empire. East–West trade flourished, however, along the caravan routes through Mongol lands and on the sea-lanes controlled by the Arabs.

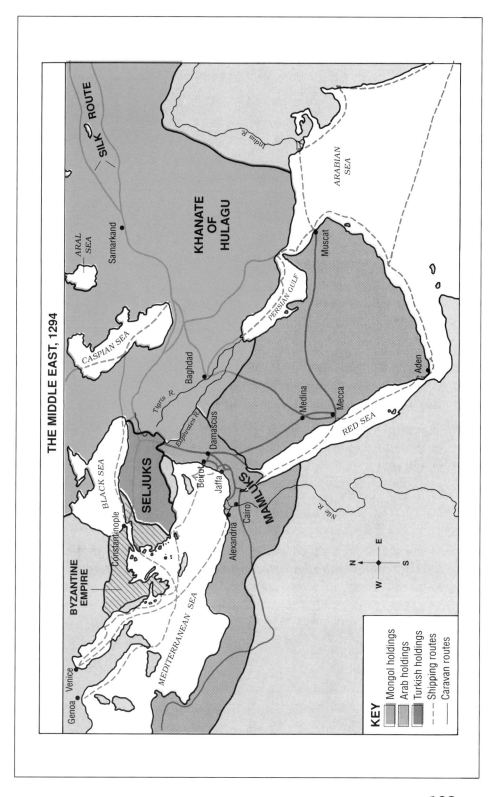

THE MIDDLE EAST, 1294

SILK ROUTE

ARAL SEA

Samarkand

CASPIAN SEA

Indus R.

KHANATE
OF
HULAGU

ARABIAN
SEA

PERSIAN GULF

Muscat

Baghdad

Tigris R.

Medina

Mecca

Aden

RED SEA

Euphrates R.

Damascus

SELJUKS

Beirut

Jaffa

MAMLUKS

BLACK SEA

Cairo

Alexandria

Constantinople

Nile R.

BYZANTINE
EMPIRE

Venice

Genoa

MEDITERRANEAN SEA

N
W — E
S

KEY

Mongol holdings
Arab holdings
Turkish holdings
Shipping routes
Caravan routes

in the early fourteenth century when its realm stretched from the Taurus Mountains to the southern tip of the Red Sea coast, and out through Egypt into the Libyan desert. Under the Mamluks most of the land in Egypt was granted to officers who were responsible for raising a fixed number of soldiers. Thus feudalism was the basis of the Mamluk's system and the source of their military power.

Check Your Understanding

1. **a.** Who was Hulagu? **b.** How did he bring an end to the Abbasid dynasty?
2. **a.** Who were the Mamluks? **b.** How did they come to power in Egypt?
3. *Thinking Critically:* What characteristics of the Muslim Empire enabled the Mamluk dynasty to come to power?

CHAPTER REVIEW

■ **Chapter Summary**

Section 1. Beginning in A.D. 750, rule under the Abbasid caliphs brought many changes to the Muslim empire. The capital changed to Baghdad and with it the nature of Muslim rule, which became elaborate, autocratic, and awesome when the caliphs assumed the trappings of Persian rulers. Also new to the empire was an elaborate bureaucracy to administer the government under the direction of the vizier, the real ruler of the empire. Trade, which became as widespread as the empire, brought the Muslims into contact with many different cultures. By assimilating information from these cultures and adapting it to their own benefit, the Muslims developed a high level of achievement that became known as Islam's Golden Age.

Section 2. Baghdad became a center of intellectual, literary, and scientific achievement as Muslim scholars drew upon Jewish and Christian concepts, classical Greek thought, Persian traditions, and Indian accomplishments. In his writings Ibn Sina, otherwise known as Avicenna, passed on to Western scholars the ideas of Aristotle. Ibn Rushd, or Averroes, also passed on the ideas of Aristotle as did Maimonides, a Spanish-born Jewish philosopher. Muslim scholars, through their interest in alchemy, provided the basis for the modern science of chemistry. Others provided information on optics, astronomy, mathematics, and geography.

Section 3. Fine arts flourished and rose to great heights in the Golden Age of Islam. Among the notable works passed on were the tales of Shahrazad in *A Thousand and One Nights*, or *The Arabian Nights*, as they are also known. Islamic architecture, especially in the mosque, displayed a number of distinctive styles, most borrowed or adapted from other cultures. Graceful designs and geometric patterns such as the arabesque became traditional decorations because Muslim religious tradition forbade the use of any images connected with living figures. The Muslims also perfected the art of calligraphy in writing Arabic script and produced numerous handcrafted artifacts, from elegant tooled leather to intricately woven rugs and wall hangings.

Section 4. The Muslims also developed an elaborate and complicated body of law called the Sharia. The Sunna, or traditions of the Prophet, known through the Hadith, are one of its bases. The Muslims under the Abbasids also devised new law codes and a court system to cope with the variety of situations that arose after the death of the Prophet. In all, four major schools of Muslim law are recognized. Muslims who abide by these schools of Muslim law are called Sunnis or Sunnites. About 10 percent of all Muslims are Shi'a, who have their distinctive beliefs and leaders.

Section 5. The Abbasid Empire lasted from 750 to 1258, when the Mongols from Central Asia sacked Baghdad. The seclusion and isolation of the caliph from the people, the turning of the caliph into a mere figurehead, and the Muslim characteristic of assimilating new peoples and customs eventually led to the downfall of the Abbasid Empire. Persians, and then Turks, took over the administration of government, which became increasingly bureaucratic and out of touch with the people, making it easy for local rulers to establish independent states and dynasties. Important groups contributing to the decline of the Abbasid Empire were the Fatimid dynasty in Egypt, the Seljuk Turks, and the Crusaders from Christian Europe.

Section 6. The Mongols from Central Asia swept westward relentlessly under the leadership of Genghis Khan and his grandsons Kublai Khan and Hulagu Khan until they were turned back at the borders of Europe and Egypt. Hulagu Khan sacked Baghdad in 1258 bringing to an end the Abbasid dynasty. But Hulagu's further advance into Egypt was stopped by the Mamluk dynasty in Egypt, which owed its power to Middle Eastern feudalism and which flourished for several centuries.

■ Vocabulary Review

Define: diwan, wazir, arabesque, calligraphy, oral tradition, Hadith, Sunna, Sharia, qadi, mufti, ulema, sultan, feudalism

■ Places to Locate

Locate: Baghdad, Manzikert, Fatimid Empire

■ People to Know

Identify: Mansur, Harun al-Rashid, Ibn Sina (Avicenna), Ibn Rushd (Averroes), Ibn Khaldun, Isma'ilis, Buyids, Seljuks, Mongols, Hulagu Khan, Mamluks, Baybars

■ Thinking Critically

1. Why have the Muslims under the Abbasids been called great adapters and assimilators?
2. In what ways has the Muslim facility for adaptation and assimilation been an advantage to Islam? In what ways has it been a disadvantage?
3. What is the relationship between Muslim law, Muslim beliefs, and the Muslim state?
4. The Abbasid Empire reached its cultural peak during a period of political disintegration. Why was Islam's cultural peak not achieved when Islam was at the height of its power?
5. Compare the effects of the Crusades and the Mongol invasions on the Muslim empires, explaining which one had the greater impact on the Middle East and in which way or ways.

■ Extending and Applying Your Knowledge

1. Some of the Europeans who traveled with the crusading knights kept journals of their impressions of the Middle East. You might enjoy Joinville and Villehardouin's *Chroni-*

cles of the Crusades, Penguin. You might also enjoy reading an account of the Crusades written from the Muslim viewpoint in Maalouf's *The Crusades Through Arab Eyes*. Prepare a book report on either.

2. Compare pictures of Byzantine and early Islamic art. What similarities do you see? Then look at paintings done during the Abbasid period. What changes have occurred? What influences do they express? Prepare a report answering these questions.

5

The Ottoman Empire

Arab domination in the Middle East under the Umayyad dynasty gave way to the international Islamic empire presided over by the Abbasid caliphs. But the Abbasid caliphs became nothing more than figurehead rulers when they lost control of their territory in 1055 to the Seljuk Turks. The era of Turkish ascendancy over Islam was interrupted for a time by the Mongol advance under Hulagu Khan. But Turkish rule resumed when a new leader emerged from a small state on the Anatolian Peninsula toward the end of the 1200's.

The new ruler was Osman. He began building the third and last Islamic empire by first attacking Byzantium in the west and then expanding eastward and southward into Palestine and Syria. By the 1600's the empire included all of the Middle East (except for Persia and parts of the Arabian Peninsula), the Balkan Peninsula in southeastern Europe, and North Africa.

The dynasty eventually became known as the Ottomans and the territory over which the dynasty ruled became known as the Ottoman Empire. The empire's greatest achievement was in imposing a unified political order over much of the Middle East, southeastern Europe, and North Africa. The Ottomans used the title of sultan rather than caliph. As sultans, the Ottoman rulers held life-and-death power over every human being in their domain. As their power grew, however, the Ottomans became distrustful of outside influences and tried to isolate their empire from changing times and new ideas. Eventually the empire was unable to fend off the ambitious nations of Western Europe.

1. Expansion Under the Ottomans

After the Seljuks came to power in the Middle East, they allowed other groups of Turkish people to migrate into the area from Central Asia. Many of them occupied the frontier areas between the Islamic and Byzantine empires. Converted to Islam, the chieftains of these groups hired themselves and their warriors out to the Seljuk commanders who rewarded them with fiefs when their fierce fighting defeated Byzantine armies. As some chieftains became more powerful than others, they turned their fiefs into their own private strongholds. Soon they began to capture Byzantine land on their own, especially when the Seljuks became occupied with the Mongol invasions.

By 1290, one of the chieftains of these local groups became strong enough to command allegiance from the other local chiefs and to proclaim his independence from the Seljuks. This leader was Osman, the founder of the Ottoman Empire.

Osman's Success

From his father, Osman inherited the small fief of Sogut in eastern Anatolia. From this base he began laying the foundations of the empire, attacking and capturing less powerful fiefs and towns in Anatolia. Osman's soldiers, who were called **ghazis** (GAH-zeez), lived by a strict set of rules similar to the code of chivalry practiced by the knights of Western Europe. Rank in the ghazi was determined by deeds, not birth.

Later Osman's son Orkhan continued empire-building. Orkhan kept expanding the empire westward until the northwestern corner of Anatolia between the Black and Aegean seas was in

This old engraving was entitled "Ottomanus," Latin version of "Osman," founder of the state from which the Ottoman Empire developed. He is wearing a turban, the style of headdress that is still worn in some areas of the Middle East.

The Middle East Under Ottoman Rule

1290–1326	Osman, founder of Ottoman dynasty
1345	Turkish settlements in Europe
1451–1481	Mohammed II
1453	Fall of Constantinople to the Turks
1520–1566	Reign of Suleiman the Magnificent
c. 1600	Beginning of Ottoman decline

Ottoman hands. Then Orkhan crossed over to Gallipoli (guh-LIP-uh-lee) on the western side of the Dardanelles, the strait separating Europe from Asia Minor. Gallipoli fell to Orkhan in 1354. With this foothold the Ottomans began to press into the Balkan Peninsula, making inroads into territory covered by the present-day nations of Albania, Greece, Yugoslavia, Rumania, Bulgaria, and the European part of Turkey. By 1354 Ottoman peoples had begun to settle in Europe. It was at this time that Orkhan assumed the title of sultan, making it the traditional title for all Ottoman rulers.

Trouble in Asia Minor

By the end of the fourteenth century the Ottoman sultans had built their small feudal state into a major power. But they still longed to extend their control eastward throughout Asia Minor. In this area local Turkish chieftains still held power. Dreaming of uniting all the Muslim lands of Asia Minor under his rule, Bayezid I (beye-yah-ZEED), the fourth Ottoman sultan, attacked and subdued the ghazis in the east. But their Turkish chieftains, refusing to be put under Ottoman control, fled to the court of Tamerlane in Baghdad.

Tamerlane—Timur Leng, or Timur the Lame—son of a Mongol chieftain, had entered Central Asia and northern India and in 1379 swept into the Middle East to take Aleppo, Damascus, and Baghdad. Tamerlane was as fierce a marauder as Genghis and Halagu Kahn had been. When Bayezid appeared to be planning an invasion of the Mongol states, Tamerlane himself invaded Turkish territory. In 1402 at Ankara (AHNG-kuh-ruh), he defeated the Ottoman armies and took Bayezid prisoner. According to legend the captive sultan was locked in an iron cage slung between two horses and carried with the Mongol armies. Tamerlane made no serious effort, however, to hold Anatolia. The empire was divided among Bayezid's four remaining sons, who promptly began to battle among themselves for supremacy. Ultimately the youngest ruled alone. His name was Mehmed (meh-MET), which is a Turkish version of the name *Mohammed*. Other versions of the name are Mahmud, Mahmoud, Mahomet, and Muhammed.

Restoring the Empire

Mehmed was able to avoid his father's mistakes. Mehmed looked on Europe and the Balkans as regions for great and profitable conquest. This was part of the ghazi tradition and found favor with the Turkish warriors. By the time of his death the Ottoman state was once more united.

The sultans who followed Mehmed continued his policy of rewarding the old Ottoman families with lands and offices, and the civil strife that had torn Asia Minor apart under Bayezid was not repeated. Instead, the Ottomans made further inroads into the Balkans, along the northern shore of the Black Sea, and in Asia Minor. Their most important victory came, however, when Constantinople fell in 1453.

The long-anticipated attack on Constantinople began in April when 170,000 soldiers under Mehmed II and a fleet of 300 to 400 ships assaulted the Byzantine capital. For 54 days the city was under constant bombardment from the sea. Cut off, battered from every side, and abandoned by their allies, the 50,000 inhabitants of the city finally ceased their resistance and the city fell on May 29. The taking of Constantinople, a Muslim goal for centuries, had a tremendous emotional impact on Muslims, who changed the city's name to Istanbul. The once-glittering capital of the Byzantines, the symbol of Roman and Christian domination in the eastern Mediterranean area, became the capital of the Ottoman Empire. Mehmed II was widely acclaimed throughout the Middle East for his achievement and was always called "Fatih" (the Conqueror) by his subjects.

Selim I and Suleiman the Magnificent

Unlike his ancestors who had concentrated on Asia Minor and Europe, Selim I (suh-LEEM), who ruled from 1515–1520, looked south to Syria, Egypt, and the North African coast for conquests. The Ottoman armies defeated the Egyptian Mamluks in 1516 near Aleppo in Syria. Selim was victorious because the Ottomans used artillery while the Mamluks fought as cavalry.

The Treasures of Tamerlane

The great Mongol conqueror Tamerlane is remembered for his cruel methods of frightening people into submission. But this fierce warrior was also a lover of beauty and learning. As a result of his conquests, art treasures and books from all over the Middle East were collected and preserved at Samarkand, the capital of his empire, currently a city in the Soviet Union.

Tamerlane's policy was to build up Samarkand, Persia, and Afghanistan by attacking and pillaging other areas and by weakening them so drastically that counterattack was impossible. While moving into conquered territories, Tamerlane usually stole whatever treasures he could and burned the rest. He then brought the treasures he collected to Samarkand. In time the city became a richly developed center of culture and learning. But it was surrounded by barren frontier areas where Tamerlane occasionally built a palace or a mosque.

Tamerlane enjoyed having learned men around him. He carried many books back to the libraries of Samarkand himself and was a writer of merit. As he traveled he also studied architecture, and he loved planning the gardens and palaces at his capital. In Damascus he was intrigued by a new architectural form, the bulb-shaped dome. Adopting this style for a palace in India, he began a trend that culminated in the beautiful Taj Mahal built in Agra, India, in the seventeenth century. It is fitting that Tamerlane's tomb in Samarkand is one of the world's most beautiful examples of Islamic architecture.

Tamerlane was the founder of the Timurid dynasty, which continued for nearly a 150 years after Tamerlane's death. The dynasty is known for its interest in collecting fine books, carpets, armor, and works of art. Many of our Western museums contain lovely miniatures by Timurid artists. Though abandoning the desire for conquest, the descendants of Tamerlane continued the artistic tradition begun by the conqueror.

Samarkand, ancient city on the Silk Road from Asia to Europe, was destroyed by Genghis Khan in 1221 and rebuilt by Tamerlane in 1370. Tamerlane's ornate tomb, shown here, as well as other Muslim treasures attract many visitors to the city, which is in the Uzbek Republic, USSR. What distinctive characteristics of Islamic art and architecture are shown here?

Military innovations such as gunpowder and artillery also made possible a series of Ottoman victories in North Africa. After seizing Cairo in 1517, Selim demanded that the Mamluk Sultan turn over his authority as caliph, which he had acquired after the Mongols seized Baghdad and killed the last Abbasid caliph. Next, the Ottomans conquered the rest of North Africa as far as Morocco. They also seized the west coast and half the east coast of the Arabian Peninsula. Only the desert interior of the peninsula and its untamable Bedouins escaped Ottoman rule.

During the reign of Suleiman (soo–lay-MAHN; 1520–1566), the Ottomans advanced to the gates of Vienna. Greece, the Balkan Peninsula and parts of present-day Austria, Poland, Hungary, and the southern part of the Soviet Union became provinces of the empire, making the Black Sea an Ottoman lake.

Ottoman Cultural Development

The Turks of this period were master builders and poets as well as great soldiers and administrators. Ottoman architects combined the traditional style of the Islamic mosque with the domed Byzantine style. The great Christian church of Hagia Sophia (Holy Wisdom) in Istanbul was converted to a mosque and used as a model in other parts of the empire. Leaders of Ottoman society sponsored the building of impressive mosques and tombs in honor of themselves, their parents, and their relatives.

In literature as well, the Ottoman achievement was considerable. Turkish writers borrowed vocabulary, style, and themes from Arab and Persian sources. Ottoman Turkish was written with Arabic script, and its literature had a strong Islamic influence. Arab inflences were strongest in works on law and religion, while Persian classics provided the models for poetry and essay-writing. Suleiman himself was a poet of distinction and also kept a diary that is now an important historical document. The tutor of Suleiman's grandson compiled a many-volumed study of Ottoman history called *The Crown of Histories*.

Check Your Understanding

1. Who founded the Ottoman Empire, and how did he rise to power?
2. **a.** Who was Tamerlane? **b.** How did he interrupt Ottoman empire-building?
3. **a.** What three sultans were responsible for bringing the Ottoman Empire to its greatest height? **b.** How did each contribute to Ottoman success?
4. ***Thinking Critically:*** How did the Ottoman dynasty differ from the Umayyad and Abbasid dynasties in regard to political and religious control?

2. Ruling a Diverse Population

In the early days the Ottoman Turks were a vigorous and dynamic people, constantly and rapidly expanding their territory. Their warriors had two aims: fighting for the glory of Islam against Christian Byzantium and amassing personal wealth from treasures and other booty acquired in combat. The ghazis had welcomed to their ranks any warriors willing to join and able to sustain the hard life. As the empire expanded, the Ottomans ruled over many different groups of people. They accepted into the Muslim faith those who wished to embrace Islam. They also allowed a certain measure of freedom to those not embracing Islam as long as the demands of the central government for wealth and soldiers were met.

Subject Peoples

Ethnic and national groups included in the Ottoman Empire were Arabs, Kurds, Turkomans, Berbers, Albanians, Greeks, Bulgarians, and Georgians. Religious groups included Egyptian Copts, Greek and Armenian Christians, Jews, and members of Muslim sects. Turks were the majority group only in Anatolia. Elsewhere they were a minority. In the European provinces there

114

Under Suleiman I (right), the Ottoman Empire reached its greatest extent and attained its highest prestige. Suleiman is considered the greatest Ottoman sultan. European historians often refer to him as Suleiman the Magnificent because of the splendor of his court. His Muslim subjects, however, referred to him as Suleiman the Lawgiver because of his educational, legal, and military reforms.

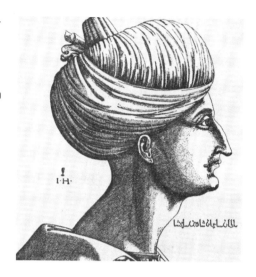

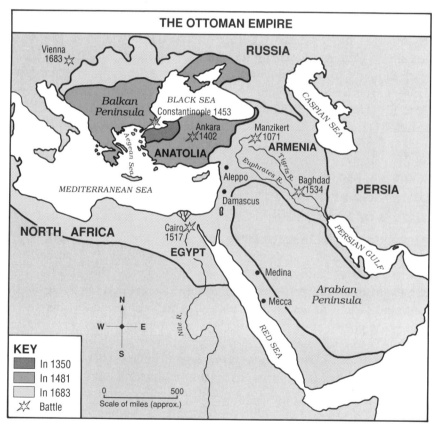

MOVEMENT: THE OTTOMAN EMPIRE. From a strategic location in Anatolia (darkest area) the Ottoman Turks spread into the Balkan Peninsula and brought the Byzantine Empire to an end in 1453. Although repulsed in Europe at Vienna, the Turks gained control of most of the Middle East.

were more Christians than Muslims. Frequent disputes between the Ottomans and their enemies occurred in the border areas of the empire. But the Turks, while a minority, were in power. The border battles usually resulted in the sending of a steady stream of slaves—chiefly Slavs, Germans, Poles, and Russians—to Istanbul and the service of the sultan.

The subject peoples were divided into religious groups called **millets** (mih-LETS). Muslims were separated from non-Muslims, maintaining a long-standing Islamic principle. The chief non-Muslim millets were Greek Orthodox, Armenian-Gregorian, and Jewish. Each millet was headed by its own religious dignitary, responsible for the payment of taxes and the good behavior of the members. Each maintained its own courts, which tried all cases except those involving public security and crime. A non-Muslim was required to appear before a Muslim or Ottoman court only when engaged in a legal dispute with a Muslim.

The Ottoman system of allowing religious groups to govern themselves has had far-reaching effects. The division of the non-Muslims into religious millets has developed an attitude that carries over to the present. Separatism based on religion has been a recurring problem in the Middle East for many years. But identity with religion began to change under western influences in the nineteenth and twentieth centuries as nationalist ideas penetrated the area and appealed to many ethnic groups. While religious identity has not vanished, in most areas national identities have gained a greater hold on peoples' loyalties.

Rights of Foreigners

The Ottoman sultans guaranteed the rights of foreigners in **capitulations**. The first capitulation was signed by Francis I of France and Suleiman the Magnificent early in the 1500's. The capitulation ensured equal treatment to French and Ottoman merchants selling goods and establishing residences in the territories of either monarch. Subjects of one monarch were to be exempt from taxation in the other monarch's territory and were to be subject only to their own religious laws. The Ottomans signed similar agreements with the monarchs of England and Holland in the 1500's and with still other monarchs much later. Both parties to the agreements thought of themselves as equals and as great powers, a status that was conceded to them by the principal nations of Europe. But European merchants profited much more from the capitulations than Turks because few Ottomans engaged in trade and commerce. In time the agreements lost their original meaning and became the means by which European companies gained privileges in the sultan's domain. In other words, they were used by Europeans as a means of gaining control over non-Europeans.

The Role of the Sultan

The sultan was both the ruler of the empire and the head of Islam, though in religious matters the Chief Mufti (see pages 122–123) could overrule any sultan who violated Muslim law. The sultan presided in Istanbul from a great palace called the Sublime Porte, or high gate, or simply the Porte.

The Ottoman leaders called themselves sultans to emphasize their secular authority. (*Sultan* means "he with authority;" *caliph* means "successor to the Prophet.") In the beginning the Ottoman leaders did not claim to be Mohammed's successors, as did the first four caliphs. Later the sultans claimed the title of caliph as well, assuming responsibility for the protection and growth of the Islamic domain. Like the Umayyads and the Abbasids, the Turks favored the dynastic concept, keeping **sovereignty** in a single family.

To prevent conflict among heirs to the throne of the sultan, the Ottomans adopted the practice of fratricide. Thus, the brother who was selected as heir to the sultan's throne because his talent and ability was considered greater than that of any of his brothers was to put his brothers to death. Support for this practice was found in the Koran, which states that discord is worse than killing. By the seventeenth century, however, the practice of fratricide had been replaced. Young princes no longer were sent at the age of 14 to govern the provinces where their talent and ability could be observed. Instead all sons of a sultan remained at the imperial court in Istanbul, and the oldest son, regardless of ability, became the heir to the sultan's throne.

Check For Understanding

1. How did the Ottomans rule over their diverse population?
2. What lasting effect did the division of the population into millets have on the Ottoman Empire?
3. *Thinking Critically:* How did the Ottoman idea of sultanate differ from the earlier Muslim idea of the caliphate? How was this a strength?

3. The Ruling Institution

The Ottoman Ruling Institution, one of the most celebrated governmental systems in history, managed civil and military affairs for the sultanate. It depended for its efficiency on the services of a vast number of trained civil servants and military officers, most of whom were technically, in the early days of the empire, slaves of the sultan. The Ruling Institution consisted of the officers of the royal household, the major officials of the government, the standing army, young men in training, and the feudal lords and knights.

The center of the Ruling Institution was the imperial household. The imperial household consisted of the palace, the sultan's residence; dormitories for young men in training; and the **haram**, quarters set aside exclusively for the women of the sultan's family. In the haram, which means "sanctuary" in Arabic, the sultan's word was law. The haram included the sultan's consorts; his mother, daughters, and young sons; and the haram's servants and entertainers. In all, several hundred people resided in the haram.

The Ottomans became known for skillfully managing their empire through the development of a staff of trained palace and government officials. The staffing of the imperial organization began with a levy, or tax, called the devshirme. The devshirme was imposed on the Christian population of the empire after 1430. Every five years representatives of the sultan traveled through the European provinces selecting the healthiest and most intelligent Christian boys aged 12 to 20. After being converted to Islam and taught Turkish, they were assigned to military units. The cream of the levy was brought to the royal palace for more advanced training in preparation for service in the sultan's bodyguard.

At the Palace Schools, young men were trained to govern the empire. They were taught Arabic, Persian, and Turkish, Muslim law, mathematics, music, Turkish history, calligraphy, taxation, finance, and military science. The lower bureaucratic positions were filled by those students who showed no particular promise or special talents. Students with military capabilities were assigned to military units. These students could eventually rise in the ranks to great wealth and prominence. The outstanding students became the elite of the Ottoman governmental system. However, they always remained servants of the sultan and at the mercy of the most powerful official of the Ottoman Empire.

The Grand Vizier

The second most powerful official in the Ottoman Empire was the grand **vizier** (vih-ZEER). The word *vizier* comes from the Arabic *wazir* and means "chief deputy." Before the conquest of Constantinople in 1453, the vizier was usually a Muslim noble. After the conquest, the grand vizier was sometimes selected from the group of palace officials who had been captured as youths or were products of the devshirme.

After the sixteenth century, when the sultans abandoned direct involvement in the government's daily affairs, the position of the grand vizier became even more powerful. A distinguished sixteenth-century grand vizier, Lutfi Pasha, who was an historian as well as a government official, wrote:

> First and foremost, he who is grand vizier must have no private purpose or spite. Everything he does should be . . . for the sake of God, for above this there is no higher rank to which he could attain. He should speak to the sovereign, without hesitation, of what is necessary in the affairs of both religion and the state, and should not be held back by fear of dismissal. It is better to be dismissed and respected among men than to render dishonest service. [Bernard Lewis, *Istanbul and the Civilization of the Ottoman Empire.*]

Several other viziers served as advisers on peace and war, administration and justice, and bore the title of **pasha** (pah-SHAH) in Turkey. Together with other officials and judges, the pashas took part in the meetings of the Imperial Council, or *Divan* (dee-VAHN), the Turkish word for sofa. The council received this name because the council members were seated on a long sofa that stretched around three sides of the room.

Treasurers, secretaries, military commanders, provincial governors, and other officials assisted in keeping order, collecting taxes, expanding the frontiers of the empire, or defending existing boundaries. The empire was decentralized in financial matters. Provincial governors collected and disbursed their own funds. Other civil affairs were generally left to the millets.

A Strong Military Base

The strength of the Ottoman forces was based on the **janissary** (JAN-uh-sayr-ee) corps. Their Turkish name was *yeni cheri*, or "new force," which Europeans made into janissary. In the early

IMPERIAL OFFICIALS. These drawings depict leading figures in the Ottoman Empire: top left, the grand vizier with mace and sword, as he appeared in 1749; top right, the Chief Mufti of Istanbul, chief religious official of the empire, about 1700; bottom, one of the janissaries.

years this body probably developed from slaves captured in battle and were trained as a special force by feudal officers. The janissaries were feared adversaries on the battlefield. Eventually the janissaries became a formidable standing army, numbering at the most about 14,000 in the time of Suleiman. Many of these fighting men rose from the ranks to become officers or civil officials in the empire. As a major political influence in the Ruling Institution, officials who came from the ranks of the janissaries played a major part in the making and unmaking of sultans.

Another important element in the Ottoman military organization was the Muslim cavalry, called *sipahis*. In return for the revenues collected from their feudal estates, the sipahis were required to furnish specified numbers of armed men for the sultan's campaigns.

Check Your Understanding

1. **a.** How did the Ottomans rule their vast empire?
   b. Explain the role of the Ruling Institution.
2. What part did the devshirme play in the Ruling Institution?
3. What were the major duties of the grand vizier?
4. What role did the janissaries and sipahis play in the empire?
5. *Thinking Critically:* In what way or ways might the Ruling Institution be considered a major strength of the Ottoman Empire? In what way or ways might it be considered a weakness?

4. The Muslim Institution

Two major organizations shared the administration of the Ottoman Empire. The Ruling Institution, as you have just read, had the responsibility for the political and military order of the empire. The other major organization was the Muslim Institution. It had the responsibility for administering religion, law, and education throughout the empire. The two institutions were joined at the top in the person of the sultan and touched at many other places as well.

In a sense the Muslim Institution was the more important unifying force. It served to weld the Muslims of the empire under one kind of law and one system of education. Its high-ranking members interpreted the Sharia, or sacred law, and handed down decisions that shaped not only religious practice but social and imperial development as well. A talented Muslim boy could advance through the ranks of the Muslim Institution just as an individual could rise in the Ruling Institution.

The Educational System

Every city in the empire was dotted with mosques, many of which were complexes containing the house of worship together with schools, colleges, law schools, hospitals, and asylums. At one time in Istanbul there were 275 mosque-connected colleges where students studied Islamic law and the Muslim religion. The financial support for these many institutions came from the *vaqf*, or religious endowment, consisting of land set aside by the government for this purpose. The farmers who worked these

121

religious lands were reputed to be better treated than the peasants who worked the fiefs of local lords.

Schools providing both basic and more advanced education
were associated with mosques. Although education was free,
only a small percentage of Muslim youths in Ottoman times ever
completed the basic stage. The curriculum and teaching methods used a strong emphasis on rote learning, especially of long
passages from the Koran. At the upper levels of the educational
system, the course of study focused on religion and law, although some attention was given to natural history, astronomy,
and mathematics. Excellent in some ways, Ottoman education
was handicapped by rigidity and resistance to change. Its failure
to absorb new ideas and discoveries meant that Ottoman students were left far behind those in the West.

The education of the Christian and Jewish communities was
under the guidance of their respective leaders. Thus there was
no centralized educational system, but various schools existing
side by side. Because only the schools of the Muslim Institution
sought to instill loyalty to Ottoman institutions, a split developed
based on religious differences. The separation of education was
probably one of the causes of the nationalist movements that
later developed in the empire.

Those students who passed through the upper level of the
Muslim educational system constituted the ulema, or learned
men, the staff of the Muslim Institution. The ulema fulfilled
various religious and civil duties, were supported by the vaqf,
and were free from taxation. Periodically the sultans issued sets
of rules called Kanun (kah-NOON), collections of administrative
regulations, or codes of existing law based on Sharia, Ottoman
custom, and royal decree. So many Kanun were issued during
the reign of Suleiman the Magnificent that he became known
as Suleiman Kanuni.

The Chief Mufti of Istanbul

An elaborate system of Judgeships was needed to interpret and
enforce the ulema's rulings. There were several classes of judgeships, highest of which was the qadi. The qadis were assisted
by experts in sacred law called muftis, who were appointed for
life and held in high esteem. The mufti's function was to deliver
"answers" in cases requiring detailed knowledge of the Sharia.
In ordinary cities qadis outranked muftis, but in Istanbul the
mufti was the "Leader of Islam," and was called the Chief Mufti
with the right to appoint all other muftis of the empire. Theoreti-

cally no sultan could issue a law or administrative decision without the approval of the Chief Mufti. The Chief Mufti was also the final authority in the interpretation of Mohammed's teachings.

Often the Chief Mufti and the sultan disagreed. For example, Selim I decided he could achieve unity in his western dominions by ordering all Christians there to accept Islam on pain of death. The Chief Mufti intervened and instructed the leader of the Christian millet that Muslim law provided that all who accepted Muslim rule and paid their taxes should be left unmolested. Selim was forced to abandon his plan. It was often said: "The Turk shows the mufti the greatest reverence because he represents justice and the image of God."

Check For Understanding

1. What was the Muslim Institution, and who were its members?
2. How did the Muslim Institution assist in the education of Muslims?
3. Who were the ulema, and why were they powerful?
4. What system of judgeship developed in the empire?
5. *Thinking Critically:* Why could the Chief Mufti challenge the authority of the sultan?

5. Decline of the Ottoman Empire

Ten great sultans governed the Ottoman empire from its rise to power until the end of the sixteenth century. During that era the empire was called a "daily increasing flame." It grew in size, wealth, influence, and cultural attainments. Proper functioning of the whole system depended on the ruler's character and determination. Although some responsibilities were delegated to the grand vizier, this was done only with the approval and consent of the sultan. He was the crown and head of the empire. Toward the end of the sixteenth century, however, corruption began to creep into the daily life of the Ottoman sultans and into the Ruling Institution. The strength of the empire declined until by the eighteenth century, it was on the retreat before the aggressive new nation-states of Europe.

Some idea of the pleasant life of the Ottoman court may be gained by studying details from this miniature painting of the late sixteenth century. The sultan sits comfortably on his cushions, separated from his courtiers by a patterned screen. Musicians perform, poets read their latest works, and rosewater in elaborate bottles scents the air.

Erosion of the Sultan's Power

As the empire grew in territorial size, new responsibilities increased the complexities and problems of administering the vast territory. Even under Suleiman, many of the new duties and the power that went with them were turned over to the grand vizier. When these advisers were competent and honorable, the government functioned well. But during the seventeenth century many of the sultans were minors or easily influenced by subordinates or members of their family. Often the sultans were persuaded to appoint their chief officers on the basis of favoritism rather than merit.

The sultans themselves had less opportunity to develop into able rulers. Beginning with the seventeenth century, the heir of the dynasty was kept in strict seclusion during his childhood and early adulthood. He no longer received the rigorous education that earlier sultans had received and gained no experience in handling the administration of his empire. Instead, the sultans of the seventeenth century were given every luxury and indulgence and were surrounded with slaves, jugglers, musicians, and astrologers. Pleasures rather than duties occupied their waking hours.

Governmental Decay

In the Ruling Institution, bribery replaced the principle of merit. For centuries Muslims had jealously eyed the top posts in government, then monopolized by Christian slaves converted to Islam. After the seventeenth century Muslims were able to buy entrance into the elite administrative and military corps, either for themselves or their relatives. The new recruits were not always as bright, nor as highly trained and disciplined as the youths recruited through the devshirme. When put to the test in wartime, the large standing army of the sultan often proved to be an undisciplined rabble.

Two military groups that had been the backbone of Ottoman power, the janissaries and the sipahis, now became a challenge to the sultan's authority. The sultan could no longer command respect from his servants, and the servants, realizing the sultan's dependence on them, often dictated policy. In the provinces rivalries between different branches of the army or the government often erupted in revolts or minor civil wars.

Merit as a basis for appointments and promotions in the Muslim Institution was also abandoned. Important posts were sold, and Ottoman justice, once so admired by Europeans, became a mockery. A palace official, writing in 1630, stated that even the imperial household had become contaminated:

> . . . contrary to the law, . . . men with no religion and no faith, tricksters and topers [drunkards], and city riff-raff of no known nation or religion, Turcomans, gypsies, Tats [Tatars], Kurds, foreigners, . . . nomads, muleteers and camel drivers, porters, syrup-vendors, and all kinds of others [have entered government service] so that order and discipline have been ruined, laws and standards have ceased to exist. . . . [Bernard Lewis, *Istanbul and the Civilization of the Ottoman Empire.*]

The Turkish proverb, *The fish stinks from the head*, aptly illustrated what was happening. When the upper ranks of government were corrupted, Ottoman society began to degenerate.

Loss of Territorial Control

Outlying provinces such as Egypt, Yemen, the coastal regions of the Arabian Peninsula, the Kurdish provinces in eastern Anatolia, and Moldavia and Wallachia in Europe soon became semi-independent. From the time of their inclusion in the Ottoman Empire, many of these regions were permitted a great deal of self-government. Only lightly controlled from Istanbul, they had been allowed to keep their hereditary rulers as long as they made regular tax payments. With the easing of control and the growth of corruption at the center, the sultans soon lost what little authority they had had in these areas. Only when Turkish armies were sent to put down uprisings did such provinces acknowledge the sultan's supremacy.

Challenges by Foreign Powers

During the seventeenth century the Ottoman Empire met increasing opposition from foreign powers. Turkey and Austria competed for the Balkan region. Although beset by internal corruption and financial instability, the Ottoman Turks still strove to expand in eastern Europe during the seventeenth century. Their efforts, however, were met by the counterthrusts of the Austrian Hapsburgs who wanted to add Hungary to their own empire. Under the reforming Grand Vizier, Fazil Ahmed, Turkish forces wrested most of Hungary from the Austrians. In 1683 the Turkish armies surrounded and besieged Vienna. But the other European powers, although willing to dismember each other, could not permit the fall of one of their number to the Turkish outsiders. The Poles came to Austria's aid, and the siege was lifted. After intermittent fighting that lasted 16 years, Turkish aspirations in Europe were clipped. By the Treaty of Karlowitz of 1699 the Turks yielded most of Hungary to the Hapsburgs.

In the Middle East a new, powerful, Persian dynasty, the Safavids, blocked the Turkish advance toward India during the sixteenth century. On the sea, the Ottoman fleet was swept from the Indian Ocean and cut off from trade with the East Indies and the Far East by the Portuguese. On the Mediterranean, the Venetian navy gradually overcame Turkish supremacy. For a time they even **blockaded** the Dardanelles. And in Egypt, one of the wealthiest provinces of the empire, Mamluk advisers usurped much of the Turkish ruler's power and administered the land for their own profit.

After 1700 Russia, a formidable new rival, became another threat to the Ottoman Empire. Under Catherine the Great (1762–1796) the expanding Russian empire began to carve increasingly large pieces of territory from the sultan's domain. After a series of wars, the Turks were forced in 1774 to sign away a major part of their holdings in the Black Sea area to Russia. By the Treaty of Kuchuk Kainarji (koo-CHOOK keye-nahr-JIH, 1774) Turkey not only gave Russia a long stretch of territory along the Black Sea but also free passage to the Mediterranean through the Turkish Straits, a major goal of Russian **foreign policy** ever since. Later, on the basis of this treaty,

Russia also claimed the right to protect Greek Orthodox subjects of the sultan.

Effects on Industry and Commerce

Whereas the Ottomans had once been leaders in military science, they now fell behind the Europeans. When the empire ceased to expand, Ottoman society became increasingly closed to non-Muslims, and a false sense of security pervaded the government. Europe, on the other hand, was going through a period of rapid change, developing new forms of government, new theories of science and philosophy, and new military techniques. Revolutionary economic changes were causing many European countries to seek new markets and new sources of raw material in the East. Western businesspeople and merchants were penetrating the Ottoman Empire. At the same time Turks clung to their traditional occupations as soldiers, government officials, and farmers. Turkish merchants and craftsworkers clung to traditional methods in industry and commerce. Most Turks looked down on trade and commerce as a livelihood and left banking, importing, and exporting to Greeks, Armenians, Jews, and other non-Muslims. Like the Manchus in China, the Ottomans regarded Europeans as uncultured people from whom there was nothing to learn and little to fear. Consequently, the Ottomans were unprepared for the menace waiting at their doorstep.

Check Your Understanding

1. What changes took place in the sultanate that led to a loss of authority for the sultan?
2. What effect did bribery have on the Ruling and Muslim Institutions?
3. What caused Ottoman justice to be looked on as a mockery?
4. What foreign powers challenged Ottoman supremacy along its borders?
5. What effects did resistance to change have on the Ottoman economy?
6. *Thinking Critically*: How does the Turkish proverb, *The fish stinks from the head*, apply to Ottoman society in the seventeenth century?

CHAPTER REVIEW

■ Chapter Summary

Section 1. The Ottoman Empire began when Osman initiated a dynasty in territory in northwestern Anatolia. His successors expanded into Europe after crossing the Dardanelles in 1345 and then turned eastward to conquer the rest of the Anatolian Peninsula, Syria, and Palestine in the 1500's. Their eastward advance was halted temporarily by Tamerlane, but under Mehmed, expansion of the empire continued. His successors defeated the Byzantines at Constantinople in 1453, renaming the city Istanbul and making it the capital of the empire. Selim I defeated the Mamluks in Egypt, adding caliph to his title of sultan, and expanded into North Africa. Suleiman the Magnificent continued the expansion, again moving into Europe where his advance was halted at the gates of Vienna. Cultural expansion continued as the Ottomans became known as master builders, efficient government organizers, and poets and writers of distinction.

Section 2. The Ottomans ruled a diverse group of people of many languages, religions, and ethnic backgrounds. The people were divided into religious groups called millets, subject to the Ottoman sultan, but each governed by its own leaders. The Ottoman rulers preferred the term *sultan* to *caliph* and continued the dynastic concept of successors being chosen from the descendants of a single family. In matters concerning violations of Muslim law only, the sultan could be overruled by the Chief Mufti of Istanbul.

Section 3. The empire's civil and military affairs were managed by the Ruling Institution, which was composed of the sultan, officers of the sultan's household, the grand vizier and other major officials of the government, the standing army, and feudal lords. The Imperial Council, or Divan, headed by the grand vizier managed the empire's daily affairs. Also important to the empire's administration were the janissaries and the sipahis. Many janissaries as well as viziers and other government officials were trained from youth after their conscription from Christian communities. The sipahis made up the empire's hard-driving cavalry. They collected revenues from their feudal estates to furnish troops for the sultan's campaigns.

Section 4. The Muslim Institution paralleled the Ruling Institution in importance, but had a stronger influence on the makeup of the empire by uniting it under the Sharia and one system of education. Schools were associated with mosques. Graduates of the university law schools constituted the ulema, the learned men, who handed down rulings on Muslim life. Judges called qadis interpreted the ulema's rulings. They were assisted by experts in sacred law called muftis. The Chief Mufti was the leader of Islam. He resided in Istanbul and was the final authority in the interpretation of Mohammed's teachings.

Section 5. The Ottoman Empire began to decline in the seventeenth century. Internal corruption and decay in government led to erosion of the sultan's power. Abandonment of merit as a principal of promotion led to a weakening of the governmental system. Challenges from foreign powers contributed to loss of territories and further weakened the governmental system. Also instrumental in Ottoman decline were Muslim attitudes of superiority toward foreigners, their disdain of commerce and trade, and their resistance to new inventions and other changes in general.

■ **Vocabulary Review**

Define: ghazi, millet, capitulation, devshirme, haram, vizier, pasha, janissary, sipahi, ulema, qadi, mufti

■ **Places to Locate**

Locate: Anatolia, Black Sea, Aegean Sea, Dardanelles, Balkan Peninsula, Constantinople (Istanbul), Vienna

■ **People to Know**

Identify: Osman, Orkhan, Bayezid, Mehmed, Tamerlane, Selim I, Suleiman the Magnificent

■ **Thinking Critically**

1. Why was the capture of Constantinople important for the Turks?
2. What influence has the millet system had on present-day Middle East attitudes?
3. *A chain is only as strong as its weakest link.* How does this statement apply to the Ottoman Empire in its declining years?

■ Extending and Applying Your Knowledge

1. Give evidence of the diverse ethnic makeup of the Ottoman Empire by color-coding a map to show the location of each ethnic group.

2. Prepare an oral or written report on Suleiman the Magnificent, comparing his accomplishments and character with those of Tamerlane.

6

Modern Turkey

Modern Turkey began in 1922 after World War I had left the Ottoman Empire confined to the Anatolian Plateau and the European side of the Turkish Straits. Much of Turkey's history during the last 150 years can be written in terms of two forces—**Westernization** and **nationalism.**

Westernization was the attempt by many reformers to introduce into the empire the kinds of changes that had transformed the countries of Western Europe into modern industrialized **democracies.** Western political theories attracted Turkish students who wanted to see them applied at home. Nationalism caused various ethnic groups in the Balkan Peninsula to rebel against Ottoman control and demand their political rights. Both Westernization and nationalism helped bring about the breakup of the Ottoman Empire and the birth of modern Turkey. But other forces were also at work, including the struggle for power among the nations of Europe.

Today Turkey is a nation of contradictions beset by many problems. Its economy is stifled by an excess of imports over exports, insufficient resources to support a rapidly growing population, and a sense of traditionalism among farmers and other rural workers that hinder acceptance of social change. But Turkey has set an example for other nations trying to develop democratic ways. Because its people have always shown determination for achieving their goals, Turkey is making progress toward modernizing its ways and industrializing its economy.

1. Early Efforts at Reform

The Ottoman Empire thought of itself as the sword of Islam, conquering Europe for the Islamic faith. In Turkish eyes the Christian civilization of Europe was immensely inferior to Ottoman culture. But when the empire reached its territorial limits in the sixteenth century, it began to be challenged by European armies that surpassed its army in strength.

Reforms Under Selim III

Ottoman reformers became convinced that their country must adopt European military techniques and equipment. Among the first to reach this conclusion was Sultan Selim III, who ascended the throne in 1789 shortly before the outbreak of the French Revolution. Selim decided to create a new infantry trained and equipped along European lines. French officers arrived to organize the new forces and to give instruction to young Turkish officers at military and naval schools that Selim had established. Recognizing the importance of education, the sultan had printing plants built and encouraged the translation of Western books. He also opened embassies in European countries to gather information about the West.

Many Ottomans, particularly the janissary officers, opposed Selim's reforms. They believed that Western influence had grown too strong, and in 1807 military leaders supported a rebellion against the sultan. Selim was forced to abdicate, and reformers at the royal court were murdered.

Reforms Under Mahmud II

Mahmud II (mah-MOOD), who came to the throne in 1808, had been influenced by the ideas of his cousin Selim. Like his cousin, Mahmud turned first to military reform. He created a new armed force, a move that the janissaries resented, and in 1826 they mutinied. This time, however, the sultan was ready. Troops loyal to the sultan surrounded the janissary barracks and opened fire. Both in the capital and throughout the country the janissaries and their allies were killed by the thousands. Thus, the hard core of resistance to military reform was smashed.

Mahmud knew that much of the authority of the sultan had slipped into the hands of the army, the ulema, and the provincial sipahis. Mahmud intended to regain the sultan's lost authority. As we have seen, his first step was to reform the army and break the power of the janissaries. His second was to abolish the military fiefs, pension off the sipahis, and lease the land

TIMETABLE

From Empire to Modern Republic

1789	The beginning of Westernization
1829	Greek independence
1853–1856	The Crimean War
1876	Adoption of first Constitution
1878	Independence for Serbia, Rumania, Montenegro
1908	Young Turk revolution
1910	Bulgarian independence
1919–1922	Kemal's nationalist movement
1922	End of sultanate
1923	The Republic of Turkey
1928	Alphabet reform
1934	Surname adoption
	National suffrage for women
1938	Death of President Atatürk
1950	Formation of Democrat Party
1961	First coalition government
1982	Adoption of third constitution
1987	Election of Prime Minister Turgut Ozal

to tax farmers. A third measure was to eliminate the independence of the ulema and the Chief Mufti. No longer was the Chief Mufti to have complete control over legal revenues or the appointment of judges and teachers.

Mahmud's military reforms increased the pace of Westernization. To modernize and improve the army, Mahmud relied on education. Hundreds of students entered the military colleges, where they learned European techniques and languages. Even more affected by Western ideas were the young cadets whom Mahmud sent to European capitals to study. There many young men became acquainted with the writings of Western philosophers and political thinkers.

Mahmud hoped to introduce Western practices to his subjects as well as to his soldiers. Besides sending students to Europe, he also supported printing and translating because these were important means of spreading new ideas. Turkey's first newspapers were published during the 1820's. Mahmud even tried to change the outward appearance of his Muslim subjects. The turban was replaced by the fez, a red felt brimless cap of North African origin and beards were shaven to conform to European practices.

But the peasants who lived in isolated villages remained untouched by the changes introduced by Mahmud. Religious opposition and peasant failure to understand the conditions underlying social reform and the demands of a modern economy held back real change in the Ottoman Empire.

The Tanzimat

The reform movement continued after Mahmud's death. By sending young men to study in Europe and by improving the education of those entering the civil service, Mahmud created a new generation of reformers prepared to continue his policies of Westernization. Their ideas were put into edicts, called the Tanzimat (tan-ZEE-maht), the Reorganization.

A few months after Mahmud's death in 1839, his successor issued the first great reform edict, the *Hatti Sherif of Gülhane.* It consolidated many of the reforms enacted in the previous three decades by Mahmud. A second reform edict, issued in 1856, banned religious discrimination, modernized penalties for violations of criminal law, and provided for prison reform. But efforts of Ottoman reformers to carry out these decrees were often checked by the same obstacles that had blocked earlier attempts. The old ruling group resented the imposition of practices borrowed from Christian Europe. Their antagonism was fanned by the growth of nationalism among the Slavic Christian minorities of the Balkan Peninsula. Many of the reform measures had been designed to protect these Balkan minorities. (See pages 135-137.)

Check Your Understanding

1. What reform did Selim III begin, and how was his reform received?
2. What steps did Mahmud II take to restore the power to the sultanate?
3. What opposition to reforms arose within the empire?
4. *Thinking Critically:* How would Mahmud II's reforms have helped to Westernize Ottoman subjects?

2. The Effects of European Rivalry on the Empire

In the eyes of most European leaders in the nineteenth century, the Ottoman Empire was near collapse. They called it "the Sick Man of Europe" and were ready to dismember it if the opportunity arose. Only their rivalries with other European nations and individual national interests prevented a unified European attack on the empire. Instead, Britain, France, Austria–Hungary, and Russia competed for indirect influence in the Balkans. Often this meant meddling in the internal affairs of the empire. It also meant that the empire's problems with its Balkan provinces might easily turn into international crises.

The Eastern Question

Each European power tried to win the upper hand in the Balkans, and their efforts at working out a solution to the problem was called the "Eastern Question." The states of Europe debated whether to divide the provinces of the empire among themselves or to keep the empire alive but weak. Alive, the Balkan provinces could be a buffer state between the conflicting aims of Russia and Austria-Hungary and a roadblock against Russian penetration in the Middle East.

Britain as the Empire's Protector

In 1798 a French force landed in Egypt, but was forced out by the Ottomans and the British. After France's ouster, which had sought to further its commercial interests by becoming protector of the Roman Catholic Church in Ottoman lands, Britain assumed the role of the empire's protector. It thereby gained an important voice in settling conflicts that arose in the Middle East and in driving out rivals who offered challenges to the British position.

Britain's goal in the Middle East was to maintain a **balance of power.** Its overall foreign policy was aimed at preventing any one country from dominating the area. To accomplish their goal and keep a balance of power in the Middle East, Britain's foreign ministers were forced to protect the Ottoman Empire and oppose its breakup.

The Russian Threat

All during the nineteenth century the Russians attempted to gain a foothold south of the Black Sea. At times they tried to replace Britain as the empire's protector and thus win concessions to further their own interests. But more often Russia sup-

The original caption on this cartoon, which appeared in a German newspaper in 1895, read: "The Sick Man: But gentlemen, I am not dead yet." The patient is, of course, the Ottoman Empire, and the undertakers thrusting funeral bills in his face are (left to right) Britain, Russia, France, and Italy. Why might a German newspaper have printed a cartoon favoring the Ottomans?

ported minority groups within the empire in hopes that dissension would tear the empire apart. When the Greek subjects of the sultan revolted in 1821, Russia took on the role of protector and sided with the Greek rebels, who were Greek Orthodox Christians. The rebels eventually gained independence for a Greek state in 1829. Russian foreign policy also played on the growing nationalist sentiments of the Balkan Slavs and encouraged their efforts to break away from the empire.

The Crimean War

Mounting tension between millets, each supported by one of the European powers, led to violence in Jerusalem during the 1840's and 1850's. In 1853, after Russian forces moved to the borders of two Turkish provinces, the czar sent an ultimatum to the Ottoman sultan demanding exclusive rights for Russia to protect Orthodox Christians in the empire. When the Ottoman government rejected the demand, Russia declared war.

The once fierce Turks were no longer a match for the Russian fighting forces, and the czar's navy quickly destroyed the Ottoman fleet on the Black Sea. Recognizing that the Ottoman Empire was in danger of collapse and the balance of power in the area was about to be destroyed, Britain and France hurried to the empire's rescue. When the Russians refused to withdraw from the Crimean Peninsula on the Black Sea, the European powers declared war on Russia.

The Crimean War with Russia fighting Britain, France, Sardinia, and Turkey raged from 1853 to 1856. Both sides finally accepted a **compromise** that was incorporated in the Peace of Paris, 1856. The **status quo** was restored except for minor changes granting autonomy to the Ottoman Christians in the Balkans. (The minor changes referred to here had nothing to do with the edict of 1856 that is mentioned on page 134. That edict was forced on the Ottomans by the British, French, and Austrian ambassadors.) The treaty also called for the Black Sea to be neutralized and the Bosporus and the Dardanelles were closed to all warships. (See map, page 144.) Although the Crimean War prevented Russia from gaining direct access to the Mediterranean Sea, access to the Turkish Straits and control of the city of Istanbul remained a major Russian foreign policy objective.

Russian Intrigue in the Balkans

Czar Alexander II (1855–1881), objecting to the restrictions that the Treaty of Paris imposed on Russian aspirations, was determined to stir the boiling pot of Balkan nationalism. Russian agents aroused Balkan Slavs against their Turkish rulers. A Russian-supported Slavic movement encouraged revolt against the Ottomans and incited demands for independence under Russian protection. "All Slavs are brothers!" became the rallying cry. After arousing the Slavic peoples in the Ottoman Empire's Balkan provinces to revolt, Russia claimed the right to intervene to protect "Russian security." Another Russo–Turkish war resulted in Ottoman defeat. At San Stefano in 1878 the czar forced a treaty upon the Ottomans that provided for a larger and self-governing Bulgaria and decreed independence for Serbia, Rumania, and Montenegro.

Check Your Understanding

1. What was the Eastern Question?
2. How did Britain acquire its role as protector of the Ottoman Empire?
3. **a.** What were Russia's goals in the Middle East?
   b. What methods did Russia use in trying to achieve its goals?
4. **Thinking Critically:** Citing evidence from the textbook, illustrate the stand taken by Britain, Russia, and France on the Eastern Question.

3. The Seeds of Revolution

During the second half of the nineteenth century, a widening gulf developed between younger Turks who studied and traveled throughout Europe and the older men of the Tanzimat. The younger men, influenced by the democratic governments of Great Britain and France, criticized the **autocratic** rule of the Ottoman sultans.

Young Reformers

An important leader of the young reformers was Namik Kemal. Namik Kemal was a dramatist and political writer familiar with the writings of European political thinkers. Their ideas concerning liberty, rule by law, and the protection of property led Kemal to believe that the progress and prosperity of the European nations were due in large part to their parliamentary and constitutional forms of government. If Turkey was to match the European achievement, it too must establish a **constitutional government.**

Kemal and the young thinkers who agreed with him expressed their ideas and criticisms in **radical** journals and newspapers. Many of these young reformers were forced into exile, but they continued their attacks in foreign publications. Most, however, were allowed to return to Turkey in 1871, just as the Ottoman government was entering a period of severe crisis.

The Last Ottoman Reformer

In 1871 the Grand Vizier, Ali Pasha, who had given Turkey honest, efficient government, died. Because of weak advisers and the extravagance of the new sultan, the Ottoman government was led to the brink of bankruptcy. On top of this, a rebellion broke out in the Christian provinces of Bosnia and Herzegovina (her-t'zuh-goh-VEE-nuh) and spread to Bulgaria, where it was brutally suppressed by Ottoman forces. For a time it looked as if the European powers would again intervene.

At this point, Midhat Pasha, a former government official, emerged from retirement. Fearing foreign intervention, he organized in 1876 a successful **coup** to depose the sultan. When a new sultan, Abdul Hamid II (ahb-DOOL hah-MEED), came to the throne, reformers expected great things from a ruler who had traveled in the West and been exposed to European ideas. The sultan appointed Midhat Grand Vizier, and together they proclaimed the country's first **constitution.** Although Islam was the official religion, all subjects of the sultan once again were declared to be free and equal. A two-chamber **parliament** was given the power to approve laws presented by the sultan's council of ministers. Provincial and municipal councils were established to deal with local matters. The country's minorities and intellectuals rejoiced when this constitution was proclaimed. They believed that a new era was dawning, one that would bring life in their country closer to Westernization.

The Return of Repressive Rule

Abdul Hamid resented Midhat's great popularity and the growing independence of parliament. Taking advantage of an emergency provision in the constitution, he soon suspended that document. Abdul Hamid next exiled Midhat and dismissed parliament. In 1881 the sultan again ordered Midhat's arrest and banished him along with several other reformers.

To divert attention from his repressive acts, the sultan tried to arouse nationalist feelings and to promote an Islamic revival. The title of caliph, long in disuse, was reinstated so that Abdul Hamid might assume the role of the leader of Islam. This tactic was particularly successful in whipping up Muslim fervor against the Balkan Christian nationalists. To prevent plotting against his **dictatorship,** the sultan sent spies to all parts of the empire to hunt out his enemies. Rigid press **censorship** was imposed, unfriendly newspapers suppressed, and outspoken editors driven into exile.

Rise of the Young Turks

Hundreds of **liberals** fled the country, and their writings were smuggled into the empire from abroad. Despite secret police, spies, and terrorism, Western ideas infiltrated the empire. At home young army officers conspired with students in schools and colleges to overthrow the sultan. These young revolutionaries remained in contact with the Turks in exile. Together they were known as the Young Turks.

The immediate problems facing the Young Turks were Balkan and Turkish nationalism and the role that Christian minorities should have in the Ottoman Empire. One group of Young Turks favored Ottomanism, the formation of a multinational empire similar to Austria-Hungary. All subjects, regardless of race, nationality, or religion were to be equal. Another group, the Pan-Turanists, pressed for a "Turks First" policy that would put minorities in their place. This group, looking for a justification of its policy, sought to find in ancient times the "pure" origins of Turkish blood. According to the Pan-Turanists, the Ottoman

Turks were an offshoot of a great Turanian race that had once inhabited Russia, Central Asia, and western China. Other revolutionary groups favored a strongly centralized government. Still others proposed **autonomy** for the various nationalities of the Ottoman Empire.

Those who supported Turkish nationalism and called for greater centralization formed the Society of Union and Progress. General direction was provided by the society's Committee of Union and Progress (CUP) with headquarters in Paris, but with branches throughout the Ottoman Empire. Government officials and professionals, especially army officers, formed the backbone of this secret society.

The Young Turks in Power

Young Turk propaganda won many converts within the military forces and among army officers in the empire. These converts feared that the empire was about to collapse under the external pressure of European intervention and the internal pressure of Balkan nationalism. In 1908 their fears led to a general revolt. The CUP supported the revolt and demanded that the sultan restore the constitution of 1876. In the cities peoples of all races and religions rejoiced at the end of Abdul Hamid's authoritarian rule.

Working in secret, the CUP soon came to dominate the newly convened parliament. Instead of multinationalism, the Young Turks of the CUP advocated ultra-Turkish nationalism. Their aim seemed to be to "Turkify" the country rather than to further the hope of Albanians, Armenians, Bulgarians, Greeks, Kurds, and Arabs.

The **conservatives** in the Muslim clergy found fault with the Young Turks, calling their leaders godless. Before long a counter-revolutionary organization, the League of Mohammed, was set up to fight CUP godlessness. With Abdul Hamid's backing, the League succeeded in overthrowing the CUP government for a few days in 1909. But less than two weeks later the Young Turks returned to power. Deposing Abdul Hamid in favor of a younger brother, the CUP eliminated its chief opponents.

Continuing Problems in the Balkans

Taking advantage of the upheaval produced by the revolution of 1908, Bulgaria declared its independence. Crete announced its union with Greece. Austria annexed Bosnia and Herzegovina. The Young Turks now abandoned all pretense of reform and

The Armenian Genocide

The Armenians, an ancient Middle Eastern people, converted to Christianity soon after its founding. The largest concentration of Armenians lived in the Anatolian region of the Ottoman Empire. In the 1890's, along with other non-Muslim and non-Turkish minorities in the empire, the Armenians developed a strong spirit of nationalism. In the forefront of the Armenian nationalist movement were the leaders of the three Armenian religious communities—Gregorian, Catholic, and Protestant. Like other nationalist groups, the Armenians organized secret revolutionary societies, or organizations, that worked to achieve cultural independence and a greater recognition of Armenian rights.

During the 1890's, the Ottoman authorities attacked Armenian villages in Turkey's eastern provinces, charging that the villagers were committing treason by receiving assistance from the Russians and collaborating with them. In these attacks, at least 100,000 Armenians were killed.

During World War I an even greater number of Armenians lost their lives. Beginning in 1915, Armenian soldiers in the Ottoman army were stripped of their weapons and put to work in forced labor camps, or shot. In eastern Turkey, groups of Armenians rebelled with the aid of Russia, leading to further killing. By June 1915, the Ottoman government deported all non-Muslims, moving them away from military zones and lines of communication. All non-Muslims in the armed services were sent to unarmed service units.

Between 1915 and 1917, nearly all Armenians (an estimated 1,500,000) were driven from Anatolia, most across the Syrian desert where hundreds of thousands died from starvation, exhaustion, and exposure. In the Turkish War for Independence (1920–1922) additional numbers of Armenians were killed. Estimates of the total number of Armenians who had perished by the end of 1922 range from 600,000 to nearly two million. The Armenian **genocide** remains one of the most controversial issues in modern Middle Eastern history.

Soldiers of the Young Turks ride in triumph after the success of the 1908 revolution that deposed Abdul Hamid II. They carry the crescent moon-and-star banner, which had been an Ottoman symbol since Mehmed II captured Constantinople in 1453. The moon-and-star symbol also appears on the flags of the Republic of Turkey and other Muslim states.

equal treatment for non-Muslims and non-Turks. They declared their aim was to "Turkify" the empire and to destroy all other national movements. They had little success, however. In the next few years the Balkans became the most dangerous trouble spot in Europe. Greece, Bulgaria, Albania, Serbia, and Montenegro quarreled among themselves and with Turkey over densely populated Balkan lands. In North Africa, Italy seized Tripoli (now Libya) from the Ottoman Empire, while the Arabs revolted in Syria and Yemen. In eastern Turkey the Ottomans suppressed an Armenian nationalist movement. (See page 141.)

The Failure of Political Solutions

Despite the efforts of early military reformers, the Tanzimat, and the Young Turks, the problems of the empire were too far-reaching to be eliminated. By the outbreak of World War I Slavic nationalism in the Balkans had completely undermined Ottoman authority. The Turks, who had always been outnumbered by the many ethnic groups they ruled, were now unable to prevent these people from creating their own intellectual and cultural ways of life.

Although the Turkish reformers realized that their empire urgently needed to change, their understanding and imitation of Western methods were often inadequate. For example, the reformers failed to see that much of Europe's prosperity and progress was the result of the Industrial Revolution and its creation of an ever-expanding economy. Blinded by the traditional Ottoman attitude toward trade and business, the reformers tried to solve Turkey's problems with political solutions instead of encouraging new industries or modernizing agriculture. Many reforms proclaimed in Istanbul never reached the distant peasant villages. The conservative Muslim clergy sought to protect the faithful from modernization, calling all changes introduced from the West "Christian" innovations and "works of the devil." As the ulema became increasingly suspicious and hostile to non-Muslims, many Ottoman officials came to share their views.

Check Your Understanding

1. What did Namik Kemal and other reformers want for the empire?
2. What reforms occurred under Midhat Pasha?
3. How did Abud Hamid react to Midhat's liberal reforms?
4. **a.** Who were the Young Turks? **b.** Which group of Young Turks emerged as leaders of the revolution?
5. *Thinking Critically:* How did Balkan nationalism and traditional Turkish attitudes affect the success of the Young Turks' Revolution?

4. Collapse of the Ottoman Empire

Rivalries and intrigues among the great powers for positions of influence in the decaying Ottoman Empire played an important part in events leading up to the outbreak of World War I. Russia had long insisted on intervening in the region to "protect the interests" of fellow Slavs and fellow Christians against their Muslim rulers. Britain and France countered Russian moves vigorously until the appearance of a more formidable competitor, Germany.

Beginnings of World War I

Slavic nationalism reached a fever pitch in the opening years of the twentieth century. The situation was complicated by the jealousy various Slavic peoples felt for each other, by the intrigues carried on by Russia and Austria-Hungary for influence in the Balkans, and by the system of **alliances** into which the

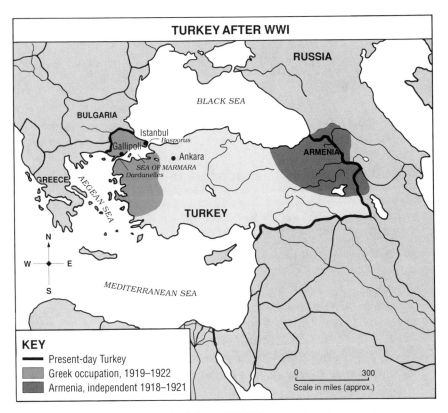

TURKEY AFTER WWI

RUSSIA

BLACK SEA

BULGARIA

Istanbul
Bosporus
Gallipoli
● Ankara
SEA OF MARMARA
Dardanelles

ARMENIA

GREECE

AEGEAN SEA

TURKEY

N
W ◆ E
S

MEDITERRANEAN SEA

KEY
— Present-day Turkey
Greek occupation, 1919–1922
Armenia, independent 1918–1921

0   300
Scale in miles (approx.)

PLACE: TURKEY AFTER WORLD WAR I. The Greek occupation in Turkey began in 1919, even before the Treaty of Sèvres (1920). Armenia's existence as an independent republic died with the Treaty of Lausanne in 1923, which recognized Turkey's independence and set its boundaries.

countries of Europe had locked themselves. On one side was the Triple Alliance of Austria-Hungary, Germany, and Italy. On the other side was the Triple Entente of Britain, France, and Russia. Any conflict involving one of them would inevitably involve the others. A particular troublespot was the Austrian-held provinces of Bosnia and Herzegovina that Serbia coveted.

On June 28, 1914, the Archduke Franz Ferdinand, heir to the throne of Austria-Hungary, was murdered in Sarajevo (sahr-ah-YAY-voh), capital of the province of Bosnia. The assassin was a young Bosnian who sympathized with Serbia. The Austrians used the murder of their crown prince as an excuse to crush the Serbs, who called on Russia for support. On July 30 Russia mobilized its troops; on August 3 Germany declared war on France; on August 4 Great Britain declared war on Germany. World War I was underway.

Turkish Participation

Regarding the Russians as a greater threat than the Germans, the Ottoman Empire joined the war on the side of the Central Powers. This side consisted of the former Triple Alliance nations of Germany, Austria-Hungary and Bulgaria. Lined up against the Central Powers were the Allies. The Allies consisted of the Triple Entente nations of Great Britain, France, and Russia along with Serbia and Italy, who was a former member of the Triple Alliance.

Turkey's greatest moment in the war came in 1915. A large British land and sea force had for several months been attempting to open the Dardanelles to Allied shipping, but they were continually met with stubborn and effective resistance from the Turks. When the British decided to evacuate their troops from the Gallipoli Peninsula near the Straits, the passageway to the Bosporus and the Black Sea (see map, page 144) remained closed to the much-needed supplies that might have been of considerable aid to Russia in its desperate struggle on the Eastern Front. The retreat from Gallipoli, which still rankles in British memories, is a source of national pride and satisfaction to the people of Turkey.

By the end of the war Turkey was overrun by Allied troops, and even Istanbul was occupied. In 1920 the Allies imposed the humiliating Treaty of Sèvres on the Turks. The occupied Ottoman provinces were divided among Great Britain, France, Italy, and Greece. An independent Armenia and an autonomous Kurdish state were carved out of eastern Anatolia. The Turkish Straits and the country's government, including its armed forces, finances, and what was left of its territory were placed under Allied control. Turkey became a powerless vassal state, subject to European domination.

The major problems facing postwar Turkey were to prevent total collapse and further loss of territory from Greek nationalists, who were eager to revive their ancient Hellenic empire at Turkey's expense. In 1919 a Greek army landed in Anatolia at Smyrna, which the Turks later changed to Izmir (IZ-mir). Protected by Allied warships, the Turks' traditional enemy began to advance eastward with the intention of annexing Western Anatolia.

Organized Resistance

Many Turks resented the degrading treatment imposed by the victorious Allies. Among the Turks was a young army officer named Mustafa Kemal (moos-tah-FAH keh-MAHL), who had helped turn back the British in their attempt to seize control of the Turkish Straits. A few days after the invasion of Smyrna, Kemal organized an army to fight the Greeks. He also organized a resistance movement among the people of Anatolia. He then summoned delegates to a congress to plan strategy for the ensuing struggle.

Soon the resistance army was fighting both the Greeks and the authorities in Istanbul, who feared that the nationalist movement under Kemal might oust the sultan. But the war against Greece aroused a spirit of nationalism among the Turkish people. The struggle had religious overtones, since many Turks regarded the war as a fight to save their homeland from Christian control. Before long Turks everywhere, as well as the Allies, began to look on Kemal's nationalists as Turkey's true government.

The Nationalists in Power

Victory over the Greeks was assured in 1922 when the Greek army was driven from Anatolia. The war had shown that Kemal and the nationalists had the support of the people. During the war Mustafa Kemal had made the declaration that **sovereignty** belonged to the people. In 1922, at the urging of Kemal, the National Assembly separated the offices of sultan and caliph and then abolished the sultanate. The following year Turkey was declared a **republic** and Ankara became its capital. After 500 years of imperial rule, the Ottoman Empire came to an end.

Check Your Understanding

1. What role did the Balkans play in bringing about World War I?
2. Why did Turkey align itself with the Central Powers during World War I?
3. What was the result of Turkish participation in the war?
4. Who was Mustafa Kemal, and how did he come to power?
5. **Thinking Critically:** Explain how nationalism was both an advantage and a disadvantage for the Turkish people.

5. The Founding of Modern Turkey

The traditions that held the Turks to the past had to be broken if a modern Turkey was to rise from the ashes of the Ottoman Empire. Mustafa Kemal, the new republic's first president, set about changing the people's culture and attitudes as well as their political institutions. He did this through his tight control of the Republican People's Party (RPP), first formed in the early days of the resistance.

The Republican People's Party

Kemal's forceful personality, strong sense of mission, and astute political skill enabled him to hold power until his death in 1938. While Kemal lived, only members of the RPP, which included most of the country's leading nationalists, held office. The RPP dominated the National Assembly and monopolized all important positions.

Kemal believed that without tight control he could not modernize Turkey. Like other reformers before and since, he felt that only a benevolent dictatorship could prepare the way for democracy. In the first years of his presidency, Kemal jailed his opponents, torturing some and executing others. Later, however, he no longer needed to use repression to maintain a stable government. Most Turks felt that Kemal had saved the independence of their country. As a result, his government and the RPP had widespread popular support.

The RPP program had six goals: republicanism, nationalism, **populism**, **statism**, **secularism**, and reformism. In other words Turkey was to be a republic. It was to be guided by Turkish nationalism for the benefit of the people (populism) with a state-controlled economy (statism). It was to be free from religious domination (secularism), and it was to be motivated by a spirit of reform. The RPP moved quickly to implement these goals.

Establishing a Secular State

In 1924 the National Assembly abolished the caliphate. The break with Islam reflected Kemal's conviction that religious conservatives were the greatest obstacle to progress in Turkey. Kemal was opposed to mixing religious and non-religious affairs. He sought to "Turkify" the Muslim faith by ridding it of Arab influences. Use of Arabic was banned in public ceremonies, and the Koran was translated into Turkish. All public education was placed under a secular Ministry of Public Instruction in order to end the domination of education by the conservative Muslim clergy.

When the Ministry of Religious Affairs and its privileges were abolished, Islam's official status as a state religion came to an end. Sharia courts were closed, their jurisdiction turned over to secular courts, using legal codes adopted from the West. Muslim religious orders were outlawed.

Kemal also ordered other changes aimed at undermining Turkish ties to traditional practices. In 1925 he ordered the Assembly to pass a law forbidding men to wear the fez. In announcing the law, Kemal said: "We are going to adopt the civilized international mode of dress, including a headdress with a brim; this I wish to say openly. The name of this headdress is 'hat'."

Villagers protested that Western-style hats interfered with the performance of their religious duties. They said the brim made it impossible to touch the forehead to the ground during prayers. Kemal also attacked the veiling of women, although he did not actually ban the use of the veil.

Language Reform

Language reform was closely related to the numerous other changes in tradition instituted by Kemal and the National Assembly. In 1928 a new alphabet replaced the traditional Arabic script in which Turkish had always been written. The replacement of this script with a Westernized alphabet struck another blow at the conservative opponents of change. But the new alphabet also promoted literacy by simplifying reading and writing. With the new alphabet, it was possible to print books more rapidly and it was easier for people to learn writing. Literacy in the new alphabet was also made a requirement for public office. Within a few months of the alphabet's introduction, books, newspapers, public documents, and all signs were printed in the new letters. During the next decades literacy increased throughout the nation.

Economic Reforms

In an effort to reduce the influence of Europeans and other non-Muslims in the economy, Kemal introduced a system of state socialism to ensure an independent Turkish economy. "We shall create," declared Kemal, "every industry, great or small, for which there are in our land the economic conditions necessary to its work and development." While state banks were established to finance government-controlled enterprises, Turkish industry never reached its hoped-for importance. Government bureaucracy, red tape, and poor planning hampered efforts to make Turkey into an industrialized nation.

Reaching the People

Village life changed little during Kemal's lifetime. Most villagers, or peasants, who made up about 75 percent of Turkey's population, remained illiterate and superstitious. They retained a deep longing for old Muslim customs and traditions. This continued despite the government's efforts during the 1930's to bring reforms to all parts of the country through the establishment of People's Houses and Village Institutes.

The main purpose of the People's Houses was to educate the villagers and to acquaint them with the best of the new Turkish culture. They were also used to strengthen the influence of the RPP. The Village Institutes were schools that trained secondary school graduates to become teachers for rural areas. Reforms proved more effective, however, in the larger cities where government supervision was more direct.

One reform that affected everyone in Turkey was contained in a law passed in 1934. This law required everyone in Turkey to adopt a surname, or last name. Kemal led the way by adopting Atatürk, which meant "First and Foremost Turk" or "Father of the Turks." With the adoption of Atatürk, Kemal became known as Kemal Atatürk.

Before the law requiring the adoption of a surname, a Turkish baby received only one name. This was sufficient identification among villagers. But more precise names were needed as more people moved to cities, the cities grew, and people learned how to read and write. Many Turks found it difficult to decide on a surname, and some took as long as two years to make their decision. A few people made nicknames their official surnames. Others chose a name derived from the father's name or occupation. The majority of Turks, however, chose their names from a list provided by the government. Among the most popular were Sturdy, Bright, Whitesoul, and Trueturk.

Ismet İnönü

Atatürk died in 1938 at the age of 57. He was deeply mourned throughout the republic he had helped create, and his tomb was declared a national monument. Ismet İnönü—a close friend, army comrade, and political associate of Atatürk—was chosen

SHAPER OF A NATION. Atatürk's intense desire to modernize his country led him to push his reforms at every opportunity. Here he teaches the new Latin alphabet at a park in Istanbul in 1928. Below, the splendid mausoleum and memorial to Turkey's first president dominates a vast plaza in Ankara, the city he chose for the republic's capital. Turks regard the building as a national shrine.

as the new president of Turkey by unanimous vote of the National Assembly.

Inönü, who took as his surname the name of the town where he had fought in an important Turkish victory over the Greeks, governed Turkey during World War II. He kept his nation neutral in the war until 1945, when it became obvious who the winner was going to be. Then he declared war against Germany and the other Axis powers. In aligning Turkey with the Allies, Inönü avoided a repetition of the mistake made by Turkey in World War I.

Check Your Understanding

1. What were the goals of Kemal's Republican People's Party, or RPP?
2. **a.** Which goal was a top priority for Kemal? **b.** How did he implement this goal?
3. How was language reform tied to secularism?
4. What prevented Turkish industry from surpassing agriculture in the national economy?
5. **a.** How did Kemal come to acquire the surname Atatürk? **b.** Why was this name change significant?
6. Who succeeded to the presidency of Turkey after Atatürk's death?
7. **Thinking Critically:** Cite evidence from the text to prove or disprove the statement: *Atatürk gave Turkey a modern, Western image.*

6. Government Since 1945

In the early days of the republic, Atatürk's ruling style had prevented the formation of more than one political party. During World War II, Inönü maintained Atatürk's one-party political system. But once World War II had ended with an Allied victory and democracy was proclaimed a national ideal, Inönü permitted new political parties to form. The entire postwar period has been marked by political struggles for dominance within the multiparty system.

The Democrat Party

Celâl Bayar and Adnan Menderes (men-DEH-rez), two RPP members who were unhappy with RPP policies, founded the Democrat Party in 1945. Between 1946 and 1950, the Democrats worked hard to build their party organization in the many small towns and farming villages of rural Turkey, capitalizing on the growing discontent with RPP policies and one-party rule. Farmers resented the neglect of rural areas and the falling prices for agricultural products. Students and intellectuals disliked the restraints on the press and on political organizations. People in business hoped for less governmental control of the economy, the lowering of import barriers, and an end to the maze of complicated government regulations. Religious conservatives dreamed of the return of outlawed Muslim practices and the restoration of more authority to Islamic leaders.

In the election of 1950, Turkey's first free election, the Democrat Party was swept into office. Menderes became the **prime minister** and made that post the real center of government. Bayar remained in the background as president. Many restrictions on business were lifted. **Trade unions** were permitted. Above all, much greater attention was paid to the needs of the long-neglected Turkish peasants.

With American aid, roads were built to link rural areas to cities where produce could be marketed. The number of schools increased, and greater numbers of girls attended them. New roads and schools brought modern ideas into remote rural regions. Mass-circulation newspapers and radios kept people in the rural areas informed about developments in the capital and other urban areas of the country. Some land reform occurred. In addition, tractors, other kinds of farm machinery, and modern methods of agriculture were widely introduced.

Criticism and Overthrow

By 1956 Turkey's economy suffered a downturn, and the nation hovered on the edge of bankruptcy. Criticism of the Democrat Party increased. Critics charged that the reforms undertaken by Menderes were not always considered carefully, that programs seemed more for show than for real improvement, and that only a small segment of the population received any benefit from them. Menderes reacted to the mounting disapproval by trying to silence public criticism. One by one he closed opposition newspapers. He clamped down on the universities, dismissing outspoken professors. Developing a new **authoritarianism,** Menderes began to use the military to support his political machine. He established a committee to investigate, try, and imprison outspoken members of the RPP and other political parties. When former President Inönü was expelled from parliament for criticiz-

Menderes showed his new authoritarianism by using the military to support his political machine and to suppress criticism of his strong-arm tactics. In this photo mounted police in Istanbul in 1960 are putting down an anti-Menderes demonstration by university students. Why would Menderes have considered university students a threat to his rule?

ing the Menderes dictatorship, a storm of protest swept the country.

On May 27, 1960, the Turkish army staged a bloodless coup, the most important upheaval in Turkish history since the time of Atatürk. President Bayar, Prime Minister Menderes, all cabinet members, and about 400 members of the Democrat Party were arrested and later tried. Menderes was executed and Bayar sentenced to life imprisonment. A **military junta** called the National Unity Committee (NUC) took over the government. The junta, promising to "work for nothing else than the welfare of the nation," ruled until a new constitution was approved by the voters in a public referendum.

Government Under the 1960 Constitution

The new constitution, which replaced the one in force since 1924, guaranteed social and political security to all citizens. It established a bicameral, or two-chamber, parliament composed of a National Assembly and a Senate, both elected by popular vote. All legislation passed by parliament had to be approved by a new 15-member Constitutional Court. The Constitution also recognized a multiparty political system, attempting to avoid the kind of one-person authoritarian rule imposed by Atatürk, Inönü, and Menderes.

In the election campaign for the new parliament, the NUC recognized four political parties. These were the RPP; the Nation Party, an offshoot of the RPP formed in the 1950's; the Justice Party, the refuge of former members of the now outlawed Democrat Party; and the New Turkey Party, formed by Democrat Party members opposed to Menderes.

In order to control the government, one party had to win a majority of the seats in parliament. But with four different parties vying for seats, no party was able to win a majority. As a result, in 1961, Turkey had its first government by **coalition.** The Republican People's Party, which gained the most seats in parliament, named the prime minister. But the prime minister had to cooperate with the other parties to form the government and keep it in power.

The Justice Party and Public Unrest

The Justice Party, under the leadership of Suleyman Demirel, was the most powerful political adversary of the Republican People's Party. By attacking the RPP as the party of the elite upper classes, it attracted workers and farmers in both the urban and rural areas and people with a conservative religious outlook. In the elections of 1965 and 1969, the Justice Party won a majority of seats. It encouraged the construction of hundreds of new mosques, permitted prayers in Arabic, and authorized Islamic religious instruction in government-run schools. But the Justice Party was unable to cope effectively with Turkey's growing international indebtedness, rising inflation, and increased unemployment.

In 1970 public unrest erupted in large-scale demonstrations by students. Rival trade unions clashed in the streets. Public employees went out on strike. Anti-Americanism showed itself in terrorism, resulting in bomb attacks on United States property and in the kidnapping of American citizens.

When the army intervened in 1971, Demirel resigned. A series of broad coalition governments that included both the RPP and the Justice Party followed. **Martial law** was declared in several provinces, newspapers were supressed, strikes banned,

Between 1971 and 1980 when a military junta again took over the government, Suleyman Demirel, shown campaigning here in 1977, participated in several coalition governments as leader of the conservative, pro-Western Justice Party. Demirel's chief opponent in this election was a leftist. Why would the West have preferred Demirel's election to that of his leftist opponent?

and hundreds of radicals arrested. Political assassination and other acts of terrorism were almost daily occurrences. Victims were from all political parties and every sector of society. In September 1980 a six-officer military junta of five generals and an admiral took over the government to prevent the spread of "anarchy and terrorism."

The National Security Council

Calling themselves the National Security Council (NSC), the junta suspended parliament, banned all political parties, and imposed strict press censorship. It arrested 30,000 people, including the leaders of all major political parties. Within a year, safety and economic conditions improved. The NSC then authorized plans for drafting still another constitution, submitting it to the people in 1982.

The new constitution greatly increased the power of the president. It also outlawed all political parties that were considered either too liberal or too conservative. The objective of the constitution was to ban both Marxists and Islamic militants and to give the president power to control political dissent that occurred within the country.

By 1983 the NSC decided that the country was stable enough to permit elections for a new National Assembly. But it allowed only three hand-picked parties to participate in the election, at the same time forbidding all former political leaders to run for office. The election resulted in the victory of Turgut Ozal, a former deputy prime minister who had worked closely as an economic adviser to the NSC.

Politics Today

By 1987 the NSC finally relaxed restrictions on some 200 political leaders, allowing the former leaders of the RPP and the Justice Party to return to politics in parties with new labels. In the November 1987 parliamentary elections, seven parties vied for seats, but only three parties gained sufficient votes to be seated in the parliament. They include Ozal's Motherland Party, Demirel's True Path Party, and the former RPP, now known as the Social Democratic Party and led by Erdal Inönü, the son of Ismet Inönü.

Check Your Understanding

1. What kinds of discontent swept the Democrat Party into office in the election of 1950?
2. What kinds of criticism of Menderes led to the establishment of a military junta?
3. Why did the new constitution of 1960 establish a multiparty system?
4. What did the Justice Party accomplish?
5. Describe the operations of the National Security Council.
6. What parties were represented in the National Assembly after the 1987 elections?
7. **Thinking Critically:** How is a multiparty system both an advantage and a disadvantage to the establishment of a stable democracy?

7. Domestic and Social Policies

The return to political stability in the late 1980's gave hope that Turkey would be able to improve the social and economic conditions that gave rise to its political unheavals.

Turkey's Standard of Living

Several different statistical measures are used to determine a country's standard of living. Two of the chief measures are the **gross national product** and the **per capita income.** The gross national product (GNP) is the total value of all of the goods and services produced in a country in a year. The gross national product divided by the country's population gives the per capita income. Turkey's per capita income is approximately $1,300 U.S. dollars, a figure that is about half that of Syria, but much lower than the per capita incomes of the oil-rich nations of the Middle East.

One reason for Turkey's low per capita income is Turkey's population, which is growing at the rate of approximately a million people a year. Four out of every ten people are under the age of 15, but only six out of 100 are 60 years of age or older. Turkey's low standard of living takes its toll on its inhabitants. Life expectancy, the average number of years a baby can be expected to live, is 57.

Population Distribution

Another reason for Turkey's low per capita income is the distribution of its labor force. More than half of its labor force (58 percent) is engaged in agriculture. Yet only 34 percent of Turkey's land is suitable for agriculture. With insufficient land in rural areas to provide a living, many farm families are moving to the cities, thus increasing the urban population. In 1945 the urban population of Turkey was only 25 percent. Today it is 55 percent. Millions of Turks are now crammed into *gecekondu,* vast urban slums built of tin shacks, surrounding Instanbul, Ankara, and Izmir. Others have left Turkey to find employment as low-paid unskilled workers in West Germany and other Western European cities.

Outside the major urban areas, many of Turkey's 40,000 villages have been little affected by modernization. In some rural areas the wooden plow is still very much in use. Turkey's economic growth has been hampered by the heavy burden of government restrictions and controls, a heritage from the Atatürk era when the economy was state directed. With the burden only recently lifted, the new regime under Turgut Ozal has begun experiments with **free enterprise,** selling to private investors many of the state economic enterprises that were established under Atatürk. It has also removed government currency and import controls.

Literacy, Education, and the Status of Women

Raising the level of literacy and removing from women the restraints imposed on them by Islamic traditions and beliefs was an important aspect of Kemal Atatürk's program to modernize Turkey. During one of his campaign speeches in 1925, he observed:

> A society or nation consists of two kinds of people called men and women. Can we shut our eyes to one portion of a group, while advancing the other, and still bring progress to the whole group? Can half a community ascend to the skies, while the other half remains chained in the dust? The road of progress must be trodden by both sexes together, marching arm in arm as comrades. . . .

To assure the equality of the sexes, Kemal Atatürk changed the legal status of women in Turkish society by adopting Western legal codes. Polygamy was banned, and wives attained the same legal rights as their husbands in divorce proceedings. Women were also granted suffrage, first in local elections. By 1934 they had received the right to run for office and to vote in national elections.

Atatürk changed other customs as well, such as permitting women to appear in public without a face veil and giving them access to public education. Today Turkey has one of the highest percentages of university-educated women in the Middle East. The number of women professionals—lawyers, physicians, professors, bankers, and business managers—is greater than in any other Muslim country and even than in some European nations. Several women are among modern Turkey's most notable novelists. One of the most outstanding is Adalet Agaoglu.

In rural areas, however, women are often closely guarded and subjected to severe penalties for any lapse in the traditional Islamic moral code. Few attend school, keeping Turkey's literacy rate from rising higher than 70 percent. In urban areas, it is increasingly difficult for secondary school graduates of both sexes to gain acceptance at a university. Because of the high number of applicants for university education, only a small percentage of the applicants is accepted. Even then, many of

MODERNIZATION IN TURKEY. Contrasts between technology and tradition (top, and bottom left) are still evident throughout urban and rural Turkey. In the modern factory, shown below, workers install motors in Renaults. An increasing number of Turkish women are becoming part of modern technology. These women (bottom, right) attend the Middle East Technical University in Ankara.

the graduates of universities are unable to find employment in the fields for which they are trained.

Much has already been said about the impact of Muslim religious teachings on the values of the people of Turkey, especially those outside the more liberal urban areas. More than 50 years of exposure to Western ideas has not been enough to counteract the centuries of Turkish adherence to traditional practices and values. Nonetheless, Turkey continues its march toward modernization and industrialization.

Check Your Understanding

1. What is Turkey's standard of living?
2. How does population growth make it difficult for Turkey to improve its standard of living?
3. How does distribution of the labor force affect employment?
4. What efforts were made to improve literacy and the status of women?
5. *Thinking Critically:* What remnants from Turkey's past have hampered its economic and social growth?

8. Foreign Policy Since 1945

Throughout the postwar period Turkey has been friendly with Western countries. While it remained neutral for most of World War II, it entered the war on the side of the Allies just before the war ended. It also became a founding member of the United Nations, signing the United Nations Charter in 1945.

Resisting Soviet Pressure

Three centuries of hostility and several wars with Russia, now called the Soviet Union, made Turkey a natural ally of the United States in its cold war against the spread of communism throughout the world. Turkey was one of the first countries to receive large-scale American economic and military assistance after World War II. The assistance began in 1947 with the announcement by President Truman of a massive aid program for Greece and Turkey. Called the Truman Doctrine, the program was aimed at helping Greece and Turkey resist Soviet attempts to reassert old claims to the Black Sea, and the Bosporus and Dardanelles.

During the Korean War in 1950, Turkish troops joined United Nations forces in fighting Communist North Korea. The massive economic, military, and technical assistance programs from the United States soon led to an influx of Americans stationed in Turkey. After 1952, the United States urged Turkey to become a member of the North Atlantic Treaty Organization (NATO), which was pledged to defend its member nations against aggression from the Soviet Union. As a result of Turkey's membership in NATO, the United States established a number of military bases in the country.

Since joining NATO in the 1950's, Turkey has sought to become increasingly identified as a Western nation. Several obstacles have prevented Turkey's full acceptance by countries of Western Europe. Cultural differences have played a role in Turkey's exclusion from Europe. So have Turkey's human rights violations in the treatment of political opposition both within Turkey and on Cyprus. (See page 162.) But also at work have been European fears of competition, including a fear of Turkish unskilled laborers flooding European countries.

Anti-Americanism

By the late 1960's and 1970's, the deteriorating economic and social conditions mentioned earlier led many young Turks to criticize their country for its close ties to the United States. (See page 154.) Many of these radicals felt that the United States was exercising too much influence in the country. Some radicals called for Turkey to maintain a neutral policy toward the United States and the Soviet Union.

In reaction to a perceived overreliance on the United States, efforts were made to improve relations with the Communist world and with surrounding Arab countries. In 1969, the Soviet Union negotiated a trade agreement with Turkey. In 1971, Turkey recognized the People's Republic of China, sending an ambassador to Beijing. In 1972, the Soviets offered to renew a non-aggression pact that had been canceled in 1945.

Middle East Policies

Turkey is one of the few Muslim countries that maintains diplomatic ties with Israel. Popular sentiment, however, favors the Arabs in the Arab–Israeli conflict. On several occasions the Turkish National Assembly has passed resolutions that are critical of Israeli policies toward the Arabs. In the United Nations General Assembly, Turkey usually supports resolutions that are critical of Israel.

Ethnic and political divisions in Cyprus are evident in this photo of Tokni, a village in the Greek zone of Cyprus. Half of the village is Greek, half Turkish. The woman at the right stands on the Greek side while the barber does business on the Turkish side. How does Cyprus exemplify United States–Soviet Union relations?

Both nations in the Iran–Iraq war adjoin Turkey's borders. (See page 254.) Turkey carefully maintains its neutrality in the conflict, but it has actually profited from the war. Its sales of agricultural commodities and other supplies to Iran and Iraq have increased. When Iran cut off Iraq's access to the Persian Gulf, Iraq constructed several new oil pipelines through Turkey to give it access to ports on the Mediterranean.

The Cyprus Question

Disappointment over the United States' failure to support Turkey's position on the Cyprus question was a major cause of the widespread anti-Americanism that spread through Turkey. The anti-American sentiment intensified even further because the Soviet Union seemed to support Turkey's position instead of Greece's position.

When Greek Cypriots under the control of Athens staged a military coup in 1974, Turkey sent its troops into Cyprus to protect the island's Turkish minority. United Nations peacekeeping forces on the island were unable to halt the Turkish advance that brought the northern 40 percent of the island under Turkish control. Each group attempted to "purify" itself of the opposing ethnic **faction**, essentially dividing the island into two opposing groups. In 1975, the northern sector proclaimed itself the Turkish Federated State of Cyprus (TFSC). It was governed by Turkish Cypriots with support from the Turkish government. In 1983, the TFSC Assembly declared independence, calling their state the Turkish Republic of Northern Cyprus. Only Turkey has recognized their independence, however, and little contact exists between the two parts of Cyprus.

Major effects of the Cyprus conflict in Turkey have been to renew zealous Turkish nationalism, to cool Turkish–American relations, and to improve Soviet–Turkish relations. For Western Europe, the renewal of Turkish–Soviet ties has weakened NATO's eastern flank.

Check Your Understanding

1. Why was Turkey a natural ally of the United States in its cold war with the Soviet Union?
2. What conditions led to the development of anti-Americanism in Turkey?
3. What are Turkey's Middle Eastern policies?
4. **a.** What is the Cyprus Question? **b.** What have been some of its major effects on Turkey?
5. *Thinking Critically:* How has Turkey's desire to be treated as a Western nation helped to determine its foreign policy since 1945?

CHAPTER REVIEW

■ Chapter Summary

Section 1. Efforts at modernizing the Ottoman Empire along Western lines began as early as 1789 with Selim III and continued intermittently thereafter. The military was the first Turkish institution to be reformed. Then attempts were made to break the power of the conservative Muslim clergy. But efforts to bring reform to rural areas met with little success

163

because of peasant resistance to change and the intervention of the Muslim clergy.

Section 2. Calling the Ottoman Empire the "Sick Man of Europe," Western nations had a hard time deciding to attack or to protect it. Britain, for the most part, helped maintain the balance of power by acting as the empire's protector. In this role it blocked Russia's attempts to secure access to the Mediterranean through control of the Turkish Straits in the Crimean War and again in the Russo–Turkish War. But by stirring up nationalism in the Balkans, Russia helped Bulgaria become an autonomous region and Serbia, Rumania, and Montenegro became independent states by 1878.

Section 3. Reform efforts continued throughout the nineteenth century. The reformers helped to make Abdul Hamid become sultan and Midhat Pasha, Grand Vizier. But when Midhat's reforms brought him great popularity, the sultan exiled him and turned to repressive rule. A new group of reformers, called the Young Turks, deposed the sultan in 1909, set up a new sultan, and became the dominant group in the legislature. But the Young Turks failed to bring about solid economic and social reform and sought only political solutions to the empire's minority problems. Soon the Young Turks abandoned multi-nationalism and worked to "Turkify" the empire by suppressing national movements.

Section 4. The rivalries and intrigues of European nations in the Balkans and the system of alliances that had been formed led to World War I. Russia, Britain, France, and Serbia as the Allies fought against the Central Powers of Germany, Bulgaria, Austria–Hungary, and Turkey. The war brought about the total collapse of the Ottoman Empire and the rise of Mustafa Kemal, who organized a nationalist movement to resist Greek invaders. From this resistance movement, with its capital at Ankara, the Republic of Turkey was born, proclaiming its existence in 1923.

Section 5. As Turkey's first president, Kemal, who later took the surname Atatürk, ruled through the Republican People's Party (RPP) and exercised tight control over the government. The party's six goals were republicanism, nationalism, populism, statism, secularism, and reformism—all of which he achieved to some degree. But Atatürk met the same resistance to change from villagers all over Turkey that reformers before him had met. When Atatürk died in 1938, Ismet Inönü carried on the goals of the RPP.

Section 6. Since 1945 Turkey has had a multiparty political system. The parties have changed labels and leaders several times in the process of establishing stable democratic government in Turkey. Several times in the past, as each coalition or single-party government has encountered problems it could not solve, the military has stepped in to form a military junta as a temporary ruling group. When political stability seems to have returned, it then has reinstated constitutional government, sometimes with a new constitution. Turkey's present government was elected in 1987.

Section 7. Turkey's political problems seem to rest on the pace of its social and economic reforms. Its literacy level has increased about 25 percent from its 1955 level of 50 percent. But its standard of living has been affected by the million people it adds to its population each year. The majority of its people still make their living in agriculture although only 34 percent of Turkey's land is suited for farming. The lack of arable land forces many rural people to look for work in the cities where they live in crowded slums. Turkey's most significant reforms are in its efforts to assure equality, to raise the status of women, and to educate the villagers to the demands of an industrialized nation.

Section 8. Since the end of World War II, Turkey's foreign policy seems to have undergone three stages. First it resisted Soviet pressures by aligning itself with the United States. During this stage, American aid brought massive economic, military, and technical assistance to Turkey, a charter member of the United Nations. Then a period of anti-Americanism set in, beginning in the 1960's when postwar aid slowed down and Turkey's economy took a downturn. Today Turkey is more neutral, sometimes favoring the Soviet Union and sometimes the United States. Turkey's major foreign policy problem has been protecting the Turkish minority on Cyprus.

■ **Vocabulary Review**

Define: Westernization, nationalism, democracy, balance of power, compromise, status quo, autocratic, constitutional government, radical, coup, constitution, parliament, dictatorship, censorship, liberal, autonomy, genocide, conservative, alliance, sovereignty, republic, populism, statism, secularism, prime minister, trade union, authoritarianism, military junta, coalition, martial law, gross national product, per capita income, free enterprise, faction

■ Places to Locate

Locate: Balkan Peninsula, Bosnia, Herzegovina, Serbia, Bulgaria, Rumania, Montenegro, Bosporus, Dardanelles, Cyprus

■ People to Know

Identify: Selim III, Mahmud II, Namik Kemal, Midhat Pasha, Abdul Hamid, Young Turks, Kemal Atatürk, Ismet Inönü, Adnan Menderes, Suleyman Demirel, Turgut Ozal, Adalet Agaoglu

■ Thinking Critically

1. Compare early efforts at reform with the reform efforts of Atatürk and later leaders of Turkey.
2. Cite evidence from the chapter on religion, culture, and government to prove or disprove the following statement: *Modern Turkey straddles East and West.*
3. Classify the major reforms undertaken in Turkey since the days of Selim III. Determine which ones were made by revolution and which by constitutional change.
4. Assess the effects of nationalism, European rivalries, and autocratic rule on the collapse of the Ottoman Empire. Then rank each in order from most to least responsible.
5. Why did Atatürk seek to separate church and state?

■ Extending and Applying Your Knowledge

1. Prepare a conversation on the successes and failures of the Menderes government, taking the part of an Ankara businessperson, a university professor, or a Turkish Cypriot.
2. Prepare a report on the importance of tradition to Turkish villagers after reading *A Village in Anatolia,* by Mahmut Makal.

7

Modern Egypt

Egypt is strategically located in the center of the Arab world between North Africa and Southwest Asia. Its central location is also symbolic of its ties to the ancient past and the modern present. Modern Egyptian history begins when the land acquired a distinctive identity as a separate Arab country early in the 1800's, after 300 years of Ottoman rule. This occurred in Egypt almost a century before similar experiences in other Arab countries. In 1952, Egypt produced the first major political, economic, and social revolution in the Arab world, setting an example for similar changes elsewhere in the next few years. In the process, Egypt's capital city of Cairo became a center for Arab education and political thought.

Egypt's political leadership in the Arab world is matched by its leadership in many other areas of life. Broadcasts from Radio Cairo are listened to far more widely than broadcasts from other Arab countries. The Egyptian press is widely circulated in other Arab countries. The first and only Arab writer to win the Nobel Prize for literature was an Egyptian novelist.

Nonetheless, Egypt has its problems. It is among the poorest of the Arab countries. It is also the Arab country with the most people, the majority of whom live within a few miles of the Nile River, its major resource. About 90 percent of Egyptian territory is desert land unsuited to cultivation. Egypt is thus a land of contrasts. It mixes antiquity with modernity and extremes of poverty and illiteracy with great wealth and high cultural achievements.

1. Western Domination in Egypt

In the first half of the nineteenth century Egypt freed itself from Ottoman control and turned toward the West. Following Napoleon's invasion, Egypt's rulers embarked on a program of westernization and empire building. Their efforts, however, were only partially successful, and they soon found themselves restrained by the demands of their European backers, whose interests in the Middle East developed into **colonialism.**

Early French Influences

In the years when France and Britain were still contesting each other for a mercantile empire in India, France had gained concessions from the Ottoman sultan for trading privileges in Alexandria and Cairo. As Britain won supremacy in India, however, the British challenged French traders in Egypt by carrying their goods from India to Suez and from there overland to the Mediterranean.

When war broke out between France and Britain following the French Revolution (1789), the French government made plans to strike at the British by occupying Egypt. Once established there it might be possible to move into the Middle East and threaten India. Napoleon's invasion force disembarked in Egypt in July, 1798.

The French soon captured Alexandria and advanced on Cairo. Near that city Napoleon decisively defeated the Mamluk cavalry. To administer the country, he established provincial governments, each composed of a French military governor assisted by Egyptian advisers. Egyptians were named to all posts from which Mamluks had been ousted, and a regular tax system was introduced. Napoleon also brought with him a group of scholars to study ancient Egyptian remains and a corps of French engineers to plan a canal through the Isthmus of Suez that would link the Red Sea with the Mediterranean.

Unfortunately for the French, the situation in the Middle East worsened. On August 1, a British force destroyed the fleet that had brought Napoleon to Egypt. Encouraged by this victory, the Ottoman sultan declared war on the French. Napoleon briefly invaded Syria, but was forced to withdraw when his army was stricken with the plague. Nonetheless he was able to defeat a Turkish force that invaded Egypt in 1799. Problems in Europe, however, made Napoleon's return home necessary in the fall of 1799. Two years later Napoleon's army in Egypt surrendered to the British.

The Modernization of Egypt

1798	Napoleon's invasion of Egypt
1805–1848	Mohammed Ali's rule
1875	Sale of Suez Canal to Britain
1882–1954	British occupation of Egypt
1922	Egyptian independence and establishment of monarchy
1948	War with Israel
1952	Overthrow of monarchy and establishment of republic
1956	Nasser's election as president
	Nationalization of Suez Canal
	British, French, and Israeli invasion
1967	Six–Day War with Israel
1973	Surprise attack on Israel
1979	Egypt–Israel Peace Treaty
1981	Assassination of Sadat
1981–	Mubarak's presidency

The Founding of a New Dynasty

The vacuum of leadership left by the return of Napoleon's army to France was filled by Mohammed Ali (ah-LIH), a junior officer in the Ottoman army that was sent to Egypt. Taking advantage of the squabbles between the Ottomans and the Mamluks, he installed himself in power in 1805. Appointed by the sultan to be governor of Egypt with the title of pasha, he became Egypt's strongest political figure. In 1811 he ended any possible threat to his leadership by luring 300 Mamluk chiefs to Cairo and massacring them at a banquet given in their honor. With all opposition removed, the pasha centralized his authority and within a few years transformed Egypt into the most powerful country in the Middle East.

Provincial governors reported directly to the central government in Cairo on affairs in each village under their jurisdiction. Government departments of war, navy, agriculture, finance, commerce, education, police, and foreign affairs were organized.

169

The traditional Muslim Sharia courts were supplemented with a court system based on modern French civil law. For the first time in centuries minorities were free to practice their religions openly and to build places of worship. Because they were better treated, these minorities were better able to help develop the country. Thus, Armenians were active in government, Jews in finance, and Syrian Christian Arabs in commerce and business.

Modernizing Egypt

The pasha's ambition was to transform Egypt into a modern country. His internal reforms, moreover, were closely linked with his ambition to establish a Middle Eastern empire reaching south into the Sudan and northwards into Syria and Palestine. But he shrewdly realized that the military might needed for such conquests called for the recruitment of technicians, teachers, engineers, and skilled craftsworkers. Therefore, Egypt's governor invited Westerners, particularly people of France, to settle in the country. French officers trained Egyptian soldiers, French engineers designed Egyptian dockyards, and French managers ran new Egyptian factories. Many young Egyptians were sent to study in France. French schools and libraries were opened in Cairo, and members of the Egyptian middle class began to study French and accepted it as a second language.

Before Mohammed Ali's time, the average Egyptian had no access to secular schooling. The traditional Muslim mosque schools concentrated on Arabic and religious subjects. Mohammed Ali, therefore, established a French school system to teach science and other secular subjects. But only Egyptians living in urban areas benefited from the reforms.

French physicians introduced modern medicine in Egypt and brought the annual outbreaks of cholera and bubonic plague under control. In Alexandria a sanitation board was established to enforce rigid quarantines. While modern medicine greatly reduced the death rate, it also was responsible for increases in population. Ever since, rapid population growth has been Egypt's most critical problem.

Changes in Agriculture and Industry

Egyptian agriculture was revolutionized by long-staple cotton, which has longer fibers than ordinary cotton and makes better quality cloth. This variety introduced in 1820 by a French engineer soon became Egypt's primary export. The growing European demand raised the price paid for this product and made it the backbone of the Egyptian economy. A canal was dug in

1819 to link the port of Alexandria with the Nile Valley, where long-staple cotton was grown. The first dams were also built on the Nile to store the flood waters of the river for later use during the dry summers.

The Egyptian peasant profited little from improvement in the nation's economy. All Egypt's land theoretically belonged to the Ottoman sultan. But actually Mohammed Ali controlled all land and reaped much of the profit from its use. Large tracts were set aside for the pasha and members of his family, making them the country's greatest landlords. Local officials determined the size of plots peasants were to till and the crop to be grown. They also supplied the peasants with farm tools, work animals, and seed. After taxes and other fees had been paid, the peasant was left with only about one-sixth of the produce. Harvests were stored in government warehouses to be sold when market prices were highest. The **corvée** (kore-VAY) ensured a supply of cheap labor. Like the ancient pharaohs, Mohammed Ali actually controlled all of Egypt's resources and was the chief distributor of the necessities of daily life.

Egyptians had little knowledge of modern industrial techniques, and local handicrafts could not compete with more efficiently manufactured European goods. To free his country from dependence upon European-made products, the pasha began a program of industrialization. When wealthy Egyptians were unwilling to invest in new types of enterprise, the government itself established new industries. It brought in European experts to build these plants and mills, and to operate them until trained Egyptians could take over. Soon Mohammed Ali's government had established iron foundries, a sugar refinery, a glass factory, a munitions plant, a shipyard, and cotton spinning and weaving mills. By the 1830's local textile mills were producing all the cheap cotton and cotton cloth needed for the local market.

Attempts to Conquer an Empire

Almost from the time he came to power, Mohammed Ali followed an aggressive foreign policy. Though technically the Ottoman sultan's governor of Egypt, the pasha followed a completely independent foreign policy. His regime became so strong that the sultan even called upon him to help suppress revolts in the Arabian Peninsula and in Greece.

One of Mohammed Ali's most important military ventures was in the Sudan. Beginning in the 1820's Egyptian troops were sent to invade the Upper Nile Valley to give Egypt access to the profitable African trade in slaves and ivory.

In 1830 Mohammed Ali turned on the Ottoman sultan. Over-running Syria and Anatolia, the pasha threatened to capture Istanbul, depose the sultan, and establish his own dynasty. The European powers intervened, afraid that Egyptian conquests would destroy the balance of power in the Middle East. They forced Mohammed Ali to withdraw his armies from Anatolia. In compensation, the British and French compelled the sultan to make Mohammed Ali governor of Syria and Palestine.

When the Egyptian ruler in 1838 again attempted to expand his empire and to destroy the sultan, Great Britain convened a conference of the major European powers to deal with the situation. Mohammed Ali was warned to withdraw from Syria and to place "the desert between his troops and authorities of the sultan." When he ignored this demand, a naval blockade was imposed on Egypt. The pasha not only had to withdraw to Egypt but to return territory east of Suez that he had seized from the sultan. But in 1841, as compensation, the sultan agreed to make hereditary Mohammed Ali's governorship of Egypt.

The Suez Canal

Mohammed Ali's son, Said (sah-EED), became the new pasha in 1854. Extravagant and shortsighted, Said was attracted by the profits French promoters promised him if he allowed them to build a canal through the Isthmus of Suez. In 1856 Said granted Ferdinand de Lesseps a concession that allowed him to form a company to construct the canal. Under the terms of the agreement, however, Egypt had to bear the major construction costs of the canal, which took almost 10 years to build.

After the canal opened in 1870, it was used primarily by British shipping, and soon it became one of Britain's most vital waterways. Because Benjamin Disraeli, Britain's prime minister, recognized the canal's importance, he tried to secure its control. The opportunity came in 1875 when the Egyptian ruler, now called the **khedive** (keh-DEEV), in great need of ready cash, accepted Disraeli's offer of 4 million pounds (about $20,000,000 U.S. dollars) for the shares of the canal that he owned, which was about 44 percent of all canal shares.

Expansion Under Ismail

Said's nephew, Ismail, wished to make Egypt the showplace of the Middle East, just like his uncle. Gas and water works were built in Cairo and Alexandria. A railway and telegraph system linked Egypt with the Sudan. The Nile River system was im-

DIGGING THE CANAL. When work on the canal started in 1859, 25,000 Egyptians were employed in digging the waterway. Later the use of mechanical dredgers reduced the number of diggers. On November 17, 1869, the 103-mile waterway was opened with a procession of ships (right) watched by 6,000 foreign guests, who were lavishly entertained.

proved, and thousands of miles of new canals brought water to formerly barren lands. Alexandria's port was made one of the best in the Mediterranean while Ismail acquired control of shipping and converted it into a government enterprise. By 1873 the shipping line made Egypt crucial to Mediterranean navigation.

British and Swiss specialists were hired to teach in the primary, secondary, and higher educational institutions that were opened. The first girls' school was established, attended by daughters of upper-class families. A teacher-training institute was also founded. During Ismail's reign the number of government schools increased from 185 to nearly 5,000. A larger percentage of Egyptian males were attending school than in many European nations.

To conquer territory and to explore the sources of the Nile were the goals of Egyptian expeditions that probed southward to Ethiopia, present-day Kenya, and Zaïre. These expeditions included hired soldiers called **mercenaries** who served as officers. Some were Europeans, others were Americans who had fought in the Civil War.

Ismail's schemes cost money. Egypt managed to stay financially solvent from 1861 to 1865 when the American Civil War was in progress. England traditionally bought cotton for its textile mills from the American South. But during the war the Union blockade kept the South from shipping cotton to England. As a result Egypt's cotton was in great demand in England and commanded high prices. But with the end of the war, the demand for Egyptian cotton lessened and prices fell. Egypt faced financial ruin as huge debts came due. The need to borrow heavily from British and French financiers forced Ismail to grant certain privileges to Europeans. They were allowed to transact business without paying taxes. They were also exempted from being tried in Egyptian courts. So great was Egypt's debt that the sale of canal shares to Great Britain in 1875 made little impact on reducing it.

In 1876 European creditors created a commission to manage Egypt's financial condition, and Ismail appointed two European experts to a new advisory cabinet established at European insistence. When the country went bankrupt in 1879, Egypt's European creditors demanded that Ismail be deposed and replaced by his son Tewfik. They hoped by this action to get a ruler they could easily control.

Check Your Understanding

1. How did French influence become an important part of Egypt's modernization and expansion?
2. What improvements did Ali make in Egypt's social and cultural life?
3. Who benefited most from the improvements in agriculture and in the nation's industries?
4. What prevented Mohammed Ali from realizing his ambition of expanding his empire beyond Egypt?
5. How did the problems Ismail inherit affect Egypt?
6. *Thinking Critically:* Using evidence presented in Section 1, determine whether France or Britain contributed most to early efforts to modernize Egypt.

2. The British Occupation of Egypt

Foreign interference in Egyptian affairs aroused nationalist feeling. So did the increasingly inept government. In 1882 Colonel Ahmed Arabi (uh-RAH-bih) was appointed Egypt's war minister. He belonged to a secret society of nationalist officers who believed foreigners were receiving preferment in the Egyptian army. Following the society's goals, Arabi demanded an end to favoritism and improvements in army life. He also supported the society's demands for a representative assembly.

Europeans tended to regard Arabi and his followers as dangerous radicals rather than as patriots. The alarmed British and French governments found an opportunity for direct intervention when riots broke out in Alexandria. When Arabi ignored a British ultimatum to cease fortifying Alexandria, British ships bombarded the city and British troops were put ashore. Within a few weeks Egypt had become, for all practical purposes, a British **protectorate.**

British Officials

Although Great Britain maintained troops and kept government officials in Egypt for many years after 1882, the country never became a colony. Throughout these years the "occupation" was described as "temporary." Until World War I, Egypt in theory was an Ottoman province administered by the khedive. But in actuality, Egypt was controlled by the British agent and consul-general.

British rule brought a number of improvements to Egypt. Sir Evelyn Baring (Lord Cromer), who held the post of agent and consul-general from 1883 to 1907, left a permanent imprint on modern Egypt. By creating a modern tax system and an efficient financial administration, British experts saved Egypt from economic collapse. The civil service was improved, and irrigation works were expanded. In 1902 the predecessor of the present Aswan High Dam was constructed in upper Egypt. The lot of the peasant was improved when slavery and forced labor were banned. Improved medical and sanitation services greatly reduced the mortality rate.

Cromer discouraged major social change in Egypt. A small group of landowners were the principal beneficiaries of British reforms. Little was done to improve public education and the status of women, or to give Egyptians a meaningful role in their government. Expenditures for education were smaller under Cromer than under Ismail. Industry was neglected because Brit-

When this wood engraving of Ahmed Arabi appeared in an English newspaper in 1882, the caption that accompanied it called the Pasha a "would-be dictator." How might an Egyptian nationalist view the Pasha?

ish policy was to develop Egypt as a source of raw cotton for English textile mills. Despite Cromer's improvements, opposition to Great Britain increased among the middle classes.

Nationalist Demands

In 1895 Mustafa Kamel, an Egyptian journalist, formed the Nationalist Party in an effort to rid Egypt of its colonial masters. The rallying cry was, "Egypt for the Egyptians." After Kamel's death, a second nationalist leader, Saad Zaghlul (zugh-LOOL), formulated demands for a constitutional government and for Egyptian independence. At first the British governors ignored the demands, but in 1913 the first steps were taken to give Egyptians a greater voice in the affairs of their nation. Nationalist demands, however, were soon set aside because of the outbreak of World War I.

Check Your Understanding

1. What were the reasons for Great Britain's intervention in Egypt?
2. What improvements did British "protection" bring to Egypt?
3. What were the demands of the Nationalist Party and why were they set aside?
4. *Thinking Critically:* Why do most demands for reform come from groups in the middle class rather than the lower or thc upper classes?

3. The Struggle for Independence

The nationalist movement in Egypt gained momentum after World War I. Although Britain had provided for constitutional government in Egypt's internal affairs, it also had interests in British East Africa and the Sudan that precluded British withdrawal from Egypt. Conditions worsened after World War II when political unrest became widespread. By 1952 the stage was set for revolution.

During World War I Egypt was a major base for British operations against the Ottoman Empire. The presence of thousands of British troops and British pressures upon Egypt for labor, supplies, and support antagonized many Egyptians. By the war's end Zaghlul's nationalist group was demanding independence in accord with Allied promises of **self-determination** for colonial peoples. Called the Egyptian Delegation, or Wafd (WAHFD), this nationalist group presented its case before the Versailles Peace Conference. Upon the group's return to Egypt several of its leaders were imprisoned by the British, an action that only made the Wafd's cause more popular among Egyptians.

The Clamor for Independence

In 1922 Britain issued a treaty making Egypt a **constitutional monarchy.** Control over Egypt's foreign affairs, however, was retained by the British to ensure protection of the Suez Canal, Britain's life line with India, and control over the Sudan.

In the elections of 1923 the Wafd became Egypt's largest and most popular political party, leading the struggle for independence. The King and the British tried to strengthen their positions by outmaneuvering each other and the Wafd.

Egyptian politicians seeking mass support continued to use the slogan, "Egypt for the Egyptians." Their goal was to rid the Nile Valley of British control and to take possession of the Suez Canal, the Sudan, and British bases in Egypt. In 1936 a new Treaty of Alliance resolved most of the outstanding problems between Egypt and Britain and gave Egypt greater self-government. With the outbreak of World War II shortly thereafter, the clamor for independence temporarily subsided. The war also prevented full implementation of the treaty's terms. When Egypt became an Allied base, the terms related to withdrawing British troops from the country were delayed. At one point the Germans, under General Erwin Rommel, threatened to overrun Egypt and push on into the Middle East, but were stopped at the battle of El Alamein in Egypt's western desert.

A farm worker from the agricultural station at Izmir steers a tractor through rows of young crops, spraying insecticide to keep crops healthy until harvest time. Such advances in technology have helped Egypt increase food production.

Conditions Under King Faruq

A handsome slim young man when he became king in 1936, Faruq (fah-ROOK) was a national idol. But within a few years he became monstrously fat and was accused of squandering millions on yachts, lavish parties, rare postage stamps, and jewels. Royal interference infected the whole political system and seriously reduced the efficiency of Egypt's army. Faruq, with the reputation of an international playboy, came to symbolize the evils of the old regime.

A huge gap separated Egypt's upper class from the masses. The elite upper class, about one percent of the population, lived in ostentatious luxury. The great mass of people, on the other hand, were among the most impoverished in the world. A few very wealthy families controlled Egypt, its politics, economy, and every other important aspect of national life. They were wealthy because they owned much of Egypt's best agricultural land. Most of the cotton exported from Egypt was grown on their estates. In Egypt the middle class was small in numbers and unimportant in a political sense.

Egypt's wretched peasants, who were called **fellaheen** (fel-uh-HEEN) and who constituted 80 percent of the population, lived on the verge of starvation. Shortly after World War II, a shocked observer reported:

> To speak of housing conditions is to exaggerate . . . the fellaheen inhabit mud huts, built by making a framework of sticks, usually cotton sticks, and plastering it with mud.

The hut is a small enclosed yard, where the family and the buffalo live together, with a smaller inner room with a roof but no window and a sleeping roof where chickens, rabbits, and goats are kept. [Doreen Warriner, *Land and Poverty in the Middle East.*]

Disease made most peasants aged at 40. Nearly four out of five men of draft age had to be rejected for military service because of poor health. Polluted water from the Nile and irrigation canals, used both for drinking and washing, was a major source of disease. Unskilled workers earned the equivalent of about five cents for a twelve-hour day.

A major cause of poverty was the rapid increase in population. The annual rate of increase in population was higher than that for the nation's economy. Nearly all Egyptians lived in the Nile Valley, a narrow fertile strip on each side of the river, stretching from the Sudan northward. Only four percent of Egypt's 386,650 square miles could be cultivated because water was not available to irrigate more.

Defeat in Palestine

Egypt had few ties with the Palestinian Arabs who opposed the **partition** of Palestine between Arabs and Israelis. (See page 212.) But it had joined the Arab League, created in 1945, and united with Arab nations in attacking Israel in 1948–1949. The defeat suffered by Egyptian troops embittered junior officers against their commanders. In his *Philosophy of the Revolution,* Gamal Abdel Nasser (juh-MAHL ub-dool NAH-sur), himself then a junior officer, described his feelings.

> We are fighting in Palestine, but all our thoughts were concentrated on Egypt . . . left an easy prey to hungry wolves . . . . We have been duped—pushed into a battle for which we were unprepared. Vile ambitions, [and] insidious intrigues . . . are toying with our destinies, and we are left under fire unarmed.

Tension between Great Britain and Egypt continued to mount. The number of British troops, which after World War II were withdrawn from Alexandria and Cairo to the Suez Canal zone, increased. Guerrilla attacks were launched against the British in the canal zone. On January 26, 1952, rioters set fire to foreign-owned stores and homes in Cairo. The free Officers Society continued to prepare for the day when it could seize control of Egypt's government. At midnight on July 22, 1952,

General Neguib (seated) rides through the streets of Cairo soon after the forced abdication of King Faruq. Right, Nasser, just appointed premier, and President Neguib confer concerning union between Egypt and the Sudan.

members of the secret Free Officers Society swooped down on army headquarters and seized the national radio station. By morning they had gained control of the government.

The Revolutionary Command Council

The powers of government authority rested with a Revolutionary Command Council (RCC) made up of officers of the society. Although Colonel Nasser was the most important RCC member, the Council named 51-year-old General Mohammed Neguib (neh-GEEB) as commander-in-chief. Neguib was chosen to head the Council because the RCC thought that an older man would have a better chance of making its actions seem acceptable to the public. In 1953 when the Egyptians proclaimed a republic, Neguib became Egypt's premier and first president.

The officers of the RCC wanted at first only to rid the country of Faruq's influence and to establish reputable and competent civilian government. But RCC attempts to purge political parties of corrupt leaders and to end the power of the great landlords led to a break with leaders in the civilian government. The young officers wanted to bring about major reforms quickly. Dozens of them were assigned to supervise the day-to-day work of civilian ministries and to watch for corruption and inefficiency. The revolutionary council soon became disillusioned with both the civil government and the people as a whole. Discussing the July revolution in *Philosophy of the Revolution* Nasser wrote:

The masses did come. But how different is fiction from facts! . . . They came straggling in groups. The Holy March to the Great Goal was halted. . . . It was only then that I realized, with an embittered heart torn with grief, that the vanguard's [RCC] mission did not end at that hour. . . . We were in need of unity, but found nothing but disunity. We were in need of work, but found nothing but indolence and inactivity. Hence the Motto of the Revolution—Discipline, Unity, and Work.

A Struggle for Power

Two main currents of thought about the revolution emerged among the officers. General Neguib represented those who favored reform of the country's established institutions. He and his supporters wanted to hold elections; to retain but reform the existing parliament and political parties; and to revise rather than to discard the constitution. Nasser and his followers believed that more drastic changes were needed. Democracy for the people, Nasser claimed, was a matter of making available things that directly affected their lives, such as better schools, improved health, and a higher standard of living. Instead of parliamentary democracy, Nasser advocated "guided democracy" in which the people would be led by the revolutionary leaders to a better life.

Neguib resented what he regarded as meddling by the young officers. On the other hand, the young officers charged that Neguib wanted to be a dictator. In 1954, Nasser removed Neguib and became premier. He was elected president in 1956. He remained Egypt's all-powerful and widely popular ruler until his death in 1970.

Check Your Understanding

1. Why did demands for independence increase after World War II?
2. What were the goals of the Wafd?
3. What conditions existed in Egypt under King Faruq?
4. What led to the overthrow of the Egyptian monarchy and its replacement by the Revolutionary Command Council?
5. **Thinking Critically:** How did Neguib's ideas about ruling Egypt differ from Nasser's ideas?

4. Egyptian Politics—1952 to the Present

In the period since 1952, Egypt has undergone two phases in its political relations, especially with the rest of the world. Under Nasser, Egypt's geographical position, its control of the Suez Canal, and its role as the first Middle Eastern nation to undergo a successful political revolution put it in a position of leadership among the Arab nations of the Middle East. Its relations with nations outside the Arab world, especially the United States and Great Britain, turned on its many past experiences with Western **imperialism.** The distrust created by the West's past imperialist policies led Egypt to take a generally cool position toward the United States and Great Britain and to assert its right to accept aid from any country, including the Soviet Union and other Communist nations. Resentment toward Israel, which Egypt viewed since its formation as an outpost of Western imperialism, led to a feeling of solidarity among Arab nations often at odds on other issues.

But Egypt followed a different course after Sadat came to power. When Sadat's overtures to Israel after the 1973 war resulted in a 1979 peace treaty between Egypt and Israel, the rest of the Arab world rejected Egypt's leadership. The coolness toward the West that Egypt once took also disappeared, with the result that Egypt was one of the major recipients of United States' foreign aid in recent years.

Nasser's Leadership

Many parts of the Arab world looked on Egypt's 1952 revolution as a model for change, especially after Nasser's leadership brought political stability to the country.

Radical Arab nationalists regarded Nasser as a hero because he was the first to overthrow an Arab monarchy. With agricultural reforms and his program of **Arab socialism,** he was the first to institute extensive social, economic, and political reforms. (See page 190.) He was also the first to break openly with the West by accepting economic and military aid from the Soviet **bloc.** In other Arab countries, many advocates of change listened to Nasser's radio broadcasts and followed the lead of Egyptian secret agents who conducted subversive activities and stirred up unrest. After 1952 Syria, Iraq, and Yemen experienced revolutions similar to Egypt's.

From 1958 to 1961 Egypt and Syria united to form a single country, the United Arab Republic (UAR) with Nasser as president. But after three years, many Syrians became disillusioned, claiming that Egypt treated Syria as nothing more than an Egyptian **satellite.** They resented the political domination of Egyptian officials in the union and the restrictions placed on free enterprise in the economy. The two countries severed their union in 1961 with Syria calling itself the Syrian Arab Republic. Egypt continued to call itself the United Arab Republic until 1971 when it officially changed its name to the Arab Republic of Egypt.

Even before Nasser, attempts had been made to forge a common bond among Arab nations. Despite similarities in language and religion, it has proved difficult to overcome other cultural differences, although a regional organization of Arab countries called the Arab League has functioned since 1945. (See page 259.)

Nasser's Foreign Policy

After World War II, the nations of the world became aligned into three blocs. One bloc—the West—consisted of those nations that aligned themselves with the United States and other traditional Western nations. Another group—the Communist bloc—consisted of those nations that aligned themselves with the Soviet Union. A third bloc consisted of many newly independent nations and other nations struggling to industrialize and improve their standards of living. This bloc of nations, which emerged in force during the 1970's, is sometimes called the **Third World.** Many Third World nations refrained from aligning themselves with either the West or the Communist bloc. Thus they became known as **nonaligned nations.**

Nasser formed close ties with nonaligned nations. He also showed an increased concern for Africa, partly to counteract Israel's close ties with African nations and partly to strengthen Egypt's position in the Third World. Thousands of African students came to study in Egypt. Hundreds of African rebel leaders found haven there. During the Algerian revolution (1954–1962) against France, Nasser supplied the Algerian rebels with arms and equipment. Nasser also aided other revolutionary movements in Africa and Asia.

Nasser's overtures to the Soviet Union brought him into conflict with the Western powers. In 1956 the United States withdrew its offer of economic assistance in building the Aswan High Dam because it believed Egypt was pro-Soviet in its domestic and foreign policies. In retaliation for the withdrawal of Western economic aid, Nasser **nationalized** the Suez Canal, which was an Egyptian corporation owned mainly by European stockhold-

The Suez Canal

The importance of a waterway linking the Mediterranean and Red seas was recognized long before Ferdinand de Lessups approached Mohammed Ali's son, Said Pasha, in 1854 with his plan for the Suez Canal. In ancient times a canal linked the Mediterranean with the Red Sea from about the twentieth century B.C. until about the eighth century A.D. At that time the waterway fell into complete disrepair and was closed.

Since construction began in 1859, the Suez Canal has played an important role in Egyptian history. Millions of dollars were spent in its construction, and thousands of Egyptians worked as forced laborers. The working conditions were so dangerous that as many as 120,000 Egyptians laborers lost their lives. From the canal's opening in 1869 to its shut down by Nasser in 1956, the canal was one of the world's most strategic waterways.

In 1956, however, Nasser nationalized the canal. The act promoted Egyptian nationalism and solidified Nasser's position of leadership in the Arab world. Nationalization also put Egypt into the international spotlight when the UN intervened in the Suez War to keep the act of retaliation by Britain, France, and Israel from erupting into a large-scale conflict.

But the role of the canal has changed since the 1967 war with Israel. At that time Nasser again shut down the canal and clogged it with mines and sunken ships. Not until June 5, 1975, was the canal cleared of its obstructions and reopened. During the period when it was closed to all shipping, major changes had taken place in ocean transportation. The reopened canal was unable to accommodate the huge tankers that were built to carry oil from the Persian Gulf states to Europe and the Americas. Pipelines to the Mediterranean also took away business. Nonetheless in 1983 more than 22,000 ships used the canal, bringing revenues of close to $990 million in U.S. dollars to Egypt's economy. Plans to deepen the canal and to keep it a strategically important waterway are in progress.

ers. Egypt's nationalization of the canal led to an armed attack by France and Great Britain in collaboration with Israel. All three nations were greatly concerned about the consequences of Egyptian control of the canal. Great Britain especially distrusted Nasser. Also, France resented Egypt's aid to Algerian rebels, and Israel felt threatened by Egypt's growing military strength and its refusal to recognize Israel's right to exist. The three nations attacked Egypt but failed to overthrow Nasser. The situation was brought under control through the efforts of the United States, the Soviet Union, and the United Nations, but tensions between Egypt and Israel remained high.

In 1967 Nasser closed the Strait of Tiran to Israeli shipping and mobilized troops along Egypt's border with Israel. Israel then launched a surprise air attack in early June. Even though Syria and Jordan came to Egypt's aid, Israeli forces defeated the Arab armies in less than a week. As a result of the conflict, which is called the Six–Day War, Israel occupied territory in Egypt, Jordan, and Syria, including the entire Sinai Peninsula.

Nasser submitted his resignation. But after public acclaim opposed it, he withdrew his resignation and continued in office until his death in 1970. He was succeeded by Anwar Sadat (sah-DAT). While a ceasefire had been declared in the Six–Day War, negotiations for peace became stalemated by the conflicting demands of both sides. Efforts by the United Nations, the two **superpowers**, and other countries failed to bring about a final settlement and a withdrawal of Israeli troops from the occupied territories.

Sadat's Foreign Policy

After Anwar Sadat became president, receiving more than 90 percent of the vote in a national referendum, power remained concentrated in the hands of a few individuals. But Sadat soon outmaneuvered other competitors for power, becoming the dominant figure in the government until his assassination late in 1981.

A major objective of Sadat was to recover the Sinai Peninsula from Israel. Egypt sorely missed the income from the valuable oil resources that the peninsula contained. It also missed the income from the Suez Canal, which had been closed since the Six–Day War in 1967. Between 1970 and 1973 Sadat attempted unsuccessfully to negotiate the return of the territory to Egyptian control. Finally he decided on war.

In October 1973 Syria and Egypt launched simultaneous surprise attacks on Israel's northern and southern borders, respectively. (The **neutral** world press refers to this war as the October War, while the Israelis call it the Yom Kippur War and the Arabs the Ramadan War.) Initially both countries penetrated Israel's defensive lines, crossing into territory Israel had seized in 1967. Syria retook part of the Golan Heights, and Egypt crossed the Suez Canal into the Sinai. But again the superpowers and the United Nations intervened with a cease-fire after three weeks of fighting before either side could declare a complete victory. Sadat, however, felt that Egyptian successes in the war were enough to declare an Egyptian victory and sanction his efforts to keep seeking a peace settlement with Israel. But again there was no formal peace settlement.

Direct Negotiations with Israel

In 1974 Sadat signed the Sinai I agreement and in 1975 the Sinai II agreement. These agreements returned much of the Sinai to Egypt and secured commitments for foreign aid from Egypt's allies. But when further efforts at securing Arab and Israeli cooperation slowed, Sadat made a dramatic move. In November 1977 Sadat surprised his fellow Egyptians, the superpowers, and the other nations of the world by announcing that he would fly to Jerusalem to negotiate directly with Israel's leaders for a peace treaty. During his visit to Jerusalem, Sadat met all of Israel's leaders and addressed the Knesset, Israel's parliament, explaining why peace was both necessary and possible.

Following Sadat's Jerusalem visit, direct negotiations for peace continued, but they were long and difficult. Meetings between Sadat and Menachem Begin (Muh-NACKH-uhm BAY-guhn), Israel's prime minister, were strained and frequently came to a breaking point. But President Jimmy Carter of the United States personally assisted in the negotiations, arranging a 12-day meeting between Sadat and Begin at a presidential retreat near Washington, D.C., called Camp David. At Camp David, Sadat and Begin signed preliminary agreements called the Camp David Accords, that led to the signing of the Egypt–Israel Peace Treaty in 1979.

The treaty recognized Israel's right to exist. It also called for the withdrawal of Israeli armed forces and civilians from the Sinai within three years. It also created special security arrangements in the Sinai and a United Nations buffer zone along Israel's border with the Sinai. It left open for further negotiation the question of Israel's occupation of the West Bank and the Gaza Strip as well as the question of Palestinian autonomy. From Sadat's standpoint, it meant that Egypt regained control

CAMP DAVID ACCORDS.

Right, Sadat, Carter, and Begin sign the accords on September 17, 1978. The 13 days of intense negotiations at Camp David were followed by three more months of work before the official treaty was signed.

Left, Israel's Menachem Begin (with folded hands) listens to Egypt's Anwar Sadat make a point. Below, Begin and Sadat's representative receive the Nobel Peace Prize from Aase Lionaes, the committee's chairwoman.

of its lost oil fields. The Suez Canal was also reopened to international shipping. With the money from oil exports and canal fees now flowing into Egypt's economy, Egyptians expected an improvement in economic conditions, if not a return to prosperity. Because these expectations went unmet, Sadat's popularity was severely eroded. (See page 195.) He was assassinated in October 1981 by radical Muslims. Hosni Mubarak (HAHZ-nee moo-BAHR-ahk), the vice president, succeeded Sadat.

Mubarak's Leadership

A former commander of the Egyptian air force, Mubarak ruled with a style that was quite different from Sadat's. In his personal approach he lived a lifestyle that was simple compared to Sadat's. Mubarak was low key and not given to making many public speeches or personal appearances. Much more conciliatory toward his critics, he sought to reach an accommodation with them rather than overpowering them. In an early gesture of goodwill, he released many of the opponents who had been jailed by Sadat. At times, it seemed that Mubarak wanted to stand above politics rather than enter the bitter disputes that plagued the country.

Mubarak made no sudden changes. He kept intact the many enterprises nationalized during Nasser's era of Arab socialism. He also permitted private owners to retain the properties that Sadat had denationalized. He fostered the multi-party political system that Sadat had initiated, but without the tokenism that was part of Sadat's policy. He did this by distancing himself in national elections from the National Democratic Party (NDP) that had dominated Egyptian politics under Sadat and by encouraging opposition parties. He promised them full freedom of expression and honest elections, even intervening to assist one new opposition party in obtaining a place in parliament.

By 1987 opposition parties were well represented in parliament. The NDP still outnumbered the opposition parties, but their presence in parliament meant an open discussion of the country's problems. In addition, Mubarak allowed a fairly free and open press to exist. This meant that Egypt was the least authoritarian Arab nation in the Middle East.

Mubarak's Israeli Policy

Mubarak also insisted on keeping Egypt's peace commitments to Israel. He continued contacts with Israeli leaders in an effort to achieve a wider peace settlement with other Arab states. On several occasions, Mubarak acted as an intermediary between

Hosni Mubarak, Egypt's President, addresses an international conference of non-aligned nations at New Delhi, India. Why do many non-aligned nations look to Egypt for leadership in international affairs?

Israel and his fellow Arabs. His role as a go-between helped overcome the charge that Egypt had betrayed Arab interests in negotiating a peace treaty with Israel. By 1988 Egypt had been readmitted to several subsidiary organizations of the Arab League and was given assurance that in the near future it would regain full membership.

Egypt continues to follow a path in world politics that serves its own best interests. Whether it will also serve the interests of the Arab world, is a question only Egypt's future actions can answer.

Check Your Understanding

1. **a.** Why did radical Arab nationalists regard Nasser as a hero? **b.** What attempts were made to forge a unified Arab state?
2. **a.** Why did Nasser form close ties with nonaligned nations of the Third World? **b.** What consequences resulted from Nasser's overtures to the Soviet Union?
3. **a.** What was a major foreign policy goal of Anwar Sadat? **b.** Why did Sadat change his tactics after the October War?
4. ***Thinking Critically:*** Compare Sadat's and Mubarak's leadership of Egypt. In which area did they differ most—domestic politics or foreign politics? Explain.

5. Social and Economic Reforms—1952 to the Present

The men who carried out the military coup of 1952 were committed to improving the life of Egypt's poverty-ridden people. President Nasser had studied the economic and political systems of countries, such as Britain, Sweden, and Yugoslavia, in which government planning was extensive. The result of Nasser's studies was Arab socialism, a series of programs in economic planning, education, and welfare.

Agricultural Reform

President Nasser claimed that his objective was to make Egypt a "democratic, socialist, cooperative society." One of the first socialist measures was the Agricultural Reform Decree of 1952. It obliged landowners to sell and accept government compensation for all holdings that were over two hundred acres. Rents were also reduced. This aided the peasants who did not own any land and who lived in perpetual debt to the landowners. Compulsory cooperatives for supplying seed, tools, and loans were established to enable the new owners to work their land. Later some of the cooperatives began to provide health and educational services. In 1961 the maximum land permitted any landowner was further reduced to about 100 acres, and reduced again in 1969 to 50 acres. But even then Egyptian farmland was scarce.

In a further effort to improve agricultural productivity, Egyptian leaders made plans to build a new dam on the Nile near the Aswan Dam constructed earlier in the century by the British. In 1959 major work began on the new dam, which would provide more land for farming through irrigation. After the Aswan High Dam began to operate in 1968, more than a million acres of farmland was added to Egypt's arable land. Egyptian farmers now had access to the Nile's water throughout the year, not just during the Nile's annual flood, because the lake created by the dam stored enough water for the entire year. The dam also created enough hydroelectric power to supply Egypt's present and future needs.

The United States, Great Britain, and the World Bank initially planned to assist Egypt in building the dam. But political and economic differences between Egypt and the United States caused the latter to withdraw from the project. The Soviet Union then came to Egypt's rescue, supplying the necessary loans and technical assistance.

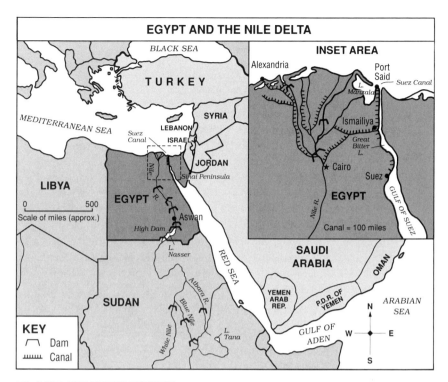

EGYPT AND THE NILE DELTA

BLACK SEA

TURKEY

MEDITERRANEAN SEA

SYRIA

LEBANON

Suez Canal

ISRAEL

JORDAN

Sinai Peninsula

LIBYA

0   500
Scale of miles (approx.)

EGYPT

Nile R.

Aswan

High Dam

L. Nasser

Atbara R.

Blue Nile

White Nile

SUDAN

RED SEA

L. Tana

KEY
⌐ Dam
ᴜᴜᴜᴜ Canal

INSET AREA

Alexandria

Port Said

Suez Canal

L. Manzala

Ismailiya

Great Bitter L.

★ Cairo

Suez

EGYPT

Nile R.

Canal = 100 miles

GULF OF SUEZ

SAUDI ARABIA

OMAN

YEMEN ARAB REP.

P.D.R. OF YEMEN

ARABIAN SEA

GULF OF ADEN

N
W ◆ E
S

PLACE: MODERN EGYPT. Egyptian crops depend on Nile River water, controlled by a series of dams and distributed through a system of irrigation canals in the Delta. Note that several of the dams are in another country.

Other areas where reclamation projects were carried on are the Western Valley Desert oases, the marshlands along Lake Maryut (MAHR-yoot) southeast of Alexandria, and in Fayum (fay-YOOM) Province southwest of Cairo.

Industrialization Efforts

Economic planning after the revolution took the form of Five-Year Plans that were designed to accomplish three things: (1) to create new jobs for the Egyptian people, (2) to diversify Egypt's one-crop economy by freeing it from its dependence on cotton, and (3) to make the nation less dependent on industrial imports. In 1956–1957 the government began to take over foreign-owned businesses and industries. Most large-scale, Egyptian-owned businesses were also nationalized. The owners were given compensation in the form of government bonds. In consequence, the non-agricultural sector of Egypt's economy became largely government-owned, -managed, and -operated. These steps were necessary, said Nasser, because private busi-

191

The Aswan High Dam

Egyptians proudly point to the Aswan High Dam as a proof of Egypt's remarkable progress toward modernization. With this dam, equal in size to 17 Great Pyramids, the ancient Pharaohs' dreams of conquering the Nile River were finally realized. The dam, which is 310 feet high and two miles wide at the top, created Lake Nasser. One of the world's largest artificially formed lakes, Lake Nasser is 300 miles long. Extending southward into the Sudan, it covered the ancient land of Nubia, thereby forcing thousands of Nubians to leave their homeland. Many archaeological treasures either had to be moved or were permanently submerged as the lake waters covered them.

In 1972 and 1973, the dam saved Egypt from one of the most severe droughts ever experienced in the Middle East. With its controlled water flow, the dam produces enough hydroelectricity to meet all of Egypt's needs. By providing irrigation for more than a million acres of farmland, it has also increased crop yields, leading to a major increase in Egypt's total food production.

Although the dam has solved some problems, it has created others. Only a third of the expected electric power has been produced, and only a fraction of the new lands the dam was expected to reclaim has been irrigated. Because of population growth, the ratio of farmers to cultivated land is approximately the same as when the dam was started. In addition, the dam now deprives downstream land of the vital soil deposits previously laid down during the Nile's annual flooding. Much silt remains behind the dam, filling up Lake Nasser. During past floods the swiftly moving river waters carried the silt far downstream. But now the volume of water moving downstream is controlled, and the river moves more slowly. The silt gets deposited in the river's channel and irrigation ditches and does not reach as far downstream as it used to. The lake and the irrigation canals have become breeding grounds for weeds and for disease-carrying parasites. On balance, however, the Aswan High Dam remains a marvel of technological achievement.

The worldwide campaign to save the monuments near Aswan resulted in many priceless remains being preserved. The photo at left shows how part of a head was cut away for transportation to a new site.

ASWAN HIGH DAM. Right, the Great Temple of Ramses II at Abu Simbel is shown in its new location 200 feet above the old. Below, the former sites of the temples are partly covered by the waters of the Nile.

ness, thinking only of profits, refused to help the government increase productivity and raise living standards.

The most important industries developed were a fertilizer plant at Aswan and a steel mill near Cairo. Textiles remain Egypt's largest industry, but chemicals, minerals, and petroleum in this early period were also important to the economy.

Social Changes Under Nasser

After the 1952 revolution many social changes took place in Egypt. Schools were opened for most children of school age. Dozens of adult educational centers were established in the Nile Valley to provide health, social welfare, and agricultural extension services to the peasants. But most social changes were more visible in the cities. Many urban workers discarded the nightgown-like *galabia* (gal-uh-BEE-yuh), a garment traditionally worn by the Egyptian lower classes. Western trousers, jackets, and open-necked shirts became fashionable. Cairo modernized transportation with new electric buses and opened a subway system in 1988. It built large white office buildings and great housing developments for workers.

Egypt failed, however, to meet the crucial challenge of keeping pace with the population explosion. Even with the establishment of new industries and the confiscation of the great estates, the growing number of Egyptians could not be provided with ways of earning a living. The government, in desperation, began to encourage family planning. But the majority of Egyptians held a strong resistance to limiting the number of children in their families. As a result, family planning programs have had only limited success in reducing Egypt's population growth.

Sadat's Liberalization Program

After Anwar Sadat became president in 1970, he began a liberalization program called the Corrective Revolution. Designed to stem a growing criticism of Nasser's authoritarian rule, this program led to greater freedom of the press and the return to private ownership of some nationalized business property. Sadat also lifted restrictions on foreign and domestic investment.

Later these measures to encourage the private sectors of the economy were called the *infitah,* or "opening." The infitah created a new wealthy middle class, called the new pashas by some people. Many of these new pashas were millionaires who speculated in real estate and commerce instead of expanding Egypt's economy by building up manufacturing and other productive basic industries.

194

Social Problems

Sadat's plans to liberalize the economy by diminishing government control and encouraging the private sector were important. But they did little to improve the basic living conditions of the majority of Egypt's population. Continuing to grow at an unprecedented rate, the population increased by a million people every nine months. By 1977 inflation and food prices were so high that riots broke out. Sadat retaliated against the rioters with mass arrests. He also outlawed many political opponents.

Islamic conservatives, who were also called **fundamentalists**, called for a return to the literal dictates of the Koran. The Muslim Brotherhood and other militant fundamentalist groups gathered the poor and students to their cause. Their slogan was "Islam is the Answer!" Sadat allowed the Muslim Brotherhood to preach its conservative doctrines, and he held frequent referendums to win public approval for his domestic and foreign policies. On the other hand, he cracked down on demonstrators and those members of the press who were critical of him.

Continuing Unrest

Sadat's difficulties in coping with Egypt's social and economic conditions continued despite his success at the negotiating table. Even before he signed the peace treaty with Israel in 1979, demonstrations over the widening gap between the rich and the poor erupted in the cities. The economy could not be revitalized fast enough to keep pace with the increases in population, even with the massive economic aid Egypt received from the United States.

Social and economic unrest continued to grow even with the removal of many of Nasser's most oppressive policies and the beginnings of a return to the multi-party system. Muslim fundamentalists became more outspoken in their attacks on Sadat. Militant Arab nationalists accused him of betraying Palestinian interests in his pursuit of peace with Israel. As a result, Egypt lost financial support from the Arab nations, and most broke diplomatic ties with Egypt. A further blow came when Egypt was expelled from the Arab League. (See page 259.)

To combat the growing unrest, to stop the demonstrations, and to still attacks from his political opponents, Sadat had more than 1,300 people arrested in September 1981. Those jailed included leaders of the Muslim fundamentalists, the leader of the Christian Coptic Church, pro-Nasserites, journalists, teachers, and business people.

Hinting that Communists were responsible for the unrest, Sadat canceled a 15-year friendship treaty with the Soviet Union that had been negotiated only two years before. He also expelled the Soviet ambassador and several staff members known to be pro-Soviet. A month later, Sadat was assassinated by Muslim radicals who accused him of betraying Islam and of trying to become a modern-day pharaoh.

Reform Under Mubarak

Mubarak also moved to accommodate the growing Islamic sentiment in the country, at the same time cracking down on the militant Islamic groups that practiced violence. Parliament acknowledged the importance of Muslim law by deciding to review all new legislation to make sure that it did not contain provisions that violated the Sharia. On the other hand, all mosques were placed under government supervision to make sure that they did not become centers of hostile action.

The Status of Women

Attempts to accommodate Islamic sentiments retarded progress in the status of women. In Egypt, women had come to play an important role after the revolution of 1952. By the 1980's nearly half the university students were women. Many women served in government, at all levels up to and including the president's cabinet. Women served in parliament, making up about a third of the total membership. Women also taught in the universities and became physicians, journalists, and owners of businesses.

But as Islamic fundamentalism gained strength in the 1980's, many women returned to wearing traditional Muslim garb—black head scarves and black dresses that covered their bodies from head to toe. In university classrooms, women were segregated from men. In response to public pressure, a 1979 law, called the "Jihan Law," was invalidated in 1985. The Jihan law, which was introduced through the influence of Jihan Sadat, required that a wife give her consent before a husband took a second wife.

Egypt seems likely to continue on its present conservative path. The revolution of 1952 took place almost a half-century ago. Economic and social gains are taking place slowly. The country still has a literacy rate of only 44 percent, not just because only primary school attendance (ages 6 to 12) is compulsory, but also because all school-age children do not attend school. Females attend primary school with males, but education is segregated at the higher levels. Females make up about

41 percent of primary-level students, 38 percent of second-ary-level students, and 33 percent of post-secondary students. Hence it is not surprising that the literacy rate for men (58 percent) is much higher than that for women (29 percent).

Check Your Understanding

1. What programs in agricultural reform did Nasser in-stitute with the aim of improving life for Egypt's poverty-ridden people?
2. **a.** How did the Aswan High Dam help to further Egypt's agricultural reform? **b.** In what way has the dam hindered agricultural reform?
3. What were Egypt's Five-Year Plans designed to accomplish?
4. What social changes took place during Nasser's years in office?
5. How did Sadat encourage the private sector of the economy?
6. How did social unrest contribute to Sadat's unpopularity?
7. *Thinking Critically:* Cite evidence from the text-book to prove or disprove the statement: *Social and economic reforms since 1952 have modernized Egypt.*

CHAPTER REVIEW

■ **Chapter Summary**

Section 1. Western domination in Egypt began in 1798 with an invading army under the leadership of Napoleon Bonaparte. After three years, French rule gave way to the founding of a new dynasty by Mohammed Ali, who ruled Egypt from 1805 to 1848 and transformed it into the most powerful country in the Middle East. Using French influence, Mohammed Ali changed the economy, government, education-al system, and other important aspects of Egyptian society. He was also determined to make Egypt an important power in the Mediterranean by conquering what remained of the Ottoman Empire. After Mohammed Ali's forces twice defeated the Sultan, European leaders intervened to save the balance of power in the Middle East and forced him to withdraw from his conquered territories. In compensation, Mohammed Ali was given a hereditary governorship of Egypt.

Under Mohammed Ali's heirs to the governorship, further improvements were made, among them the opening of the Suez Canal. But extravagant rule and military ventures plunged the country into serious debt, and brought the Canal into British ownership.

Section 2. Further disarray in Egypt in 1882 brought about British intervention that for all intents and purposes made Egypt into a British protectorate. Britain's "temporary occupation" lasted until the middle of the twentieth century. Under British rule many of the government services were reorganized and improved. The lot of the average Egyptian, however, remained much the same. After World War I, opposition to British rule was directed by the Wafd, a national movement that demanded evacuation of foreign troops and called for "Egypt for the Egyptians." From 1907 to 1911, Britain took the first steps to give Egyptians a greater voice in their own affairs. But with the outbreak of World War I, Great Britain put aside further nationalist demands.

Section 3. The clamor for independence continued after World War I. In 1922, Great Britain issued a treaty making Egypt a constitutional monarchy but retaining control in foreign affairs. In 1936 the British signed another treaty with Egypt that gave the country greater self-government than before. Britain, however, retained control of the Suez Canal zone. After World War II, conditions worsened under the playboy rule of King Faruq. Many young army officers became restive and hostile to the government. They organized an underground movement that resulted in the revolution of 1952, the overthrow of the monarchy, and the establishment of a republic. Egypt's first premier and president of the republic was Mohammed Neguib. But Gamal Abdel Nasser removed Neguib from power in 1954, and he became premier and president of Egypt, a post he held until his death in 1970.

Section 4. Under Nasser's leadership, Egypt became a powerful leader of the Arab world. Nasser attempted to unite the Arab nations by forming the United Arab Republic with Syria, a move that was shortlived. He formed close ties with nonaligned nations and made overtures to the Soviet Union that angered the United States and led to its withdrawal of aid for building the Aswan High Dam. Nasser retaliated by nationalizing the Suez Canal in 1956, an action that brought on an armed attack from Great Britain, France, and Israel. When the United States, the Soviet Union, and the United Nations forced an end to the hostilities, tensions in the area remained high. The Six–Day War erupted in 1967 as Israel launched a surprise attack against Egypt after Nasser closed the Strait of Tiran to Israeli shipping. Superpower intervention again produced a stalemate, but not until after Israeli troops had overrun the Gaza Strip, the Sinai Peninsula, the West Bank, and the Golan Heights.

Nasser was succeeded by Anwar Sadat, who was determined to recover the lost territory of the Sinai Peninsula from the Israelis. Joining with Syria, Egypt launched a surprise attack on Israel. While neither side was able to claim a complete victory, Sadat reclaimed some of the Sinai's lost territory and continued his efforts to seek peace, which eventually resulted in the Egypt–Israel Peace Treaty of 1979. When expectations of a return to prosperity never materialized, Sadat's popularity waned and he reverted to repressive measures. In 1981 Sadat was assassinated and Hosni Mubarak, his vice president, became president of Egypt.

Mubarak instituted a more open style of rule and continued Egypt's peace commitments with Israel. At the same time, he moved to improve Egypt's standing with the rest of the Arab community of nations, who were angered by Egypt's peace settlement with Israel.

Section 5. Since 1952, Egypt's leaders have tried to improve the status of Egyptian peasants. They instituted land reforms to increase the number of landowners and to make it easier for peasants to pay rent. With Soviet assistance, Egypt built the Aswan High Dam to increase the amount of its arable land by providing year-round irrigation. The dam also produced hydroelectric power to meet all of Egypt's needs. Industrialization efforts were the subject of a number of Five–Year Plans. However, most of these did not meet their goals because the population increased by a million people every nine months. The status of women improved somewhat as the westernization of Egyptian life continued after the revolution of 1952. But a recent revival of Muslim fundamentalism eroded some advances made by women.

■ **Vocabulary Review**

Define: colonialism, corvée, khedive, mercenary, protectorate, self-determination, constitutional monarchy, fellaheen, partition, imperialism, Arab socialism, bloc, satellite, Third

World, nonaligned nation, nationalize, superpower, neutral, fundamentalist

- **Places to Locate**

    Locate: Alexandria, Cairo, Sudan, Isthmus of Suez, Syria, Aswan High Dam, El Alamein, Gaza Strip, Sinai Peninsula

- **People to Know**

    Identify: Napoleon Bonaparte, Mohammed Ali, Ahmed Arabi, Said, Ismail, de Lesseps, Disraeli, Lord Cromer, King Faruq, Gamal Abdel Nasser, Mohammed Neguib, Anwar Sadat, Hosni Mubarak, Menachem Begin

- **Thinking Critically**

    1. Why might Mohammed Ali be considered a great ruler?
    2. How did imperialism help to shape Egypt's present policies?
    3. Why was it important for Nasser to court nonaligned nations in the 1960's and 1970's?
    4. Why have the superpowers and the United Nations intervened when hostilities have erupted between Egypt and Israel?
    5. Why do you think Egypt's leaders have been unable to improve noticeably the peasants' lives?

- **Extending and Applying Your Knowledge**

    1. Write a report on the Suez Canal, updating information about conditions along the canal and analyzing the importance of the canal to world trade, both in the past and in the present. Consult the *Readers' Guide to Periodical Literature* for articles in news magazines.
    2. Consult the appropriate volume of *Vital Speeches* and read Anwar Sadat's address to the Knesset. Then prepare a summary of the speech for the class.

8

Modern Israel

The republic of Israel, founded in 1948, is a small country with a land area about equal to that of New Jersey and a population of about 4.5 million. Bordered on the north by Syria and Lebanon, on the east by Jordan, and on the south by Egypt, Israel is surrounded by neighbors that, except for Egypt, are hostile to its existence. Israel's terrain can be divided roughly into three physical regions. In the west is a narrow fertile plain along the Mediterranean Sea. A hilly region occupies the north and center. In the south is the Negev, a desert that takes up more than half the country. Despite the handicaps of small size, hostile neighbors, and a scarcity of productive land, Israel has become a dynamic nation, one of the most highly industrialized in the Middle East.

The country's political and economic development has been rapid despite many obstacles. After the United Nations approved a resolution dividing Palestine into separate Jewish and Arab states and Britain announced termination of its mandate, Israel declared its independence. As a result of the ensuing war (1948–1949) between Israel and several Arab states, hundreds of thousands of Arabs were displaced. Except for Egypt, neighboring Arab states have refused to recognize Israel's right to exist. Continuing animosity between Israel and the Arab countries has led to three more wars and numerous border raids and other hostile encounters. Because of its threat to world peace the Arab–Israeli issue has been frequently raised before the United Nations. To understand the position of both sides, it is necessary to know something of the historical background of the modern state of Israel.

1. The Roots of Jewish Nationalism

Jewish attachment to Palestine, the land in which the modern state of Israel was established, originated in Biblical times. It was the place in which most of the early history of the Jewish people, also known as Hebrews and Israelites, unfolded. (See pages 47–49.) Their existence as a unified people continued for hundreds of years after Moses led them back to Palestine from bondage in Egypt. Twice thereafter they were driven from their homeland, once when the Babylonians took them into captivity in the sixth century B.C. and again when the Romans destroyed Jerusalem in the second century A.D.

Experiences in the Diaspora

The period since Rome's destruction of Jerusalem is called the Diaspora, a term that comes from the Greek word meaning "dispersed." Though a few Jews continued to live in Palestine, large Jewish communities were formed in many countries in Europe, North Africa, and the Middle East.

The position of Jews who settled in Europe was difficult. In most European countries where Christianity was the dominant religion, Jews were excluded from the mainstream of life because they were nonbelievers, or non-Christians. As nonbelievers, European Christians regarded them as outsiders. Jews were forbidden to own land and to hold political office. They were also excluded from entering most professions.

During the Crusades thousands of Jews were massacred by the Christian armies passing through the lands of Europe on their way to the Holy Land, the name given to Palestine by Christians. In Spain during the 1400's, after many Jews and Muslims had undergone forced conversion to Catholicism, the leaders of the Roman Catholic Church, with the support of the Catholic monarchs, conducted an investigation called the Inquisition to determine how loyal these converts were. Thousands suspected of secretly adhering to the practices of their original faiths were persecuted, tortured, and burned at the stake. By the end of the 1500's nearly all Jews had left Spain and were dispersed throughout North Africa and the Middle East from Morocco to the Ottoman Empire.

Barred from becoming citizens in most European countries, Jews thought of themselves as a people apart. The place many regarded as a true homeland and for which most felt a deep attachment was Palestine. They also called the land of their ancient heritage Zion, from the name for one of Jerusalem's

Israel

1897	First World Zionist Congress
1917	Balfour Declaration
1920–1948	Palestine as British mandate
1948	Israel's independence
	Arab–Israeli War
1949–1953/	David Ben–Gurion's service as Israel's
1955–1963	prime minister
1956	Suez War
1967	Six–Day War
1973	Yom Kippur War
1979	Egypt–Israel Peace Treaty
1982	Invasion of Lebanon
1987–	West Bank/Gaza Strip uprising

hills. In time Zion became a symbolic name for the land of Israel. Jews in North Africa and other parts of the Middle East share this feeling.

Yearning for a Return to Zion

Jewish folklore was full of references to the Holy Land and an eventual return to Zion. Jewish writings were studded with sayings about Palestine. "It is better to dwell in the deserts of Palestine than in places abroad." "Whoever lives in Palestine lives sinless." "The air of Palestine makes one wise." Jewish holidays commemorated such events as the Jews' wanderings in the desert under Moses (Feast of Tabernacles), the purification of the Temple in Jerusalem after its destruction (Hanukkah), and the harvest season (Feast of Firstfruits). The annual Passover festival, celebrating the Exodus from Egypt, ended with a prayer of hope, "next year in Jerusalem."

While Jews were persecuted in Christian Europe and frequently were banished from such countries as Spain, France, England, Germany, and Russia, Jews were generally permitted to practice their religion in Muslim lands. Jewish scholars and government officials contributed much to Islamic cultural and political development before the twelfth century. Indeed, until the modern era Jews played prominent roles in the countries of North Africa, in Turkey, and in Iraq.

Contrasting Treatments

The ideals of the French Revolution (1789) provided an impetus for changing the situation of the Jews in Western Europe. Under Napoleon, who seized power in 1799, much discriminatory legislation was repealed and religion was no longer a principal requirement for citizenship. These changes took place not only in France but in lands influenced by French reforms. By the late nineteenth century Jews in Western Europe were gaining their full rights of citizenship. Many of them rose to high positions in Great Britain (Benjamin Disraeli), France and Germany (the Rothschilds), and other Western nations.

In eastern Europe, where the majority of Jews lived, persecution not only continued but was intensified. In Russia, where there was an influx of Jews after the partition of Poland in the late eighteenth century, a great deal of anti-Semitic legislation was enacted. Life became increasingly miserable for thousands of Jews. They were ordered confined to a region in White Russia and Russian Poland that was called the Pale of Settlement. In the 1880's hundreds of Jews were killed and their homes and businesses looted and burned in a series of massacres called **pogroms** (POH-grums) that were carried out by anti-Semitic mobs and often condoned by the authorities. In the Pale developed the largest **ghettos** in Europe, from which at least two million Jews emigrated to find better conditions in Western Europe or North America.

Stirrings of Jewish Nationalism

Against the background of the age-old longing of Jews to return to their ancient home in Palestine, czarist oppression gave impetus to **Zionism.** Many Jews came to believe that Zionism was the only solution to their plight. Inspired by other nationalist movements in Eastern Europe through which people hoped to win independence from Ottoman or Hapsburg overlords, more and more Jews began to advocate a land of their own and a return to Palestine.

During the 1880's the first Jewish pioneers left Russia to settle in Palestine, which was then part of the Ottoman Empire. Although only about 85,000 pioneers lived in Palestine before World War I, they laid the groundwork for large-scale immigration after the war. Many of the early settlements, considered the "frontier" outposts of the Jewish state, still exist.

1. What are three events in history that brought about the displacement of Jews from Palestine?
2. Which of these events is called the Diaspora?
3. Why were European Jews often subjected to discrimination?
4. Why did Jews develop a deep attachment to Palestine?
5. Why did Jewish nationalism begin in Eastern Europe?
6. ***Thinking Critically:*** Why did Jews generally receive better treatment in Muslim lands than in Christian Europe?

2. The Quest for a Homeland

The Zionist movement was founded by Theodore Herzl (HERTZ-uhl), an Austro–Hungarian Jew. In *The Jewish State,* a pamphlet written in German and translated into many languages, Herzl outlined the blueprint for a Jewish homeland and steps for obtaining it. Herzl's ideas aroused enthusiasm among many Jews and especially those in Eastern Europe. Many regarded him as a messiah who would lead them to Palestine. When he visited Eastern Europe, he was greeted by highly emotional crowds.

The Impact of the Dreyfus Affair

Herzl's conviction that Jews could not live normal lives in non-Jewish lands was intensified by the Dreyfus (DRAY-fus) affair in France, which began in 1894. Herzl, then a newspaper correspondent, covered the trial of Dreyfus, a French Jew and a military officer accused of selling military secrets to the Germans. Sentenced to life imprisonment, Dreyfus was eventually cleared of all charges and his army rank restored. But the anti-Semitic tone of both the trial and the post-trial attempts to clear Dreyfus' name so outraged Herzl that he devoted his life to working for the establishment of a Jewish homeland.

First World Zionist Congress

Herzl's program was adopted by the first World Zionist Congress. Meeting in Basel, Switzerland, in 1897, the world Zionist Congress adopted the "Basel Program," containing the general principles that were to guide the movement until the establishment of a Jewish state. This program called for Jewish settlement in Palestine and outlined methods of raising funds to support the Zionist movement. The World Zionist Organization and the whole modern Zionist movement grew out of the Basel Congress.

Chapters of the organization were established in many countries and millions of dollars were raised to finance the undertaking. Small bands of pioneer Zionists settled in Palestine before and during World War I. The newcomers were challenged even more deeply than they had expected to be. Most were unfamiliar with conditions of life in Palestine and were shocked to learn how greatly much of the land had been neglected over the centuries. The settlers were also surprised to learn that the Arab inhabitants of the country followed a way of life different from theirs.

Jewish Attitudes Toward Settlement

The Zionist movement was directed by Europeans who had little knowledge of the Middle East. Most Jews imagined it to be, in the words of Herzl, "a land without a people waiting for a people without a land." In fact, however, an Arab nationalist movement was being born about the time of World War I. Many Arab nationalists lived in Palestine. Since that territory was part of the Ottoman Empire, its inhabitants did not consider themselves different from those who lived in the adjoining Arab regions that became the present-day nations of Syria, Lebanon, Iraq, and Jordan. Ahad Haam, a man with greater insight than many of his fellow Zionists, had observed in 1891:

> We abroad have a way of thinking that Palestine today is . . . uncultivated wilderness, and that anyone who wishes to buy land there can do so to his heart's content. But that is not in fact the case. It is difficult to find any uncultivated land anywhere in the country. . . . We abroad have a way of thinking that the Arabs are all savages, on a level with the animals, and blind to what goes on around them. But that is quite mistaken. The Arabs, especially the townsmen, [understand] . . . our aims, but they keep silence . . . because for the present they anticipate no danger to their own future from what we are about. But if the time should ever come when . . . the indigenous [native-born] population should feel more or less cramped, then they will not readily make way for us. . . . [Hans Kohn, *Nationalism and Imperialism in the Hither East*]

Zionist Pioneers

For centuries the Jews of the ghettos of eastern and central Europe had been considered either physically weak or averse to work on the land. Toward the end of the 1800's, some Jewish leaders began to advocate the formation of a new class of agricultural and industrial workers. As immigrants came to Palestine, these leaders tried to direct them to a new way of life. The elder statesman of Israel, David Ben–Gurion, says of his arrival in Palestine early in this century: "I found the environment I had sought so long. No shopkeepers or speculators. . . . These were villagers . . . burnt by the sun." (See page 208.)

Land under cultivation was purchased, but immigrants often bought tracts of wasteland. They had to build roads, clear fields of rocks, break soil, and plant crops—all backbreaking outdoor work. Financial support was furnished by the Jewish National Fund, which collected contributions from Jews all over the world. The kibbutzim (kih-but-SEEM, plural) and other frontier settlements became the pride and joy of Zionists everywhere. The kibbutzim and other agricultural communities embodied both Jewish traditions and the newer social values of Zionism.

TEL AVIV. The cornerstone of the city of Tel Aviv was laid in the year 1907. The location (below) is now a thriving metropolis (left) stretching for miles along the Mediterranean.

David Ben-Gurion

The vigorous leadership of David Ben-Gurion, Israel's first prime minister, gave Israel a head start in the critical early years of the nation's existence. His vitality seemed to characterize the spirit of the land.

Born David Green in Poland, he chose the name Ben-Gurion (son of a lion) when he went to Palestine in 1906. It is said that he chose the name because of its Biblical ring. His concern for the rights of workers led him to help establish the Palestine Workers' Party, or Mapai, from the initials of its name in Hebrew, which became a leading political force in Israel. During World War I, the Turks deported Ben-Gurion. He then went to the United States where he promoted Jewish immigration to Palestine.

Impressed by the Balfour Declaration, Ben-Gurion enlisted in the British Empire Forces in Canada and served with General Allenby against the Turks. During the period when Palestine was a British mandate, he continued to press for the establishment of a Jewish state. He helped found the Histadrut and in 1935 became the chairman of the Jewish Agency, the organization responsible for promoting immigration to Palestine. After World War II he led the struggle for independence. In 1949 he became Israel's first prime minister, leading the country through its first two wars.

Ben-Gurion's leadership was broken only by a two-year period out of office, from 1953 to 1955. During his years as prime minister, Ben-Gurion was limited by the small size of his Mapai party, which had to form coalitions with other factions to stay in power.

After a full career in politics and government, he retired in 1963, spending much time farming and studying. His interest in philosophy once led him to extend a visit to Burma in order to take a nine-day course in Buddhism. Yet throughout his life he was faithful to Jewish traditions, constantly studying and quoting from the Bible until his death in 1973.

The first **kibbutz** (kih-BUTS, singular) was established at Degania in 1909.

Check Your Understanding

1. **a.** What was the Zionist movement? **b.** What impact did the Dreyfus Affair have on its founding?
2. How did the World Zionist Congress help to further the Zionist movement?
3. How did Jewish attitudes affect settlement in Palestine?
4. **a.** What is a kibbutz? **b.** How were the first kibbutzim developed?
5. *Thinking Critically:* Could the establishment of a Jewish homeland have been accomplished without a worldwide organization? Explain.

3. Debate over Palestine's Future

During World War I Zionism had Jewish followers in the countries of the Allies and of the Central Powers. Both the British and the Germans made promises about the future of Palestine in an effort to muster worldwide Jewish support for their respective causes. Perhaps the most significant of these statements was the so-called Balfour Declaration, which became the keystone of Jewish hopes for a national home in Palestine.

The Balfour Declaration

In 1917 Arthur Balfour, British Secretary of State for Foreign Affairs, issued a statement concerning the future of Palestine, which heartened Zionists everywhere. Balfour was probably mindful of the contributions of Dr. Chaim Weizmann (HEYE-um VYTS-mahn), a Jew born in Eastern Europe and a brilliant chemist who had placed his talents at the disposal of the British government during World War I. Britain was also eager to obtain support from Jews around the world at a difficult period in the war. The declaration promised assistance to Jews in the establishment of a homeland in Palestine. In his statement Balfour said:

> His Majesty's Government view with favor the establishment in Palestine of a national home for the Jewish people, and will use their best endeavors to facilitate the achievement

of this object, it being clearly understood that nothing shall be done which may prejudice the civil and religious rights of existing non-Jewish communities in Palestine. . . .
[Israel Cohen, *The Zionist Movement*]

However, the British had also made commitments to Arab nationalists concerning the disposition of territory in the Ottoman Empire. (See pages 242–243.) Although some British officials later insisted that their wartime promises to the Arabs excluded the area of Palestine, the assurances were vague enough to permit the Arabs to interpret them as including Palestine. The ground was thus laid for disputes that were to embitter Jews and Arabs for so many years.

At the end of the war Palestine and the former Ottoman lands south of Lebanon and Syria were in British hands. In 1920 Palestine became a British **mandate**, along with Iraq and Trans–Jordan. These former Ottoman lands were administered by Great Britain acting under a mandate by the League of Nations. The Balfour Declaration was a part of the terms of the mandate, and Britain agreed to aid immigration to Palestine and to help settle Jews when they arrived. The first British High Commissioner was Sir Herbert Samuel, a British Jew.

Arab–Jewish Confrontations

Almost immediately the British, the Zionists, and the Arab nationalists were involved in a bitter controversy about the future of Palestine. The Zionist leader Chaim Weizmann, who later became Israel's first president, attempted to work out an amicable settlement with the cooperation of Faisal (FY-sul), who later became King of Iraq. Despite several meetings, they were unable to reach an agreement and Arab–Jewish relations continued to worsen.

One reason for the increased hostility was the growth of Arab nationalism after World War I. Nationalism was especially strong in Palestine where the local Arab leaders demanded independence and opposed fulfillment of the promises to the Jews under the mandate. Despite Arab opposition, the rate of Jewish immigration was stepped up, and the number of Jews in the country increased greatly, causing fear that they would soon outnumber the Arabs.

On several occasions the British offered compromise plans calling for modified forms of self-government. But each time either the Arabs or the Jews found the British plan unacceptable. The British dilemma was compounded by frequent outbreaks of violence culminating in the Arab revolt, 1936–1939. Thousands of British troops were moved into Palestine to put down the Arab uprising.

Nazi Persecution

Nazi persecution of the Jews, beginning with **Kristallnacht** and continuing with the **Holocaust** during World War II, aroused intense feelings among Jews everywhere. Increasing pressure was put upon Great Britain to permit large-scale migration of Jews into Palestine against the wishes of the Arab majority. During World War II supporters of the Zionist movement smuggled Jews from Europe to Palestine. As Arab nationalists saw the Jewish minority grow, their fears of being outnumbered increased. During the period of the British mandate (1920–1948), the Jewish population of Palestine increased tenfold from about 65,000 to more than 650,000. The Arab population doubled to about 1,200,000.

At the end of the war the world learned about the Holocaust and the extent of its horror. The Nazis had killed some six million European Jews. One third of the world's Jewish population had been massacred in the Nazi death camps. Zionists demanded the immediate establishment of a Jewish state in Palestine. The underground movement to bring Jewish refugees to Palestine was stepped up against British and Arab wishes. When civil war again broke out in Palestine, Great Britain, recognizing its inability to formulate a settlement mutually acceptable to Jews and Arabs, referred the Palestine issue to the United Nations in 1947.

Check Your Understanding

1. What did the Balfour Declaration promise to Zionists?
2. How did the conditions of the Balfour Declaration intensify Arab–Jewish hostilities?
3. How did Arab nationalists feel about Britain's Palestinian mandate?
4. *Thinking Critically:* What effect did knowledge of Kristallnacht and the Holocaust have on worldwide sentiment toward the establishment of a Jewish state in Palestine?

4. Continuing Arab–Israeli Hostilities

Since 1922 and the establishment of the British mandate for Palestine, the question of what to do with Palestine had been a continuing problem. When Britain accepted Palestine as a mandate, it expected to establish two states: a homeland for Jews of the Diaspora despite Arab opposition. Its inability to satisfy either Arabs or Jews frustrated everyone involved. As the time approached for the actual establishment of an independent Jewish state, the Arabs continued to voice uncompromising opposition. Feeling that it had done all that one nation could do, and unwilling to risk the Arab animosity that was sure to result from partition, Britain turned to the United Nations (UN) for help.

Steps to Israeli Independence

The UN sent a commission to survey the situation in Palestine. With both Jews and Arabs demanding complete sovereignty in all of Palestine, the UN General Assembly voted to end the mandate and recommended that Palestine be partitioned into three separate areas. The first area was to be a Jewish state inhabited mostly by Jews. The second area was to be an Arab state. The third area was to be an international zone that would include Jerusalem, Bethlehem, and other nearby holy sites.

Both sides were prepared to fight for their objectives. The Palestine Arabs protested that the UN recommendation violated the principle of self-determination. They began to use force to oppose partition and the establishment of a Jewish state. Armed bands from Syria and Trans–Jordan began to infiltrate Palestine to assist the Palestinian Arabs.

The Zionists, on the other hand, received the United Nations proposal with enthusiasm and resolved to implement it regardless of Arab reaction. The Jews had previously formed a defense force called the Haganah (huh-guh-NAH), largely to protect themselves against Arab attacks. Out of the Haganah and other underground military units, the Jews of Palestine began to build a national army. At first their troops were familiar only with light arms and hit-and-run **guerrilla** tactics. Gradually, however, they were able to acquire heavier weapons from sympathetic parties.

After the UN partition resolution in November 1947, conflict between Jews and Arabs grew more intense. Raids, reprisals, and counterreprisals from both sides were frequent. Neither the British nor the UN was able to stop the fighting. The British

THE STATE OF ISRAEL. The throng celebrates Israel's Declaration of Independence. Inset: David Ben–Gurion signs the document, May 14, 1948.

mandate ended on May 14, 1948, the same day that Israel proclaimed its independence. The next day Arab armies from five neighboring Arab states (Egypt, Trans–Jordan, Iraq, Syria, and Lebanon) invaded the new Israeli state. Despite their determination, the Arab armies could not defeat the Israelis. Finally by July 1949, the UN persuaded all the invading nations except Iraq to sign separate armistice agreements with Israel.

Continuing Tensions, 1949–1956

Several issues plagued Israel's relations with Arab nations during the early years of its independence. One of these was the refugee question. About 725,000 Arabs fled Israel to settle in surrounding Arab territories. The fleeing **refugees** charged that they were driven from their homes by the Israelis. The Israelis, however, claimed that most Arab refugees fled because they were persuaded to leave by their own Arab leaders. Reacting to Israeli refusal to allow them to return to their homes, armed Palestinian groups infiltrated across Israel's borders, causing hundreds of minor and several major incidents of terrorism. Many of the Palestinian refugee population, which today numbers over two million, have continued to demand a return to their homes in Israel.

Besides demands on Israel to allow the return of Arab refugees, Arab leaders demanded compensation for property acquired by Israel and the surrender of territory held by Israel beyond its armistice frontiers. The Israelis rejected most demands for concessions. They believed that concessions would be interpreted as a sign of weakness. Charging the Arab states with trying to destroy Israel, they stated that they would never surrender territory gained in a conflict they did not start. As invaders, Israel charged, the Arab states were responsible for the flight and continuing plight of the Palestinian refugees. They further charged that permitting a return to Israel of these refugees who had been indoctrinated with a hatred of Israel would seriously jeopardize Israel's security.

A further issue complicating the search for peace in the Mideast was the tensions between the United States and the Soviet Union. The Arabs charged Israel with being a tool of Western imperialism and a means of continuing the Western presence in the Arab world. Israel's economy had been bolstered by Western funds, both from United States government sources and from many people in the United States, France, and Great Britain sympathetic to the Israeli cause. At the same time, many Arab states accepted military and economic aid from the Soviet Union and other Communist countries as well as from the United States, France, and Great Britain.

Still another issue was the presence of a UN peacekeeping force in the Middle East. The UN Truce Supervision Organization was established to carry out the provisions of the 1949 armistice agreements. Its main job was to patrol the borders between Israel and its neighbors. After Egypt's conflict with Israel, Great Britain, and France over the Suez Canal in 1956, a United Nations Emergency Force (UNEF) was set up to patrol the frontiers between Egypt and Israel. (See page 185.) But Egypt continued to bar Israeli shipping from the canal. Although the UNEF did have some success in preventing terrorist acts along the border between Israel and Egypt, such incidents continued along the Syrian and Jordanian frontiers.

Six–Day War, 1967

For some years Egypt had been receiving large supplies of arms from the Soviet Union. In May 1967 Egypt demanded that the UNEF leave its territory and began to send troops and tanks into the Sinai Peninsula to threaten Israel. Another act of provocation was the closing of the strategic Strait of Tiran, thus cutting off Israel's access to the Red Sea and preventing ships from reaching the Suez Canal. These incidents accompanied by threats to destroy Israel precipitated an Israeli attack on Egypt that quickly spread to Syria. Jordan then entered the conflict

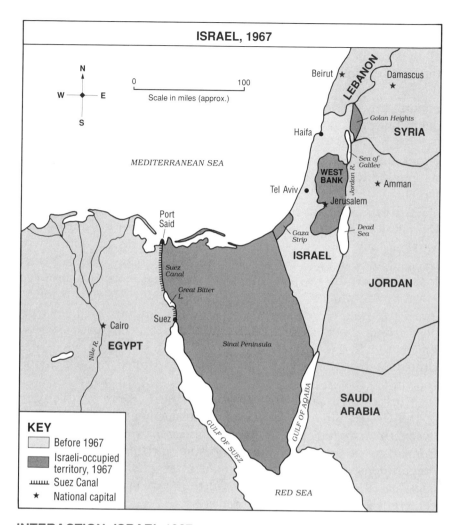

ISRAEL, 1967

N
W — E
S

0 ————— 100
Scale in miles (approx.)

MEDITERRANEAN SEA

Beirut ★ LEBANON

Damascus ★

Golan Heights

Haifa ●

SYRIA

Sea of Galilee

WEST BANK

Jordan R.

★ Amman

Tel Aviv ●

Jerusalem

Port Said

Gaza Strip

Dead Sea

Suez Canal

ISRAEL

Great Bitter L.

JORDAN

Suez

Cairo ★

EGYPT

Nile R.

Sinai Peninsula

GULF OF AQABA

SAUDI ARABIA

GULF OF SUEZ

RED SEA

KEY

Before 1967

Israeli-occupied territory, 1967

Suez Canal

★ National capital

INTERACTION: ISRAEL 1967. In 1967 Israel occupied strategic areas of three hostile Arab neighbors: the highlands of southern Syria, Jordanian territory as far as the western bank of the Jordan River, and Egypt's Sinai Peninsula.

against Israel. Within six days the Israelis had destroyed the Arab armies. Israel took the Sinai Peninsula and the Gaza Strip from Egypt; East Jerusalem and the West Bank from Jordan; and the Golan Heights from Syria. During the height of the brief war, Egypt sank ships in the Suez Canal to block traffic. The waterway remained closed long after the Six–Day War had come to an end.

For years after the Six–Day War, Israel remained in control of the areas seized from its enemies. Diplomats of the UN and several countries tried to arrange some kind of territorial concessions from both parties, but with little success.

The Yom Kippur War, 1973

Many Israelis believed that their country was the dominant military power in the Middle East. Because of this belief, they thought they would be able to maintain the status quo without making any territorial concessions. Anwar Sadat, Egypt's president, however, was determined to regain the Sinai Peninsula. (See page 186.) He convinced Syria to join him in a surprise attack on Israel during October 1973, hoping to return to international attention the question of the territories occupied by Israel.

The attack occurred on the holiest of Israel's holy days, Yom Kippur (Day of Atonement), which in 1973 occurred during the Muslim holy month of Ramadan. The war lasted only three weeks. Some of the heaviest battles fought since World War II took place on the Egyptian and Syrian fronts. More Israelis were killed in the war than in the entire period since 1948. Although Israel was taken by surprise and initially suffered setbacks on both fronts, it soon recovered and seized the offensive against Egypt and Syria. But the war ended in a stalemate when the United States, the Soviet Union, and the United Nations intervened.

During 1973 and 1974 Henry Kissinger, Secretary of State of the United States, negotiated disengagement agreements between the warring parties. Israel agreed to withdraw its forces from parts of both the Sinai Peninsula and the Golan Heights. Preparations were also made for an international peace conference to settle issues outstanding in the Arab–Israeli conflict. The conference met only once, however.

Direct Peace Talks, 1977–1979

By November 1977 Anwar Sadat had become impatient with efforts to achieve a peace settlement through an international conference and decided to take the initiative himself. In a surprise announcement he told the Egyptian parliament that he was about to fly to Jerusalem in a direct bid for peace. Sadat's visit and his address to the Israeli parliament was the first direct overture for peace by an Arab leader. It was an event that stirred great enthusiasm throughout Israel.

Despite these positive steps, the process of peace negotiations was long and difficult, taking over a year to finally reach agreement. During the year the negotiations frequently were broken off because of disagreements over the Sinai Peninsula and Jewish settlers in Arab territory. Personal conflicts between Sadat and Menachem Begin, the Israeli prime minister, also occurred. Nevertheless, the negotiations were saved from failure by the mediation of President Jimmy Carter of the United States.

In 1978 President Carter convened a meeting between Sadat and Begin at Camp David, the Presidential retreat near Washington, D.C. At the conclusion of this 12-day meeting a preliminary agreement was signed. The war between Egypt and Israel ended formally in March 1979 with the signing of a peace treaty in Washington. The treaty provided for normalization of relations between Egypt and Israel, the exchange of ambassadors, the return of the Sinai Peninsula to Egypt, and demilitarization of most of the Sinai Peninsula with an international peacekeeping force in the region. For their efforts, both Sadat and Begin were awarded the Nobel Peace Prize.

The West Bank and Gaza Strip

Israel's continued occupation of the West Bank and the Gaza Strip was not resolved by the 1979 treaty. The treaty, however, made provisions for future negotiations about the West Bank and the Gaza Strip. Ever since these territories were occupied in the 1967 war, Israelis have been divided over their disposition. Except for Jerusalem, which Israel has made its capital, many Israelis have opposed annexation of the West Bank and Gaza Strip. Those who favor annexation argue that all of Palestine belongs by historic right to the Jewish state and should not be given up, even as part of a peace settlement. Opponents feel that it is inadvisable to keep territory with such a large Arab population. They point to the high Arab birthrate and argue that Arabs would outnumber Jews in an Israel that included the West Bank and the Gaza Strip.

Lebanon Invasion

Israel's continued occupation of the West Bank and Gaza Strip stirred deep resentment among the Palestinian Arabs. By the 1980's demonstrations and protests were frequent. Most inhabitants sympathized with the Palestine Liberation Organization (PLO), the Palestinian nationalist organization that led the fight against Israel. Israeli leaders at the time believed that unrest in the occupied territories could be suppressed if the PLO's bases and headquarters in Lebanon were destroyed. They also felt that destruction of the PLO would end the terrorist attacks launched from Lebanon across Israel's northern border.

In June 1982 Israel began a massive invasion of Lebanon. The invasion was intended to destroy the PLO and to force Lebanon to sign a peace treaty with Israel. Ariel Sharon, Israel's minister of defense, confidently told his government that the fighting would be over in a few days. The fighting lasted far longer however, and Israeli forces surrounded Beirut (Lebanon's capital), pushing farther into Lebanon than was planned.

The Israelis besieged the PLO forces in Beirut for several weeks. Then through United States intervention, the fighting was ended. Thousands of civilians had been wounded, and many killed. Large-scale destruction took place in southern Lebanon and in the capital. Israel lifted the siege in August after an agreement was reached to withdraw PLO forces from Beirut.

After the PLO forces were withdrawn, Lebanese Maronite Christian militias, allies of Israel, entered two Palestinian refugee camps in Beirut and massacred hundreds of Palestinian men, women, and children. The massacre had a traumatic effect in Israel. To begin with, the war in Lebanon had been unpopular. The massacre aroused widespread criticism and mass protests against Sharon and the war. Many young men refused to serve in the occupation forces in Lebanon. Although Israel agreed to a gradual withdrawal of its forces, the opposition wanted a hastier departure. The issue of the war in Lebanon and demands that Israel end its occupation of Lebanon became major issues in the 1984 election campaign for the Knesset.

After the election, the withdrawal from Lebanon was completed except for a narrow strip of land along the Israeli border. This "security zone" is still held by Lebanese forces allied with Israel and is frequently policed by Israeli troops. None of Israel's major objectives in the 1982 invasion were achieved. Syrian forces remained in Lebanon, which refused to sign a peace treaty with Israel. After several months, PLO forces returned to Lebanon.

Palestinian Uprising

In December 1987 a major uprising of Palestinians in the occupied West Bank and Gaza Strip occurred. More than half the inhabitants in these territories had lived all their lives under Israeli military control. They had become resentful of the restrictions imposed on them by the Israeli army. These included frequent curfews, deportation of many politically active leaders, arrests without trial for hundreds suspected of terrorist acts, school and university closings, and interference in daily life.

Although the uprising began as a spontaneous demonstration, it soon became an organized movement with an underground leadership that demanded an end to Israeli occupation,

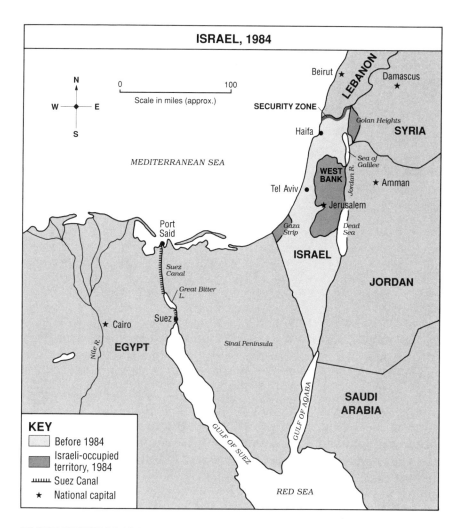

ISRAEL, 1984

N
W — E
S

0 —————— 100
Scale in miles (approx.)

MEDITERRANEAN SEA

Beirut ★   LEBANON   Damascus ★

SECURITY ZONE

Haifa ●   Golan Heights   SYRIA

Sea of Galilee

WEST BANK   Jordan R.

Tel Aviv ●   ★ Amman

★ Jerusalem

Gaza Strip   Dead Sea

ISRAEL

Port Said

Suez Canal

Great Bitter L.

Cairo ★   Suez

JORDAN

EGYPT   Nile R.   Sinai Peninsula

GULF OF SUEZ   GULF OF AQABA

SAUDI ARABIA

RED SEA

KEY
- Before 1984
- Israeli-occupied territory, 1984
- Suez Canal
- ★ National capital

ENVIRONMENT: ISRAEL, 1984. Compare this map with one on page 215. What territories has Israel continued to occupy? How has the continued occupation of these territories affected Israeli and Mideast politics?

the release of all political prisoners, and the establishment of an independent Palestinian state. Most Palestinians supported the PLO as the leader of the Palestinian nationalist movement. Israel, however, never recognized the PLO, labeling it a "terrorist" organization and never allowing it to operate in its territories.

Furthermore the Israeli government opposed the establishment of a Palestinian state in the West Bank and Gaza Strip. But disagreement over what to do with the occupied territories continued. The minimum that Palestinians were willing to accept was far more than most Israelis were willing to concede. The maximum that most Israelis were willing to give was far too little

Scenes of street violence like this have been taking place in the West Bank and Gaza Strip since Israeli occupation began. What group is recognized as a leader of the Palestinian nationalist movement?

for the Palestinians. All the Arab states, including Egypt, supported Palestinian demands for an independent state.

Palestinian Independence

In November 1988 the Palestine National Council met in Algeria and issued a declaration of Palestinian independence. At the same time it indicated that it might be willing to negotiate a peace settlement with Israel. Palestinians in the occupied territories received the declaration enthusiastically. Israel rejected it, however, declaring that indirect statements about mutual recognition were too vague. It seemed that the conflict would continue and that divisions between Israelis and Palestinian Arabs would become deeper and more bitter.

Check Your Understanding

1. What was the 1947 UN recommendation regarding Palestine?
2. What issues plagued Arab-Israeli relations:
   a. between 1949 and 1956?   **b.** since 1956?
3. What are the pros and cons of Israeli annexation of the West Bank and the Gaza Strip?
4. What has complicated relations between Arabs and Israelis since 1982?
5. What reaction did Israel have to the PLO's declaration of independence?
6. *Thinking Critically:* Is the Palestinian question capable of being solved peacefully? If so, what will it take to solve it?

5. Politics and Government

Most Zionist political parties and organizations in Israel were offshoots of groups formed in Europe after the first World Zionist Congress. These institutions, many government practices established by the British during the years of the mandate, and a few laws from the Ottoman era proved helpful in creating the new Jewish government in 1948.

For example, the Israeli Knesset was the end result of the Jewish national assembly organized in the 1920's. Many of the government agencies in charge of railroads, ports, and the like had been established by the British. Matters such as marriage, divorce, and adoption of children were in part regulated by the legislation that reflected the influence of older Ottoman laws. In addition, many of the top personnel in the Israeli government were also leaders of the World Zionist Organization.

Democratic Foundations

Most Jewish settlers in Palestine before 1948 came from Europe. For this reason institutions, customs, and points of view in the Jewish community of Palestine tended to reflect European democratic ways. Democratic practices took even deeper root during the era of the British mandate.

Israel has been one of the few developing nations where democratic practices are the norm rather than the exception. Israel has always held regular free elections. The press has been uncensored except for reasons of military security. Moreover, political parties have conducted their activities without government intervention or restriction, fostering the rise of more than two dozen different political parties, some of which resemble moderate Western European Socialist parties.

Much of Israeli politics in recent years has been dominated by two major party blocs, the left-of-center Labor Party formed from Mapai and other labor groups, and the right-wing Likud bloc. Since 1977 these two major blocs have deadlocked, with minor parties gaining enough seats to swing the balance of power in the national government.

The Electoral System

The Knesset, the 120-seat parliament of Israel, takes its name from the "Great Assembly" that governed Palestine 2,000 years ago. Normally parliamentary elections are held every four years, but the parliament may dissolve itself and call for new elections anytime before the end of its term. Israeli voters cast their votes

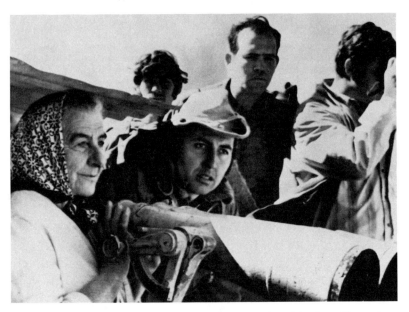

Officers briefed Prime Minister Golda Meir when she visited a military observation post in the Israeli-occupied Golan Heights in 1971.

not for individuals but for parties, each of which presents the voters with a predetermined slate of candidates.

Knesset seats are assigned in proportion to each party's percentage of the total national vote. Since Israel's founding in 1948, no single party has received enough votes to control the government, giving Israel a continuing series of coalition governments. The president of Israel, whose role is largely symbolic, is elected by the Knesset for a five-year term. After consultation with representatives of the political parties, the president calls on one of the Knesset members to serve as prime minister. Ordinarily the prime minister comes from the party holding the most seats in the parliament.

Party Politics, 1948–1977

From 1948 until 1977 Israel was governed by the Labor movement, a group of several semisocialist parties including the Mapai that united in 1968 to become the Israel Labor Party. The most notable political and military leaders of the Labor movement were David Ben–Gurion, Golda Meir, and General Moshe Dayan. Most important government posts were held by members of the movement. The powerful trade union movement, the Histadrut, controlled much of the country's economy. Many of the Labor Party's leaders came from the Histadrut.

Israel became one of the first nations to have a woman as its head of government when Golda Meir (may-AYR) was named prime minister in 1969. Earlier Meir had served in other important posts, including minister of foreign affairs, rising to become the dominant leader of the Labor Party at the age of 71. As prime minister, Meir reconciled differing factions, proving herself a strong leader. But in the 1970's Meir's popularity and the influence of the Labor Party began to decline. Many citizens criticized Meir's handling of the 1973 war and the peace negotiations that followed. They began to believe that the Labor Party had become too powerful and had been in office too long.

During the early 1970's an opposition nationalist movement began to gain strength. Called the Likud, the opposition movement attracted support from a variety of groups who wanted to annex all the territory seized by Israel in the 1967 war. One group included opponents of Labor's socialist economic policies who desired to establish a free economy. Most Jews from Asian and African countries called Oriental Jews or Sepherdim voted for Likud. They felt that Labor had discriminated against them by giving preference to Jews of European origin in government employment and in slating candidates for public office.

After Meir's resignation and the call for new elections in 1974, Likud became a major threat to Labor's control. In the 1977 elections the Likud emerged as the party with the largest number of seats in the Knesset. Thus Likud leader Menachem Begin became prime minister, forming a coalition government with several religious and non-Labor parties. Many Israelis called this sudden and unexpected political change an "earthquake."

Changing Coalitions

Begin proved to be very popular with the Sepherdim, who by the late 1970's formed a majority of the Jewish population. After the 1981 election, Begin won enough seats to form another government. But the 1984 election brought still another shift in party politics. The 1982 war in Lebanon was unpopular. Many Likud promises had not been kept, especially the one to undermine the power of the Histadrut. An inflation rate of more than 400 percent, growing unemployment, and the failure of the Likud to sell off many government-owned enterprises led to deteriorating economic conditions.

The result was a near tie between Labor and Likud in the 1984 election. With neither party strong enough to form a coalition government, the two parties decided to form a National Unity Government (NUG). In this government the two parties held the most important posts and shared the others with sever-

COALITION LEADERS. Shimon Peres (left), prime minister of Israel, is shown conferring in 1985 with Yitzak Shamir, Israel's foreign minister. In 1986, Peres switched posts with Shamir, following an agreement that was made at the time they formed the National Unity Government (NUG). Why was this agreement necessary?

al smaller parties. A unique arrangement was devised. Shimon Peres, the leader of the Labor Party, was prime minister for two years. Then he became foreign minister, switching posts with Yitzhak Shamir, who had become the new leader of the Likud after the resignation of Begin in 1983.

The NUG was only partially successful. It did manage to bring down inflation and to cope with some of the country's economic problems. But it failed to make progress in foreign policy. While Peres favored an international peace conference and concessions of territory for peace, Shamir opposed him. One consequence of the stalemate was the 1987 Arab uprising in the occupied territories. (See page 218.)

In November 1988 Israel again held elections for parliament. Although the Likud won 50 seats to Labor's 49, the biggest surprise was the 18 seats won by several religious parties. Israel had another coalition government, but the religious parties demanded major concessions from Shamir for their cooperation. Among these concessions was a stricter government control of religious affairs, including the banning of sports events, movies, and theater performances on the Sabbath. Opposition to the religious concessions by many Israelis led Shamir to form a new NUG with the Labor Party in which he became prime minister. Other cabinet posts were divided between Likud and Labor while a few were allocated to small religious parties.

Check Your Understanding

1. How have Israeli politics and government been influenced by its European roots?
2. How has the way members of Israel's parliament are elected led to coalition governments in Israel?
3. What issues separate the two major political parties in Israel?
4. **Thinking Critically:** Has coalition government been an advantage or a disadvantage for Israel?

6. Economic Development

Israel has made remarkable progress since the republic was established. Its Jewish population has increased more than 600 percent, largely through immigration. Approximately two million Jews have immigrated to Israel, mainly from Europe, Asia, and Africa. Absorbing them has been a major challenge for Israel.

The Importance of Agriculture

From its earliest days agriculture has been a mainstay of the Israeli economy. Long before Israel became a reality, Zionist pioneers labored to make the land productive. Since 1948 the amount of land under cultivation has increased through the development of sophisticated irrigation systems. Today Israel has more than one million acres of productive farmland, about 22 percent of Israel's total land area. About half of this acreage is irrigated.

The kibbutz and the moshav are two types of cooperative communities that have aided Israel's agricultural development. Fewer than 5 percent of the population of Israel are kibbutz members. But from the outset they have been esteemed as "pioneers" of Israel, the vanguard in the development of the country. Many of these pioneers, a far larger proportion than in other sectors of the population, have stood out in the country's political, cultural, and social life. Members of a kibbutz own little private property and receive no regular salaries. All their needs are covered by the kibbutz budget. All of the members participate in decision-making, including setting the budget. Once mainly agricultural, in recent years many kibbutzim have turned to industry.

The moshav is a cooperative that provides major economic and social services, but each family maintains its own house-

225

A DIVERSIFIED ECONOMY.

Starting almost from scratch, Israel has built a diversified economy in a hostile environment. Imported industrial diamonds are cut for export (top left). Salt water is made usable at a desalination plant at Elath on the Red Sea (top right). The Dead Sea is made to yield treasure at this potash plant at Sdom (left). Citrus fruit, a major export crop, is packed at a modern plant in Hadera (below left). Modern farming methods have made a showplace of the first kibbutz, established at Degania in 1909 (below right).

hold and farms its own land, which is owned publically. The average moshav has about 60 families. Decisions in the moshav are made by its governing body, which meets every six to eight weeks. About 4 percent of Israel's rural population are members of a moshav. In recent years both the kibbutzim and moshavim have gone heavily into debt and face a financial crisis.

The country has become self-sufficient in producing a large number of food crops, although it still must import bread grains and meat to satisfy the demands of its growing population, which now numbers about 4.5 million. The principal crops raised are fruits, vegetables, wheat, barley, and cotton. Grapes are also raised, and wine-making is an important industry. Israel is one of the world's largest exporters of citrus fruits. It also exports flowers, avocados, tomatoes, strawberries, melons, and cotton.

The Growth of Industry

Since 1967 economic planning has emphasized industry over agriculture. Almost 25 percent of the labor force is employed in industry contrasted with 6 percent in agriculture. Industry now accounts for more than 20 percent of the Gross National Product. Goods manufactured include machinery, tools, chemicals, electrical products, textiles, processed foods, and plastics. Exports include automobiles, refrigerators, tires, leather goods, and precision instruments. Israel is also a world leader in the diamond industry, producing about 80 percent of the world output of small polished stones. It also has 40 percent of the world's diamond-polishing industry, working on diamonds of all sizes and shapes.

Tourism is another important segment of Israel's economy. More than one million tourists visit Israel each year, staying at sleek modern hotels and eating at a variety of attractive restaurants. Many tourists travel to Israel in El Al, the Israeli-owned airline. The tourist industry contributes more than one billion dollars annually to Israel's economy.

Economic Challenges

Israel still must import raw materials and some manufacturing equipment. While efforts continue to be made to bring the country's imports and exports into balance, the cost of Israel's imports exceeds the revenues that are gained from exports by about $3.5 billion. Israel is also working to absorb thousands of immigrants into the economy by providing housing and apprentice programs.

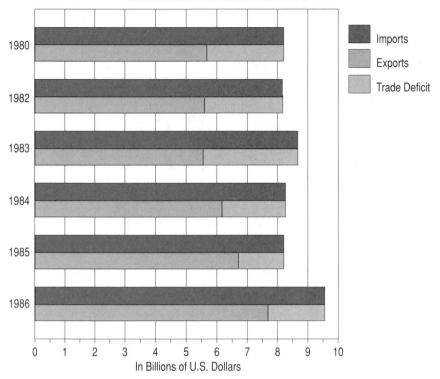

ISRAEL'S IMPORTS AND EXPORTS

Imports
Exports
Trade Deficit

1980
1982
1983
1984
1985
1986

0   1   2   3   4   5   6   7   8   9   10
In Billions of U.S. Dollars

Source: *Statesman's Year-Book,* 1988–1989

BALANCE OF TRADE. The money Israel pays for its imports consistently exceeds the revenue it obtains from its exports, creating a sizable trade deficit each year. Israel relies on its imports to meet one fourth of its food needs and almost all its petroleum needs. What are some of Israel's major exports?

Israel is also striving to develop the Negev region, which makes up about 60 percent of Israel's total land area. The Negev was once considered desolate and useless. But if water resources can be brought into the region, it can make valuable contributions to Israel's economy. Besides the arable land that could be added, valuable deposits of phosphates, potash, copper, oil, and natural gas could be extracted.

A pipeline from the Sea of Galilee went into operation in June 1964. Since then other irrigation projects have been put into operation. But the Israeli government has had difficulty persuading settlers to move into the Negev, and only about 10 percent of the people live in the southern half of the country.

The Histadrut

Founded in 1920, the General Federation of Labor, or the Histadrut (his-tuh-DROOT), is an organization that includes most of

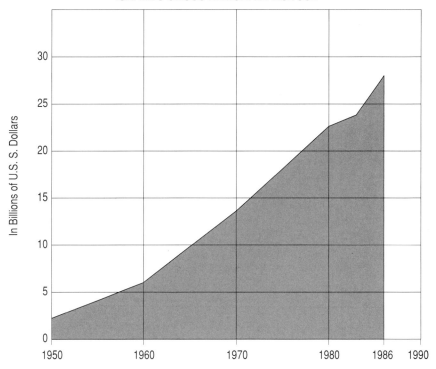

ISRAEL'S GROSS NATIONAL PRODUCT

In Billions of U.S. S. Dollars

30
25
20
15
10
5
0

1950   1960   1970   1980   1986   1990

Sources: *Facts About Israel, 1985; Information Please Almanac, 1989*

GROSS NATIONAL PRODUCT. Israel's success at developing the economic resources of its land and people is demonstrated by the continuing growth of its gross national product since 1950.

the trade unions in the country. Its almost 2 million members represent 87 percent of Israel's wage earners. Its role in the economy far exceeds that of the conventional labor union concerned mainly with collective bargaining for its members. Histadrut is owner or part owner on a cooperative basis of many industries, businesses, insurance companies, and financial institutions. It operates hospitals and convalescent homes, and publishes a newspaper and several other periodicals. It also has an affiliated women's organization that operates many cultural and social services including day-care centers, recreation facilities, and homes for older people. The Likud has attacked the Histadrut, charging that it has become inefficient and corrupt in the management of its enterprises.

Technological Achievements

The Weizmann Institute, the Haifa Technical Institute, and the Hebrew University Medical School have been internationally

229

LIFE IN ISRAEL. Fun at a modern water slide at Eliat (top left) contrasts with a farmer's moment of rest (top right) in the Hadera region. Israeli soldiers (left) stand reverently at the Western Wall in Jerusalem's Old City. Also in the Old City, an Arab and a Jew (bottom left) transact business. Yemeni artisans (lower right) represent the traditions of their ethnic group. How do these traditions differ from those of "European Jews"?

acclaimed for their contributions to the development of new agricultural, industrial, and medical techniques. Israel pioneered desalination techniques. Its first atomic reactor began operation in 1960, and its first solid-fuel rocket was launched in 1961. The United States and other countries have sought assistance from Israeli scientists and technicians. Israel has sent technical aid missions to several African and Asian countries. Ghana, Ethiopia, and Tanzania have used the services of Israeli advisers in developing communications and agriculture. Burma and Iran, before 1979, as well as several Latin American nations have also enlisted the aid of Israeli specialists.

By making assistance available, Israel hoped to win friends among nonaligned nations and break the diplomatic isolation the Arab states tried to impose on it. Many countries of Africa and Asia have preferred Israeli aid to that of the superpowers. For one thing, Israel has no "imperialist" motive. For another, many agricultural, industrial, and social experiments and programs conducted in Israel have more relevance to their own situations than those of the superpowers. During the 1970's, however, most African nations broke relations with Israel because of its continued occupation of what they consider Arab territory and its failure to recognize the rights of Palestine.

Economic Aid from Abroad

Israel has been a major recipient of United States foreign aid in the form of loans and grants. World Jewry, especially Jews in the United States, makes generous contributions to Israel. Another source of foreign aid has been reparations paid by the West German government as compensation for Jewish lives lost and property seized by the Nazis during World War II. Additional economic help has been derived from property left behind by Arabs when they fled Palestine after Israel's founding in 1948.

Check Your Understanding

1. What part did the kibbutz play in the development of Israel's agriculture?
2. What economic challenges lie ahead for Israel?
3. How has Israel assisted other nations in their economic development?
4. *Thinking Critically:* What obstacles has Israel had to overcome to be economically as successful as it is?

7. Domestic and Social Policies

Israel has had to contend with numerous social problems in its short existence as a nation. The integration of its ethnic groups is one such problem that has posed a major challenge.

Integration of Ethnic Groups

A serious internal problem for Israel is the assimilation into its social and political structure of two very different groups of people—the Arabs and the Oriental Jews. The Arabs in the West Bank and Gaza Strip remained after the creation of the Jewish state or came under Israeli jurisdiction as a result of the 1967 war and are not Israeli citizens. Oriental Jews actually constitute a majority in Israel, though their influence has been much less than that of Jews who have come from Western lands.

Sepherdim

Jews from Asia and Africa are called "Sepherdim," or Oriental Jews, to distinguish them from Jews from the Western world, who are known as "Ashkenazi." The great majority of Sepherdim, who began immigrating to Israel in large numbers in the 1950's, closely resemble both physically and culturally the populations among whom they lived before emigrating. Their presence has added new elements to the great variety of racial and ethnic types already living in Israel. These immigrants speak the languages of their native African and Asian lands. As a result Arabic is today second to Hebrew as a spoken language in Israel.

A great gap has separated most Sepherdim from the Ashkenazi. Between 1950 and the 1970's only a few Sepherdim succeeded in attaining positions of leadership in government or business. Their comparatively late arrival in Israel occurred when competition for top-level positions was already quite strong. Since the 1970's, however, the distinctions between Sepherdim and Ashkenazi have been blurred. But with their high birthrate, Sepherdim have become the majority in Israel's population. Today more than half of the Jewish population has been born in Israel, and an increase in intermarriage between Sepherdim and Ashkenazi has taken place. In addition, many Sepherdim have narrowed the education gap that once existed between them and the Ashkenazi. As a result, more Sepherdim have risen to positions of importance in Israel.

The Arab Population

More than 700,000 Arabs live in Israel and over 1.5 million in the occupied territories. Although most Israeli Arabs are citizens

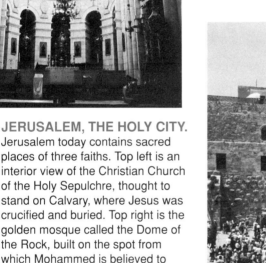

JERUSALEM, THE HOLY CITY.
Jerusalem today contains sacred places of three faiths. Top left is an interior view of the Christian Church of the Holy Sepulchre, thought to stand on Calvary, where Jesus was crucified and buried. Top right is the golden mosque called the Dome of the Rock, built on the spot from which Mohammed is believed to have risen to heaven. Nearby is the Western, or Wailing, Wall (lower right), all that survives of the Jews' holy Temple.

and many have higher living standards than Arabs in surrounding countries, they are not integrated into the nation's social and political structure. Israeli Arabs may attend the Hebrew University. While hundreds have done so, few have attained high positions in government or business. Some Israelis argue that as long as there is no peace between Israel and its Arab neighbors, Israeli Arabs cannot expect equal treatment with Jews, even in a democracy. Others argue that the second-class citizenship of the Arab minority weakens Israeli democracy.

Israel's Arab problem has taken on new significance now that there are more than 1.5 million Arabs in areas occupied during the 1967 war. This means that in the territory under Israel's jurisdiction more than a third of the population is Arab.

Israel's Standard of Living

Israel's high standard of living can be attributed to hard work and dedication. It has been furthered by Israeli mastery of scientific, technical, and managerial skills. The absorption of Arab property and large amounts of foreign aid also contributed.

Life in the cities where 89 percent of Israel's population lives resembles that in Western Europe or the United States. The Gross National Product totals about $28 billion. Its per capita income is about $6,000. Life expectancy for males is about 73 years, while for females it is almost 76 years. Among the Jewish population the literacy rate is over 90 percent, while among the Arab population it is only about 70 percent.

Education

Among the first laws passed by Israel's parliament was the Compulsory Education Law (1949), which provided free education for children ages 5–14. Since 1978, school attendance has been mandatory for children up to age 16. Free education, however, is provided for children up to age 18. Since the start of compulsory education, the main objective has been social integration of Israel's many Jewish groups into a unified people.

Israel has one of the highest rates of preschool attendance in the world with 88 percent of all three-year-olds and 97 percent of all four-year-olds attending some form of preschooling. The state system provides one year of nursery school and one of kindergarten, six years of elementary school, and six years of secondary education in grades 7–12. Five universities and two institutes provide post-secondary education to Israeli citizens.

In recognition of Israel's two major groups—Jews and Arabs—separate school systems are maintained. The Jewish system provides instruction in Hebrew and recognizes state schools, state-religious schools, and government-recognized independent schools. The Arab system provides instruction in Arabic. The Arab system, however, does not receive the same government assistance the Jewish system receives.

Status of Women

Equality of the sexes has always been a strong part of life in Israel. Jewish women participate in most facets of business, industry, and military life. Among the Arab population, women have achieved some gains as education has helped to bring their lives in line with that of the Jewish population. In 1948 only 21 percent of Arab girls attended any type of school. The percentage of girls in school had risen to 46 by 1973. By the end of the 1980's virtually all Arab girls aged 6 to 16 attended school. More professions and trades are becoming acceptable female occupations, and vocational training is increasing for all Israeli women. Nevertheless many Israeli women feel that they have a long way to go before achieving real equality.

Israel's Place in the Middle East

Israel is a new nation and much of its population has come from developing nations in Asia and Africa. But Israel is still largely European in outlook, in the origins of its leaders and institutions, and in its major international associations. While its Western ties have been a cause of deep Arab animosity, these same ties have also been Israel's source of strength.

Israel's challenges arise from this double-sided nature. Will the integration of its large and rapidly increasing Sepherdim population with the Ashkenazi continue? Will Israel's Western-style institutions and political, social, and economic outlook be modified enough to make the country a vital part of the Middle East, not just a nation located in it? Will relations between Israel and the surrounding Arab nations lead to lasting peace and regional solidarity? The answers to these questions still lie in the future.

Check Your Understanding

1. Which two ethnic groups have posed a serious assimilation problem for Israel?
2. Why has it been difficult for Israel to assimilate these two groups?
3. What statistics help to prove that Israel has a high standard of living?
4. How has Israel attempted to improve assimilation through its education system?
5. *Thinking Critically:* How do Israel's ties to the West jeopardize its efforts to assimilate its Arab population?

CHAPTER REVIEW

■ Chapter Summary

Section 1. The roots of Jewish nationalism and unity began with the Jews' return from bondage in Egypt to the "promised land" of Palestine. In the Diaspora, which began after the destruction of Jerusalem, Jewish yearnings for a return to Palestine continued through the long centuries of Jewish persecution. This oppression gave rise to Zionism and the first trickle of immigrants from Eastern Europe into Palestine.

Section 2. The Zionist movement was founded in 1897 by Theodore Herzl, a journalist outraged by prejudice and discrimination against Jews. The first World Zionist Congress, held in 1897, established the guiding principles for the development of a Jewish state in Palestine. But the stirrings of Jewish nationalism came at a time when Arabs in Palestine were also moved by a nationalism of their own. When settlers began moving into the area before and after World War I, the stage was set for confrontation between two groups wanting the same piece of territory.

Section 3. The debate over Palestine's future continued during the period when Palestine was a British mandate (1920–1948) because Britain had made conflicting promises over Palestine to both the Arabs and the Jews. Britain continually tried to reach a compromise between the growing nationalism of the Arabs in Palestine and the increasing Jewish immigration. At the end of World War II, knowledge of the Nazi persecution of the Jews and the extent of the Holocaust increased the pressure on the British to make good the promise of the Balfour Declaration. Realizing its helplessness in the face of conflicting demands and unwilling to risk the animosity of either side, Great Britain turned the Palestine question over to the United Nations in 1947.

Section 4. The day Britain ended its mandate in Palestine (May 14, 1948), Israel declared its independence. Protesting violations of self-determination, five Arab states launched an invasion of Israel that resulted in successful and determined Israeli resistance and a UN-sponsored armistice.

Between 1948 and the present, Israel has been involved in three more wars. It has occupied territory from Egypt (the Sinai Peninsula and the Gaza Strip), from Syria (the Golan Heights), and from Jordan (the West Bank). Direct talks between President Sadat of Egypt and Prime Minister Begin of Israel produced the Egypt–Israel Peace Treaty of 1979, a result of which was Israel's return of most of the Sinai Peninsula to Egypt. But Israel retained occupation of the Golan Heights, the West Bank, and the Gaza Strip.

In 1982 Israel invaded Lebanon to destroy the Palestinian Liberation Organization (PLO). In 1987 Israel faced an uprising of Palestinian nationalists in the West Bank and Gaza Strip. It has refused to make concessions regarding the Arab refugees who fled Israel into surrounding countries. After the PLO issued in 1988 a declaration of independence for an Arab state in Palestine, the tensions between Arabs and Jews seem destined to continue.

Section 5. Israel has a parliamentary form of democracy. Delegates to the 120-seat Knesset are elected by citizens who cast votes for a party's slate of candidates rather than for individuals. Since 1948 no single party has been able to dominate the parliament, giving the nation a continuing series of coalition governments. The two major parties are the Labor Party and the Likud. Minor parties often control the balance of power in the formation of a government. Politics from 1948 to 1977 were dominated by the Labor Party. From 1977 to the present, the Likud came to prominence. Strong conservative religious minorities continue to play an important swing role in forming coalition governments and in forcing concessions from the major party forming the government.

Section 6. Israel has made remarkable economic progress, developing a strong agricultural and diversified industrial economy. Six percent of the labor force is employed in agriculture, which derives its vigor from the kibbutz and the moshav. Twenty-five percent of the labor force is employed in industry, which has received priority in economic planning since 1967. Israel has developed a strong international trade, but still needs to balance imports with exports and faces many other difficult problems..

Section 7. Integration of ethnic groups, mainly the Arabs and Sepherdim, into the mainstream of Israeli life is a serious problem for Israeli social and domestic policies. Today Sepherdim make up the majority in the Jewish population. About 700,000 of Israel's population is Arab. Israel has a two-pronged education system to meet the needs of both its Jewish and its Arab populations.

■ Vocabulary Review

Define: Zionism, pogrom, ghetto, kibbutz, Holocaust, Kristallnacht, mandate, guerrilla, refugee

■ Places to Locate

Locate: Palestine, Jordan, Syria, Lebanon, Sinai Peninsula, West Bank, Gaza Strip, Suez Canal, Golan Heights, Negev

■ People to Know

Identify: Benjamin Disraeli, Theodore Herzl, David Ben-Gurion, Lord Balfour, Chaim Weizmann, Sir Herbert Samuel, Anwar Sadat, Henry Kissinger, President Jimmy Carter, Menachem Begin, Ariel Sharon, Golda Meir, Yitzhak Shamir, Shimon Peres

■ Thinking Critically

1. How did experiences of Jews of the Diaspora nurture Jewish nationalism and lead to Zionism?
2. How may early Jewish attitudes toward settlement in Palestine have influenced Arab–Jewish relations?
3. Compare Arab and Jewish attitudes today toward the presence of Israel in the Middle East with those voiced at the time of the Balfour Declaration. To what extent have attitudes changed or remained the same?
4. What do you consider Israel's most serious challenges in the areas of political, economic, and social issues?

■ Extending and Applying Your Knowledge

1. Write a report analyzing David Ben-Gurion's contributions to Israel. Given the state of affairs in Israel today, determine whether Ben-Gurion's lasting influence was negative or positive overall.
2. Read the book *My Friend, the Enemy* by Uri Avnery and give an oral report on this Israeli's impressions of the PLO and other Palestinians. Consider his point of view in determining his attitude.

9

Other Countries of the Middle East

The history of nationalism in the Middle East has been the subject of the last three chapters, spanning the period from the conclusion of World War I and the breakup of the Ottoman Empire to the present. Some of the empire's former territories established their independence at once while others became mandates of a European power, delaying their independence until after World War II.

In Chapter 6, you read about nationalist efforts of the Turkish-speaking people of the Anatolian Peninsula as they established the Republic of Turkey. In Chapter 7, you saw how the people of Egypt established a modern-day Arab republic. In Chapter 8, you learned how the aspirations of the Jewish people led to the establishment of Israel.

In Chapter 9 you will read about how other states in the Middle East arrived at independence after World War II. The struggles of Syria and Lebanon for independence began when France took them as League–of–Nations mandates after World War I. Iraq and Trans–Jordan moved from being British mandates to independent states. In the Arabian Peninsula traditional monarchies modernized or became constitutional monarchies. In Iran an Islamic Revolution in the late 1970's overthrew a constitutional monarchy that had been in existence since 1906.

While nationalism was the main impetus for these movements, it was not the only force that was shaping politics and change. Other forces included socialism, militarism, and Islamic fundamentalism.

1. Arab Nationalism in the Twentieth Century

Arab nationalism is a relatively new development in those lands bordering the eastern end of the Mediterranean and the Arabian Peninsula. Until early in the 1900's, most people in the area identified themselves with the religious community to which they belonged. In the Ottoman Empire identifying oneself as a Jew, Christian, or Muslim was encouraged by the millet system. On the other hand, the Ottoman Empire also encouraged its people to think of themselves as members of the empire rather than as members of a national group. During the nineteenth century, however, nationalism won followers among Arabs in Egypt and Syria. Until the division of the Ottoman Empire following World War I, *Syria* referred to the region of present-day Syria, Lebanon, Jordan, and Israel. When Britain and France replaced the Ottoman sultan as masters of the Middle East after World War I, Arab nationalism gradually became a powerful movement that was turned against the foreign powers.

The Fostering of Nationalism

Missionaries who came to the Middle East in the nineteenth century opened many schools. They founded the Syrian Protestant College, later called the American University of Beirut and one of the best colleges in the region. Missionaries were among the first to encourage the use of written Arabic for modern educational purposes. Their presses produced not only religious tracts but also modern literary and scientific works. Their activity sparked an Arabic literary revival. By the mid-1800's Cairo, Damascus, and Beirut had become centers of the new Arab intellectualism. Other young Arabs, sent to study in Britain or France, read the works of Western political thinkers and breathed in the spirit of nationalism that filled the air of all the European capitals.

Although many Arabs formed groups during the nineteenth century to stress their common national and cultural heritage, few Muslim Arabs advocated political independence from their Ottoman rulers. At most, they favored a process of decentralization in which Arabs would receive autonomy within the Ottoman Empire. In Beirut, however, many Christian Arabs formed secret societies for the purpose of creating an independent Arab state. Many of their young leaders were students at the American University of Beirut.

Nationalism also arose as a reaction against political repression. By the beginning of World War I, many Muslim Arabs had

Middle East Nations Since World War I

1920	Monarchy in mandate of Trans–Jordan
1922	Monarchy in mandate of Iraq
1925–1979	Pahlavi dynasty in Iran
1932	Independence of Iraq
1946	Independence of Syria and Lebanon Independence of Jordan
1951	Nationalization of Iran's oil industry
1953–	Reign of King Hussein of Jordan
1956	Suez War
1958	Republic of Iraq
1961	Independence of Kuwait
1962	Beginning of Yemen's Civil War
1967	Six–Day War Independence of South Yemen
1971	Formation of United Arab Emirates
1979	Islamic Republic of Iran
1980–1988	Iran–Iraq War
1982	Israeli invasion of Lebanon

become disillusioned and turned against their Turkish rulers, especially after the Young Turks began their process of Turkification. Soldiers joined literary men and intellectuals in underground organizations to rise against Turkish oppression.

The Beginnings of Revolt

Hussein (hoo-SAYN) Ibn Ali was Sharif of Mecca and a member of the ancient Hashemite family related to Mohammed. When in the early twentieth century, the Young Turks threatened to force centralized government on the Hejaz, the province containing Mecca and Medina, Hussein resisted. When World War I came, he accepted financial assistance and weapons from Britain, which had its own reasons for supporting Hussein. An Arab revolt would undermine Britain's Ottoman enemies and distract them from an attack on Suez. Britain also wanted to protect its trade with India and its interests in Persia. Hussein and his four sons waged guerrilla warfare against the Turks, first in the

Abdullah of the Hashemite family, member for Mecca in the Ottoman parliament, prepared the way for the Arab Revolt against the Turks. Here he is accepting the surrender of a Turkish commander in 1917.

Hejaz, then in Palestine and Syria. In return for Hussein's support, Britain agreed to the establishment of an independent Arab state in the Arabic-speaking region south of present-day Turkey.

Doubts and Fears

Not all Arabs broke with the Turks. Only small groups, mostly among the educated, were active nationalists. Many Arabs were reluctant to side with Christians against their fellow Muslims, especially since the Ottoman sultan was also Caliph of Islam. Arab peasants, who constituted the vast majority of the population, continued to be indifferent. They lived in ignorance and fear of the Turks. Even many of the British officials in the area were less than enthusiastic about the revolt. They feared that it might interrupt British plans to annex lower Iraq and might create unrest among India's 90 million Muslims, who regarded the Ottoman sultan in his role of caliph as their religious leader. Before and during the war, however, Arab nationalism gained many converts when the Ottomans took harsh measures to repress the movement in its Syrian provinces.

A Broken Promise

The close of World War I left Syria in the hands of the French, the British, and Amir Faisal (FEYE-sahl), the son of Hussein and the leader of the Arab revolt that had swept from the Arabian Peninsula into Syria by the end of the war. Arab nationalists

242

expected the Allies to keep their promise to recognize Arab independence and to withdraw their forces. But the Arab nationalists were keenly disappointed when the League of Nations failed to grant immediate independence to an Arab state. Only President Wilson of the United States opposed British and French plans to divide Ottoman lands between themselves. The King–Crane Commission, sent to the area in 1919 by President Wilson, reported:

> The territory concerned is too limited, the population too small, and the economic, geographical, racial, and language unity too manifest, to make the setting up of independent states within its boundaries desirable, if such division can possibly be avoided. The country is largely Arab in language, culture, traditions, and customs.

Instead of French and British mandates, the King–Crane Commission recommended that the former Arab provinces of the Ottoman Empire be established as a single independent state. But the 1920 Paris Peace Conference rejected the King–Crane proposals and confirmed the division of the area into British and French **spheres of influence.**

Check Your Understanding

1. Why was nationalism a late development in the area that became Syria and Lebanon?
2. Why did demands for independence come from Muslim Arabs as well as Christian Arabs?
3. Why did Great Britain support Hussein's revolt against the Ottomans?
4. What reasons did some groups have for not supporting the revolt?
5. *Thinking Critically:* How did the King–Crane Commission proposal differ from the way the League of Nations divided Syria?

2. Syria and Lebanon: From French Mandates to Independence

France had a long history of commercial and cultural associations in Syria. French commercial interest dated from the sixteenth century, and by the end of the eighteenth century

France's trade in the area was three times that of England. The Ottoman sultan had acknowledged France as protector of all Catholics within his realm. The French language was the second most widely known in the region. After World War I, French financial interests and the merchant community were eager to reestablish old and profitable ties with the Levant, an area that is generally synonomous with the Ottoman province of Syria.

Syria and Lebanon as Mandates

After the peace settlement, parts of the Ottoman province of Syria were divided into two countries. One was called Syria, the other Lebanon, both designated as a French mandate. In 1920 France agreed to Syrian independence on a condition that Faisal accept French guidance in finance and administration. The Syrian General Congress, however, refused to accept French control and declared their country an independent constitutional monarchy. The Congress demanded the evacuation of French and British forces, and chose Faisal as king. When he refused to submit to France, the French army crushed the nationalists and drove Faisal from the country. The new terms of the settlement were much harsher. France took complete control over foreign affairs, education, justice, and the economies of Syria and Lebanon. The Levant became in effect a region for French exploitation and colonization.

Because of the diverse religious and ethnic groups in Syria and Lebanon, it was easy for France to subdivide the two states into several more or less autonomous regions based on religious or ethnic differences. There were, for example, the Maronite Christians, a uniat **sect** affiliated with the Catholic Church that dates back to the fifth century. A militant people, the Maronites withstood persecution and attempts to convert them to Islam. The Muslim Alawis, a Shi'a sect, lived along the northern Mediterranean coast. The Druse sect lived in the mountains of southern Lebanon. There were also the Kurds of northern Syria and other scattered groups in the area. France gave limited authority to native Arab governments but retained tight control through a higher commissioner, usually a French general, who held absolute power.

According to the French their "divide and rule" policy was a provisional system designed to enable peoples who "politically speaking, were still minors to educate themselves so as to arrive one day at full self-government." As long as these provisional native governments carried out their functions according to instructions, the French did not intervene. But when a Lebanese or Syrian government failed to satisfy the French administrators, it was removed, and **martial law** and censorship imposed.

Because of their favored position, French businesses easily acquired financial control of the most lucrative enterprises. French companies received economic concessions, tariffs were designed to protect French rather than local business, and the local currency was linked to the French franc. Education in public institutions was conducted in French rather than in Arabic, and the official language was French.

Syria and Lebanon were divided into two separate governments, both under the same French high commissioner, or governor. Law and order were established in remote mountain areas, which were linked with the cities by roads built by the French. Health services and improved education helped to raise living standards. Beirut became the capital of Lebanon and a leading Mediterranean port, supplying the area with imports from Europe. Some Christians, especially many Maronites, who enjoyed a favored position, were happy under French rule and accommodated themselves to French culture.

Despite material improvements, the majority of the population, including many Christians, still longed for greater self-government and independence. Although the French had given Lebanon a constitution in 1926 and Syria a constitution in 1928, they kept a tight rein on both governments and suspended the constitutions in the early 1930's when agitation against outside control began to mount. There were many uprisings against the French, and revolts led to French bombardment of Damascus, the capital of Syria, on at least two occasions.

Independence for Syria and Lebanon

After the French government capitulated to the German invaders in 1940, the French officials in Syria and Lebanon were instructed to cooperate with the German war effort in the Middle East. To counteract the German threat, the Allies began their own invasion of the area. To win the support of the Arab people, General Charles de Gaulle, who had escaped from France before it fell to Germany and then became leader of the Free French Forces, was persuaded by the British to promise Syria and Lebanon their independence.

But the French were reluctant to give up their mandates. From 1941 until the end of the war, General de Gaulle struggled to maintain French control. In 1943 a crisis flared in Lebanon when strikes and rioting broke out to protest French suspension of the constitution and the arrest of the anti-French government.

In 1945 French forces landed in Syria and shelled cities. Again turmoil erupted. At last, under pressure from its Western allies and the United Nations, France agreed to withdraw its troops. In 1946 Syria and Lebanon became independent nations.

Causes of Political Instability in Syria

The problems besetting Syria's political life are the same as those troubling other Arab states. In part they reflect lack of unity among the diverse groups that make up the region. Some of the issues dividing Syria are its role within the Arab community, its relationship with other Arab states, fear of Western imperialism, hatred of Israel, and the struggle among competing **ideologies** such as capitalism, socialism, and Muslim fundamentalism.

A variety of political factions exist in Syria, and their fortunes often rise or fall with events outside the country. For example, major unrest followed the Arab defeat in the 1948 war with Israel. An army coup toppled the nationalist government that had been in power during the struggle with France. The series of military regimes that followed, however, was unable to bring stability to the nation. In the 1950's pro-Nasser and anti-Western groups flourished in Syria as Nasser successfully challenged the West. Nasser's successes in the international arena and at home, accompanied by Egyptian **propaganda,** gave him great prestige among many Syrians, long aware of Arab nationalism.

Two of the most active groups bidding for followers were the Communist Party and the Ba'ath (buh-AHTH) Party, a group with followers in several Arab countries that advocated Arab unity and socialism. The Communist Party, although legally banned, made a strong appeal because of the poverty of much of the population and because of the support the Soviet Union offered Arabs against Israel and the West. Communist strength came primarily from urban workers, a politically restless element in the cities.

Participation in the UAR

As the overtures to the Soviets increased, many Syrian leaders became concerned that the government might become Communist. To safeguard themselves against a Communist takeover, the Syrians turned to Egypt, urging President Nasser to join them in a unified state. The result was the formation of the United Arab Republic (UAR).

The union of Egypt and Syria lasted three years. Syria found itself dwarfed by Egypt, which is several times its size in area and population. After only a few months, Syrians complained that the union was more nearly an Egyptian occupation. Officers from Cairo came to Damascus to fill important posts. At the same time the Syrians were given only token posts of authority in the central UAR government in Cairo. Principal policy decisions were made by President Nasser without consulting his Syrian colleagues. Syrian merchants and the middle class in general protested when Nasser tried to impose a number of socialist measures on the Syrian economy. The experiment in unity collapsed when Syria broke away in 1961 to reestablish its own independent government and its identity as the Syrian Arab Republic.

Ba'athists in Power

The Ba'athists, aided by army officers, staged a successful coup in 1963. Later that year the petroleum and other major industries were nationalized. Soon the Ba'athists split into rival factions, and in 1966 the leftist wing overthrew the moderates. The new regime brought an increase in terrorist raids against Israel, propaganda attacks against King Hussein of Jordan, and closer ties with the Soviet Union.

Many members of the leftist wing of the Ba'ath Party were radical young army officers from the Alawite region of Syria who wanted major economic and social reforms. These officers were intensely nationalistic. The aggressive policy toward Israel that they advocated in the 1967 war led to the loss of the Golan Heights. Reaction to the defeat was an even more militant anti-Israel stance that led to Syria becoming the major antagonist of the Jewish state.

The Rise of Assad

In 1970 General Hafiz al-Assad, an Alawite from a peasant family who rose from the ranks to top command of the air force and who was a leader in the Ba'ath Party, seized power. His policies blended those of radical and of moderate Ba'athists. In 1973 Syria adopted a new constitution, giving President Assad almost unlimited power and making the Ba'ath Party dominant. By 1988 Assad had been in power longer than any other Syrian leader since the nation had won its independence.

Assad introduced a number of liberal measures to encourage foreign investment in Syria, hoping to revive an economy depleted by huge military expenditures. Despite such signs of eco-

Hafiz al–Assad of Syria reviews a parade of troops and armaments in December 1980. Behind him, with his hand raised, stands Yasir Arafat, the leader of the PLO.

nomic growth as the expansion of irrigated agricultural areas and the development of cement, textile, and new consumer goods industries, increases in the population prevented a rise in living standards. Between 1960 and 1988 the population increased from 4.5 to nearly 12 million. The population of Damascus tripled, holding 20 percent of Syria's population. Assad's measures to improve the economy, however, created a new class of wealthy **entrepreneurs** who aroused the hostility of young radicals.

Other Internal Tensions

The Syrian government has been the target of Sunni Muslim fundamentalist attacks because Assad is a member of the Alawite minority, which is looked down on by the Sunni majority. The Sunni Muslim Brotherhood has staged frequent terrorist attacks on Syrian government installations. President Assad has responded with often brutal retaliation on areas where the Muslim Brotherhood is strong.

Foreign Policy Under Assad

Assad continued Syria's aggressive policies toward Israel, and in 1973 Syria joined Egypt in its attack on Israel, hoping to regain the Golan Heights. Although small gains came through the Disengagement Agreements negotiated in 1974 with Israel

248

through the diplomacy of Secretary of State Henry Kissinger, most of the Golan Heights remained in Israeli hands. (See page 216.) Return of the territory continues to be a major goal of Syria and a major cause of tension between Syria and Israel.

Under Assad, Syria has continued to pursue an aggressive policy in Lebanon, refusing to acknowledge its separation from Syria and its existence as an independent nation. When the Lebanese Civil War began in 1975, Syria with Arab League approval sent in 30,000 troops as a peacekeeping force. These troops became involved in fighting with Israel during the 1982 invasion and remained in Lebanon. (See page 217.)

Independent Lebanon

Lebanon's large Christian population makes it different from most other Arab countries. Until the late 1960's Muslim groups were in the minority and the various Christian sects made up more than half the population. Government policy dictated a delicate balance between the country's many religious groups, a policy reflected in its tradition of legislative representation and in its unwritten constitution. According to this tradition the president was a Maronite Christian, the prime minister a Sunni Muslim, and the speaker of the parliament a Shi'a Muslim. In parliament the ratio of Christian to Muslim representatives traditionally has been six to five.

Civil War in Lebanon

The first serious threat to Lebanon's stability came in 1958 when a civil war broke out. Although the opposing sides were not divided strictly by religion, most of those who supported the government and wanted an independent, predominantly Christian Lebanon were Maronites. Opposed to the government was a coalition that included some Christians. This coalition favored Lebanon's integration with the Arab world and closer ties with the United Arab Republic. The civil war was brought to a halt after the United States was asked to intervene militarily. A reconciliation government that included representatives of most factions was organized.

But the 1958 cease-fire was only temporary. Since then tensions between the Maronite and Muslim factions in Lebanon have increased. A major cause of the tension has been a change in the population of the various religious-ethnic groups. When Lebanon became independent, the Maronite Christians were the largest faction and the diverse Christian groups constituted more than half the population. By the late 1960's the various

Muslim groups had become a slight majority in the population. The most rapidly growing sect was the Shi'a, which by 1988 constituted nearly 40 percent of the population. The Maronite Christians were now only the third largest sect in the country, and the diverse Christians as a group were a minority.

As a consequence of the shift in population, Muslim Lebanese were no longer willing to have fewer representatives in parliament than the Christians. Neither were they willing to permit Maronite Christians to control the presidency and along with it most of the country's important political posts. On the other hand Maronites, who controlled much of the country's economy and dominated its social and cultural life, were determined to prevent any changes that would undermine their control.

Renewed Fighting

Adding to the tensions between Maronites and Muslims in Lebanon was the presence of hundreds of thousands of Palestinian refugees who had fled from Israel in 1948 and in 1967. Most Muslim Lebanese sympathized with the Palestinians and wanted to help their Lebanon-based guerrilla organizations that were attacking Israel. Maronites opposed these efforts and sought to form an alliance with Israel against the Palestinians.

In 1975 fighting broke out between Palestinians and Maronites. Dozens of armed groups called militias were formed by the various religious and political factions. As the government lost control over the situation, the various militias sought to gain control of separate sectors of the country. Muslim militias fought other Muslim militias, while the Christian militias also fought among themselves.

In an attempt to restore order, the Arab League intervened and authorized the Syrian army to enter Lebanon as a peacekeeping force. Although the Syrians did from time to time restore order, fighting between the many different militias was difficult to control. Conflict erupted again and again. The Palestinians staged frequent attacks into Israel. The result was frequent counterattacks by Israel into Lebanon. Finally in an all-out effort to wipe out these bases, Israel invaded Lebanon in 1982. (See page 217.)

Since 1982 Lebanon has been in a continual state of turmoil. Even an international peacekeeping force sent in 1982 has been unable to halt the continued fighting among the various militias and the attacks by Israel. Parliament has ceased to function. In 1988 it was unable to agree on a new president. Instead two governments have been formed. A Muslim govern-

President Amin Gamayel in 1983 pays a state visit to Prime Minister Margaret Thatcher of Great Britain in her residence at No. 10 Downing Street in London. British Foreign Secretary Sir Geoffrey Howe stands at Gamayel's left.

ment took power in areas controlled by Muslim militias. In the areas controlled by Maronite and other Christian militias, a Christian government was formed. For all practical purposes, Lebanon has been divided into several small enclaves, each controlled by a different militia.

Check Your Understanding

1. What was the purpose of the French divide-and-rule policy?
2. Why was Syria's union with Egypt to form the United Arab Republic a disastrous move for Syria?
3. What domestic and foreign policies has Syria followed since the rise of Assad to power?
4. Why has civil war been a constant problem for Lebanon?
5. *Thinking Critically:* Review the excerpt from the King–Crane Commission cited on page 243. If the commissioners could have seen into the future, do you think they might have altered their final recommendation? Why or why not?

3. Iraq and Jordan: From British Mandates to Independence

After World War I, Iraq and Trans–Jordan (the southeastern portion of Ottoman Syria east of the Jordan River) became British mandates. Britain's mandate policy in Trans–Jordan and Iraq was similar to, but more subtle than, that of France in Syria and Lebanon. The British made no attempt to impose their customs or educational system on the Arabs and permitted more local autonomy.

Iraq's Independence

Iraq became independent in 1932 and was admitted to the League of Nations that year when Britain ended its mandate. But the British ambassador in Baghdad continued to exercise much influence. British troops continued to occupy strategic positions, British officials served as "advisers" in all important government posts, and major policy decisions were made in London rather than in Baghdad. One reason for the continuation of British control in Iraq was the country's rich petroleum reserves. Oil was known to exist in northern Iraq when the region was still part of the Ottoman Empire. This resource, however, was not exploited to any large extent until after World War I. Although France, Turkey, and the United States were also interested in Iraq's oil, Great Britain obtained control through deals with the other interested powers.

The British placed their World War I ally, the Amir Faisal, on the throne of Iraq after he was driven from Syria. Although Faisal came from the southern part of the Arabian Peninsula, his friendly personality and his ability to win the support of tribal chieftains, leaders in the towns, and nationalist groups, made him popular in Iraq.

Divisions and Revolt in Iraq

Iraq was divided because of diverse religious, linguistic, and ethnic groups. In the northern part of the country, the Kurds, who were Sunni Muslims, did not consider themselves to be Arabs and sought autonomy. They refused to recognize Baghdad's authority, and uprisings were frequent. Although most Iraqis were Arab, they were divided between Sunnis and Shi'as, with the latter in the majority. Since the Sunnis held most important government and military posts, the Shi'as maintained that they were the victims of discrimination.

RULING FAMILY. Left, the Amir Faisal, later king of Iraq, at the Paris Peace Conference (1919), and, right, his brother Abdullah, first king of modern Jordan.

During the 1950's opposition to the autocratic rule of the men surrounding the king gained momentum. Particularly disliked was Nuri Pasha es-Said (NOO-ree PAH-shah es-sa-EED) who became prime minister for the last time in 1954. Nuri immediately suppressed all opposition parties and newspapers and launched an attack against Communists. At the same time, many of his policies seemed designed to unite his enemies against him. He was pro-Western, pro-Turkish, and owed his position to the old, conservative, wealthy families.

Opposition turned into rebellion in 1958. Military officers staged a political coup, killing the young King Faisal II (grandson of the first Faisal) and several of his ministers. Iraq became a military republic under the hand of General Kassim.

Troubles Since 1958

In the years since the assassination of King Faisal II in 1958, Iraq has undergone several coups and countercoups. Ba'ath Socialists overthrew Kassim's dictatorship in 1963 only to find themselves purged during the same year by General Arif. Arif and his brother, who succeeded him on his death in 1966, moved Iraq into Cairo's orbit and solicited aid from the Soviet Union. In 1968 the Ba'athists once again regained power by ousting Arif, replacing him with General Ahmed Hassen al-Bakr. This shift in power meant still another change in Iraq's relationship with the rest of the Arab world.

Another problem that troubled Iraq was the continuing demand for autonomy among the Kurds in the north, which led to years of civil war. (See page 22.) After the Ba'athists took over the government in 1968, they renewed negotiations with the Kurds intending to develop a plan for autonomy in Iraq's northern Kurdish provinces. But negotiations soon collapsed and fighting was renewed between government and Kurdish guerrilla forces. The conflict between the government and the Kurdish nationalist movement has continued.

The Iran–Iraq War

In 1979 Saddam Hussein replaced al-Bakr. Hussein immediately initiated a series of purges, removing from government all potential competitors for leadership, including dozens of Hussein's former comrades.

While ruthlessly weeding out potential competitors for power, Hussein introduced a number of economic reforms that included redistributing land to peasants, opening new industries, and greatly expanding and modernizing Iraq's capital of Baghdad. He also aspired to become a leader of the Arab world and to make Iraq the dominant power in the Persian Gulf, which many Arabs called the Arab Gulf.

Following the fall of the Shah of Iran in 1979, President Hussein attacked Iran, believing that it had been greatly weakened by the Islamic Revolution. Iraq hoped to gain control of the Shatt-al-Arab, the strategic waterway that was the southern boundary between Iraq and Iran. The resulting Gulf War soon became an ideological conflict between the Arab nationalist Ba'ath Party and the Persian Islamic fundamentalists.

By the late 1980's the war had become a serious drain on Iraq's economic resources and armed forces. Estimates were that more than 100,000 Iraqi soldiers had been killed and some 500,000 wounded. War costs were greater than $1 billion a month, forcing cancellation of the country's development projects. Iraq's large oil resources should have been able to pay for the war, but the war destroyed many oil installations.

Even economic aid from other Arab countries, including Saudi Arabia and Kuwait, and military assistance from Egypt and Jordan did not prevent the danger of economic collapse. But the war was just as costly to Iran. In 1988 Iraq entered into negotiations with Iran under the auspices of the United Nations to terminate the conflict. Relations between the two countries have become so embittered over other issues, however, that future negotiations are likely to continue for years.

Trans–Jordan Under British Mandate

Abdullah, one of the Hashemite sons who had fought for the British, arrived in Trans–Jordan with an armed band after the expulsion of his brother from Syria. The local tribes agreed to accept him, and the British, afraid of rebellion, recognized him as Amir in 1920. Britain, however, still supplied the government with advisers and supplied the army and the Arab Legion with commanding officers. In 1923 Trans–Jordan was promised self-government. This promise was recognized by treaty in 1928, but Britain retained control over Trans–Jordan's finances and foreign affairs.

Abdullah's acceptance of a separate mandate from Palestine created many enemies in the Arab world. Arab nationalists in Syria, Palestine, and Trans–Jordan itself turned their attack against the Amir when he recognized the 1920 settlement that divided control in the region between Great Britain and France. This hostility and sense of betrayal fostered a division within the Arab world. Trans–Jordan (later called Jordan) remained close to the West and tended to ally itself with Iraq, also a British mandate that was ruled by a member of the Hashemite family. Egypt, Syria, and Saudi Arabia (whose ruler Ibn Sa'ud had driven Abdullah's father from Mecca in an effort to expand his kingdom) often intrigued against their Arab neighbor.

Independence for Jordan

After World War II Trans–Jordan received full independence as a constitutional monarchy in 1946 and took the name Hashemite Kingdom of Jordan in 1949. The Amir Abdullah became Jordan's first king. When war broke out in 1948 between Israel and the Arab states, Abdullah's well-trained armed forces occupied the eastern half of Jerusalem and the west bank of the Jordan River. But once other Arab troops were driven back by the Israelis, this area lay exposed to an Israeli thrust. King Abdullah attempted to create unity by joining Trans–Jordan and the west-bank areas of Palestine in a single monarchy. United with Trans–Jordan, the territory could be protected under Britain's 1949 treaty with the Hashemite Kingdom.

Egypt and Syria vigorously protested annexation of the west-bank areas of Palestine. Although Jordan participated—even to its own economic disadvantage—in the Arab boycott imposed against Israel, the Arab states, especially Syria, directed propaganda attacks against Abdullah, terming him an agent of British imperialism.

Problems Stemming from Annexation

The territory that Trans–Jordan annexed covered about 2,000 square miles. After annexation this area was called West Jordan while the region formerly known as Trans–Jordan was called East Jordan. More densely populated than East Jordan, this region contributed about two thirds of the nearly two million people of the new state. Of these over half a million were Palestinian Arab refugees who had fled from Israel during 1947 and 1948. Although these people received the necessities of life from the United Nations, it was difficult to find employment for them. Thousands were crowded into dreary refugee camps on the West Bank and left to live out their days in hopelessness.

Another problem was the integration of East and West Jordan into one nation. King Abdullah gave the West Bank Palestinians full rights as citizens, and, as a majority, they strongly influenced Trans–Jordan's political life. Their hatred of the British and desire for revenge against Israel found champions who organized strident political opposition to the king. Some did not stop at verbal criticism. On July 20, 1951, Abdullah was shot as he entered the al-Aksa mosque in Jerusalem. His assassins were Palestinians seeking vengeance for the king's ties with Britain and his attempted peace negotiations with Israel.

Jordan's Role in the Conflict

King Abdullah was succeeded by his son Talal. When the strain of ruling led to Talal's mental collapse, Hussein, Talal's 17-year-old son, was proclaimed king. Until Hussein reached his majority, however, the country was ruled by its prime minister with a small group of associates. Protests against Jordan's dependence on the West continued to mount. Pro-Egyptian and pro-Syrian groups among the refugee population won wide support while a new movement against Israel gained momentum. Torn between popular feeling and economic dependence on the West, Hussein's government faced a series of crises that tested Jordan's ability to survive.

The Arab–Israeli war of 1967 left King Hussein's government near collapse. In the 1967 war Israel captured Jordan's part of Jerusalem and the West Bank. Although this constituted only about a tenth of Jordan's territory, it contained about half the country's population, supplied nearly half its agricultural produce, was the nation's chief source of scarce foreign currency, and contained other valuable economic and political assets. Jordan's problems were compounded by the arrival of over a quarter of a million new refugees from Israeli-occupied regions. Only assistance from oil-producing Arab states on the Persian Gulf and from other foreign sources, including the United States, enabled Jordan to keep functioning as an independent country.

Since the 1967 Arab–Israeli war the Palestinian population in Jordan has increased at a rapid rate, making Palestinians the majority in the country. Palestinians also control much of Jordan's economy. King Hussein has attempted to integrate the Palestinians into Jordanian life, giving them high posts in government and drafting them into the army. The king's closest advisers, however, are still native-born east bankers. As a result much suspicion still exists between Palestinians and native-born east bankers. Palestinians in Jordan are often critical of King Hussein, with some accusing him of being too moderate in his "no-peace, no-war" relationship with Israel.

In 1970 an uprising of Palestinians against the government led by radical factions of the Palestine Liberation Organization (PLO) attempted to seize control of large sections of Amman, the capital of Jordan, and other parts of the country. The Jordanian army ruthlessly suppressed the uprising and drove the PLO militias out of the country. Ever since, relations between King Hussein and PLO leaders have been strained. Nonetheless Hussein states that he supports the efforts of Yasir Arafat (AHR-uh-faht), the PLO leader, to obtain an independent Palestinian state in the West Bank and Gaza Strip.

In 1988 Hussein announced that he was giving up all claims to the Israeli-held West Bank and that further responsibility for the territory should fall to the Palestine Liberation Organization. In effect, Hussein's announcement meant that Jordan would no longer continue to contribute financially to the assistance of Palestinians in the West Bank.

Jordan's Future

Jordan remains a developing nation, dependent mostly on agriculture and foreign aid. Industry has not grown, and the country faces serious economic problems because of its large refugee population, who are mostly dependent on economic assistance from the United Nations and foreign countries. To a large extent, its future is tied to the establishment of an independent Palestinian state in the West Bank. If such a state is established, it is expected that it will absorb many of the refugees who remain a burden on Jordan's economy.

(Continued on page 260.)

REFUGEE LIFE. Thousands of refugees (left) crossed the King Hussein Bridge (formerly the Allenby Bridge) as they fled Israel during the June 1967 war. A child (right) stands with her mother at a 1967 tent-camp near Amman, Jordan. Guerrilla-warfare training camps of the PLO have also attracted refugees.

Arab Organizations

Before World War I Arab nationalists dreamed of a vast Arab state stretching east from Morocco in North Africa, north into Syria and the lands of the Fertile Crescent, and southeast through the Arabian Peninsula. But the partition of Arab lands into British and French mandates destroyed that dream. Some 30 years later, Arab leaders then took the next best step—to form an organization that would speak with one voice for Arab interests everywhere. The organization was the League of Arab States, more popularly called the Arab League, which was founded in 1945 by seven charter members—Egypt, Saudi Arabia, Syria, Iraq, Lebanon, Jordan, and Yemen. By 1980 membership in the League had increased to 22, a number that includes Egypt, which was expelled for signing a peace treaty with Israel in 1979, but was readmitted to full membership in 1989. It also includes Mauritania, Djibouti, and Somalia.

The Arab League operates through a permanent secretariat. Its major decision-making body is its Council, on which each member state has one vote. While officially not a state, the Palestine Liberation Organization (PLO), formed in 1964 as a coordinating council for Palestinian organizations, has full status with other member states.

Until 1989 the Arab League refused to recognize Israel's right to exist. In November 1988 at the annual meeting of the PLO's 451-member National Council, Yasir Arafat—leader of the dominant Al Fatah group—declared the Israeli-occupied West Bank and Gaza Strip to be an independent state. Before a specially called meeting of the United Nations General Assembly, Arafat acknowledged Israel's right to exist and renounced terrorism in all its forms.

Check Your Understanding

1. How did Britain's mandate policy on Iraq and Trans–Jordan differ from the French policy in Syria and Lebanon?
2. What divisions existed in Iraq that led to revolt?
3. **a.** What issues have occupied Iraq's leaders since 1979? **b.** How have they attempted to deal with these issues?
4. How did ties the West affect Trans–Jordan: **a.** in its mandate period? **b.** after independence?
5. How has King Hussein attempted to solve the Palestinian problem?
6. *Thinking Critically:* Why has Jordan been unpopular with other Arab nations?

4. States of the Arabian Peninsula

Since World War II the Arabian Peninsula has emerged from one of the least known and remote regions in the world to become one of the most important international centers of world finance and business. This transformation is largely due to the expansion of its oil industry, which had begun on a small scale before World War II. Since the 1960's production has expanded on a massive scale in several countries of the region. The development and expansion of the oil industry has led to an influx of workers from all over the world—American engineers and business people, Korean and Philippine laborers, East Indian and Pakistani clerks and accountants, Egyptian and Palestinian teachers, to name a few. Former remote desert outposts and gulf ports have become large modern cities.

The Kingdom of Saudi Arabia

Originally the Saud family controlled a small desert principality of nomadic tribes in the central part of the Arabian Peninsula. Beginning in 1902, the family extended its control through warfare with other nomadic desert tribes until more than four fifths of the peninsula was theirs. The creator and namesake of Saudi Arabia was Ibn Saud of the austere Wahhabi (wah-HAH-bee) sect of Muslims.

Ibn Saud ruled the principality according to bedouin custom and tradition—a sort of tribal democracy shaped by the king's autocratic decisions. The Koran provided the guiding principles for most important decisions. Bedouins had nearly free access to the king to present their claims or request justice in person. Much of Ibn Saud's success came from his ability to win and keep the loyalty of local sheikhs.

Oil's Impact

During the 1930's American oil companies discovered great oil fields in Saudi Arabia. These were rapidly developed after World War II. At first great extravagance and corruption prevailed as each year hundreds of millions of dollars poured into the country. Millions were spent on lavish royal palaces, luxurious automobiles, gadgets of all kinds, and tribute to local sheikhs. But as the oil companies began to develop roads, build refineries and processing plants, and provide other necessary services, thousands of former nomads turned to settled employment and became skilled or semi-skilled workers.

By the 1950's, after the death of Ibn Saud, some members of the royal family realized that their country must be reorganized and modernized. Despite opposition from royal princes reluctant to surrender any of their income and privileges, revolutionary changes were brought about. Corrupt and inept, Ibn Saud's son and successor, also named Saud, was forced to transfer his executive powers to his brother Faisal. A power struggle erupted between the two brothers that continued until 1964 when Saud was deposed and Faisal became the new king.

Changes Under Faisal

Faisal imposed austerity on the country. Within a short time he had established modern government departments and services. After a 10–year absence, a visitor to Saudi Arabia reported many changes.

> Once-sleepy Jidda [on the Red Sea] is beset with traffic. The cars move bumper to bumper down the broad highway that has been driven ruthlessly through the old city, smashing the old-fashioned-wooden framed houses whose latticed windows were meant to shield the women of the house from view.
>
> New office buildings and apartment houses, new hotels dominate the skyline. In the suburbs a steel plant went into production four months ago. It makes concrete reinforcement bars with imported materials now, and the hope is that it will process local scrap iron within eight years.

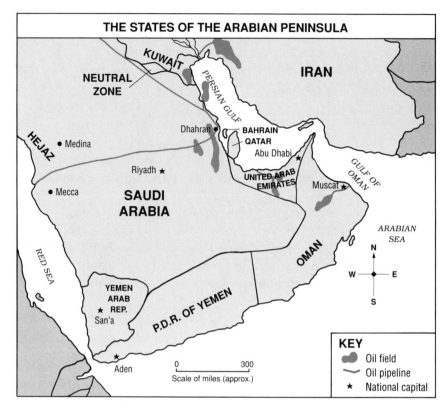

THE STATES OF THE ARABIAN PENINSULA

KUWAIT

NEUTRAL ZONE

IRAN

PERSIAN GULF

HEJAZ

• Medina

Dhahran •

BAHRAIN
QATAR
Abu Dhabi ★

Riyadh ★

UNITED ARAB EMIRATES

Muscat ★

GULF OF OMAN

• Mecca

SAUDI ARABIA

ARABIAN SEA

N
W ◆ E
S

RED SEA

OMAN

YEMEN ARAB ★ REP.
San'a

P.D.R. OF YEMEN

★ Aden

0   300
Scale of miles (approx.)

KEY
🌫️ Oil field
〜 Oil pipeline
★ National capital

PLACE: THE STATES OF THE ARABIAN PENINSULA. Most of the small states bordering the Arabian Sea and Persian Gulf have been freed from British control. Their location on major sea routes in an oil-rich region has tempted neighboring powers to intervene in their political affairs.

> Opposite the steel plant is a new oil refinery that will go into production this summer. A seawater desalinization plant supervised by Mohammed al-Faisal, second son of the King, is under construction. [© 1968 by the New York Times Company. Reprinted by permission.]

Public education was improved and expanded and for the first time made available to females. Travel time across the desert from the coast to Riyadh (ree-YAHD), the capital, was cut from three or four days to as little as six hours after the construction of modern highways.

Under King Faisal Saudi Arabia began to gain international importance as a leader of the Islamic world. He convened a number of international Islamic conferences. He supported conservative forces in the Yemen civil war against the republicans supported by Nasser. Taking advantage of his country's tremendous oil income, he helped the Arab states finance the 1967 and 1973 wars against Israel and made Saudi Arabia into one of the Arab world's most influential powers.

Saudi Arabian Foreign Policy

King Faisal was assassinated by one of his nephews in 1975 and was succeeded by his brother Prince Khalid, who died of a heart attack in 1982. Since then the country has been ruled by Khalid's half brother Fahd. Under Fahd Saudi Arabia has continued to play an important role in Middle East politics. In 1981 Fahd's peace plan became the basis for an Arab League proposal to end the Arab–Israeli conflict. Saudi Arabia has also been an intermediary on several occasions in the Lebanese civil war, as well as in other inter-Arab conflicts. In response to the tensions created by Iran in the Persian Gulf, Saudi Arabia, Kuwait, Oman, Bahrain, Qatar, and the United Arab Emirates formed the Gulf Cooperation Council as an organization for mutual protection and as a forum for discussion of regional development, economic cooperation, and other problems.

During the Gulf War between Iraq and Iran, Saudi Arabia sided with Iraq, extending several billion dollars in financial support. Its siding with Iraq greatly antagonized Iran, causing relations to deteriorate and leading Iran's leaders to label Saudi Arabia as a lackey of the United States. In 1987 pilgrims from Iran at the annual Haj in Mecca rioted. Several hundred Iranian pilgrims were killed.

The Yemen Arab Republic

Until after World War II the territory now known as the Yemen (YEH-mun) Arab Republic was one of the most isolated countries in the world. Visitors were allowed to enter only with the personal permission of the Imam, who was the country's temporal and spiritual leader. The Turks claimed the territory as early as 1536, but they were expelled by local warriors in the following century. The country remained under religious leaders until Turkey reestablished its authority in 1849. After World War I Yemen once again became an autonomous state.

Undercurrents of discontent led to growing demands for reform. Finally in 1962 the army toppled the Imam from power and established a republic. The Imam, however, gathered loyal warriors around him and fought a civil war to regain his power. In the struggle Egypt provided the republicans with troops and weapons, and Saudi Arabia gave assistance to the royalists supporting the Imam. Both the United States and the United Nations attempted unsuccessfully to mediate the dispute.

Since 1968 the various forces in Yemen have come to terms with their differences, forming compromise governments that included former representatives of both royalists and republicans. The country has remained a republic, adopting the name Yemen Arab Republic to demonstrate its ties with the Arab world.

With economic assistance from Saudi Arabia, Yemen has initiated a program of modernization in agriculture and in government organization. Yemen is one of the world's poorest countries with sparse resources, although oil was recently discovered. The amount of oil in the discovery, while not yet verified, is believed to be great. Yemen's poverty and its lack of development is underscored by the departure of about 25 percent of its population to work abroad.

One of its most serious political problems is the constant tension with South Yemen. Relations between the two countries fluctuate between negotiations for unification and open warfare. Boundary problems add to the tension. Yemen often seems caught between the conservative goals of Saudi Arabia to its north and the leftist goals of South Yemen.

People's Democratic Republic of Yemen (South Yemen)

Along the southern coast of Arabia, east of the port of Aden, were some 30 sultanates, emirates, sheikhdoms, and other tribal units, varying in size from a few hundred people and a dozen square miles to large stretches of desert populated by thousands of people. Aden and these states had been a British sphere of influence ever since the British East India Company seized the area in 1839. Aden became a British colony and an important port distributing goods to the interior area of the Arabian Peninsula and to the lands along the African coast. After the Suez Canal opened, Aden's importance in East–West trade grew rapidly. After World War II Britain established an important naval and air base in Aden.

When Arab nationalism swept the Arabian Peninsula during the late 1950's and early 1960's, the British were forced to reorganize Aden and the little protectorates into the Federation of South Arabia. The federation was administered by traditional tribal rulers guided by British colonial administrators. When the federation failed to satisfy the demand for complete independence, revolutionaries took up arms against the British. Since Great Britain was experiencing economic difficulties, the government reluctantly decided to cut back military commitments east of Suez. Thus the Federation of South Arabia was given complete independence. The new country, created in 1967, was named the People's Republic of South Yemen. It became closely allied with such other revolutionary Arab republics as Egypt, Syria, and Iraq.

In 1968 leftist forces seized control in several provinces, leading to control of the country by Marxist groups in 1969. The Marxists changed the name of the country in 1970 to the People's Democratic Republic of Yemen. The Yemen Socialist Party was the only political party allowed. It was organized and modeled on the Communist Party of the Soviet Union. Most of South Yemen's economic life was placed under state management, including agriculture, which was organized into cooperatives and state farms.

In 1986 bloody fighting erupted among differing factions of the Yemen Socialist Party, resulting in the flight of the president and his replacement with a leader of an even more militant Marxist faction. The constant internal turmoil and continuing friction with the Yemen Arab Republic to the north have been obstacles to progress in this very poor country.

Kuwait

Kuwait (koo-WAYT), a sheikhdom under British protection from 1899 to 1961 when Britain granted it complete independence, consists of 6,000 miles of barren desert. Yet it has one of the highest per capita incomes in the world because of its rich oil fields. First discovered in the 1930's, they were not developed until after World War II.

Most of Kuwait's people live in an old fortress town, also called Kuwait. During the last few decades the city has been modernized with gleaming chrome and glass air-conditioned buildings lining wide boulevards. Citizens of Kuwait enjoy television and the educational opportunities and social services of a modern Western state. So large is Kuwait's oil income that a major part of it is being invested abroad. The Kuwait Development Fund, established in the 1960's, gives economic assistance to less affluent Arab states. Funds from Kuwait, for example, helped to bolster the economies of both Egypt and Jordan after the Six–Day War with Israel in 1967. Kuwait is also one of the founding members of the Gulf Cooperation Council. (See page 263.)

Kuwait's population has expanded along with its economy, due mainly to an influx of foreign workers. Between 1968 and 1988 the population grew from about 206,000 to more than two million, a tenfold increase. Many outsiders have grown rich in

Kuwait, but they are not allowed to become citizens or to benefit from the free education, health services, and the like that the government provides its citizens. Today only 40 percent of the population are citizens. More than 400,000 are Palestinians.

In 1981 the government permitted elections for a Kuwaiti Assembly. The only individuals allowed to vote were men over 21, who could trace their Kuwaiti roots to 1920, a group that constituted only 3.5 percent of the population. In 1986, however, Kuwait's ruler, the Emir Jabir al-Sabah, suspended parliament because of growing political dissent between its members and the royal family. In foreign policy Kuwait has been an active supporter of inter-Arab causes, backing Iraq in the Gulf War, supporting Palestinian groups, and making large loans and grants to Egypt, Jordan, and other Arab countries.

Persian Gulf States

Other small countries along the Persian Gulf coast are Bahrain, (bah-RAYN) Qatar (kuh-TAR), Oman (oh-MAHN), and the United Arab Emirates, formerly called the Trucial States. Once British protectorates, these small states succumbed to the call of Arab nationalism and broke most ties with the British. The United

Kuwaitis, foreign workers, and tourists have many modern stores in which to spend their money. This jewelry store, which welcomes people who want to charge their purchases, specializes in gold ornaments of all shapes and sizes. What differences exist between Kuwaiti citizens and outsiders?

Arab Emirates was formed in 1971 from seven small sheikh-doms—Abu Dhabi, Dubai, Sharjah, Fujaira, Ras al-Khaimah, Umm al-Qaiwain, and Ajman. Abu Dhabi is by far the richest and most important of the sheikhdoms in the **federation**. Most of the federation's oil is located in Abu Dhabi, which also has about one third of the federation's population. Profits from oil are so large that per capita income is one of the highest in the world—about $19,000.

Bahrain, Qatar, and the Sultanate of Oman have oil resources as well. They have imported foreign labor, but outsiders are fewer in number than in Kuwait or Saudi Arabia. All three nations are members of the Gulf Cooperation Council and are greatly concerned about relations with Iran.

Check Your Understanding

1. What changes have transformed the region of the Arabian Peninsula from a remote and isolated area into a center of financial importance?
2. Why did civil war break out in Yemen?
3. How has the civil war exemplified inter-Arab differences?
4. Which country has a Marxist government?
5. *Thinking Critically:* What form of government is prevalent in most of these states? How does form of government reflect long-standing traditions in the peninsula?

5. The Islamic Republic of Iran

Iran is an Islamic country, but not an Arab country. About two thirds of the Iranian people speak some Persian dialect and one fifth a Turkish dialect called Azari. The country, which stands on the high Iranian Plateau, contains diverse ethnic, linguistic, and tribal groups. It covers an area larger than 600,000 square miles.

The Effects of Colonialism

During the nineteenth century Iran suffered from the territorial ambitions of the great colonial powers. From the time of Empress Catherine the Great (1762–1796) of Russia until the mid-nineteenth century, Persia and Russia were involved in diplomatic maneuvers and wars. Persia bargained with Napoleon

PUNCH, OR THE LONDON CHARIVARI.—November 30, 1878.

"SAVE ME FROM MY FRIENDS!"

"IF AT THIS MOMENT IT HAS BEEN DECIDED TO INVADE THE AMEER'S TERRITORY, WE ARE ACTING IN PURSUANCE OF A POLICY WHICH IN ITS INTENTION HAS BEEN UNIFORMLY *FRIENDLY* TO AFGHANISTAN."—*Times, Nov. 21.*

In this cartoon dealing with an 1878 confrontation between the two powers, Afghanistan is threatened by a greedy Russian bear and a grimly deter- mined British lion.

for protection against Russia, but after Napoleon abandoned his plans for the Middle East, Persia lost its chief defender. In the following decades Russia seized several Persian provinces. Many of these annexed provinces became part of the Union of Soviet Socialist Republics (USSR) after 1917. Persia also lost its rights to use the Caspian Sea.

To compensate for their losses to the Russians, the Persians claimed Afghan territory and attempted to seize parts of the country. But the British did not want Persia to take over any part of Afghanistan because Britain could not permit any nation outside its empire to control the mountain passes to India. To forestall the loss of Afghan territory, the British themselves oc- cupied parts of the country and forced Persia to surrender its claims. With Afghanistan as a base the British were able to restrict Russian penetration of Persia. London's policy was to keep both countries free, but dependent upon Britain.

Concerned with the growing strength of Germany, Britain and Russia agreed to settle their differences over Persia in 1907. Persia was divided into three spheres of influence. Russia was to have a free hand in developing its economic interests in the north. Southern Persia was to become a British sphere of influ- ence. The area between was to remain a neutral zone.

Southern Persia's value to Great Britain was underscored by the discovery of oil. The Anglo–Persian Oil Company formed in 1908, mostly with British capital, became an instrument for British influence in southern Persia. Soon after the discovery of oil, Persia became the chief supplier of fuel to the British navy. Persia thus became important to Britain as Egypt had earlier because of the Suez Canal.

During World War II Iran was occupied by British and by Russians because it provided a route for Allied supplies to Russia. After the war, the intervention of the United Nations and the United States was needed to persuade the Soviet's to evacuate the northern provinces which they had taken over in 1942.

The Pahlavi Dynasty

Reza Khan, a former army colonel seized power in 1923 and made himself **shah** in 1925, changing his name from Khan to Pahlavi (PAH-luh-vee), after an ancient Persian dynasty. Like Kemal Atatürk in Turkey, the shah was impressed with the material progress of the West. He too attempted to update his country by building factories, railways, and hospitals. Reza Shah also wanted to "modernize" the outward appearance of his subjects. Women were ordered to discard the veil and their traditional shapeless black garb. Reza Shah's efforts to achieve modernization, however, met with resistance. Conservative religious leaders claimed that these efforts threatened Islam. The tribal chiefs feared losing control over their followers. The wealthy landowners feared that their ownership of vast tracts of land was endangered.

But during World War II, Reza Shah admired the Fascists, and he was deposed by the Allies, who occupied his country. His son and successor, Mohammed Reza Pahlavi, nearly lost his throne when nationalists threatened to take over the government. However, with the backing of the United States, the Iranian army managed to keep the shah in power.

During the 1960's the shah initiated a number of economic and social reforms aimed at improving living conditions among the impoverished peasants. These efforts were taken despite opposition from groups that had opposed his father, and from nationalists who believed that their ruler was too closely identified with "Western imperialism."

Increasing Opposition to the Shah

As opposition to the shah increased, his regime became more repressive. By the early 1970's the shah dominated most impor-

The Shah of Iran presents a bundle of land titles to the chieftain of one of the semi-nomadic tribes that make up a sixth of the country's population.

tant sectors of society—the army, the landed aristocracy, the wealthy merchants, and the government bureaucracy. The shah's secret police, the State Organization for Intelligence and Security known as SAVAK from the initials of its name in Farsi, arrested thousands of dissidents, many of whom were tortured in the shah's prisons. In 1979 Amnesty International, a private organization devoted to the fostering of human rights and the elimination of political repression, reported that Iran had the highest rate of death penalties in the world, no valid system of civil courts, and its "history of torture . . . is beyond belief."

Despite reform programs in agriculture, the expansion of industry, and the growth of the educational system, Iran still had many problems. Chief among them was that only a small percentage of the population seemed to benefit from the reform programs, which the shah called the "White Revolution." As one of the largest producers of oil in the Middle East, Iran used its oil revenues to develop its resources. But most projects were grandiose schemes that did little to raise the living conditions of the average peasant. The royal family controlled much of the country's wealth. It had the largest landholdings and owned many shares in the government's newly established industries, depositing Iran's profits in investments in Europe and the

United States where the income from these investments was at the shah's private disposal.

The shah also aspired to make Iran the dominant power in the Middle East. He invested billions of dollars in the most modern sophisticated weaponry, most of it acquired from the United States. His army was thought to be the most powerful in the Gulf region. As the backbone of the shah's regime, it was considered capable of protecting the shah's government against any uprising.

But by the late 1970's it was becoming increasingly evident that neither the reforms of the White Revolution nor the repression of SAVAK could stem the rising tide of discontent. Mass demonstrations demanding either major reforms or removal of the shah erupted throughout the country. Neither the army nor the police could stop them. Workers in the oil fields resented the widening gap between the rich and the poor. Students and other intellectuals objected to censorship and restraints on the press and intellectual life. The nationalists opposed Iran's growing dependence on the United States for arms and political support. Middle class entrepreneurs feared competition from the new government-controlled industries. Finally, clergy of the Shi'a sect, a majority of Iran's Muslim population, resented the shah's efforts toward modernization.

The Islamic Revolution

Iran's Shi'a clerics traditionally were regarded by villagers and the poor as defenders of the oppressed against the ruling powers. The Shi'a clergy were particularly hostile to the shah because of his attempts at forced modernization and his schemes to return Iran's calendar, flag, and other national symbols to representations of pre-Islamic ancient Persia. The most prominent opposition leader was the Ayatollah Ruhollah Khomeini (eye-uh-TOH-luh roo-HAH-luh koh-MAY-nee), the highest ranking cleric in Iran's Islamic establishment. Khomeini, who had been exiled by the shah during the 1960's and was living in France, was still looked to for leadership by the various dissident factions in Iran.

In 1978 the shah was no longer able to keep his government together. Neither was he able to deal with the displays of civil disobedience that swept through the country. In January 1979, Shah Mohammed Reza Pahlavi, his family, and his chief advisers left for an "extended vacation." Several days after their departure, Khomeini returned from France and formed a Council of the Islamic Revolution, which took control of the country.

THE ISLAMIC REVOLUTION.

Since 1979, demonstrations (top left) have been frequent occurrences in Iran. The entrance to a cemetery (top right) honors some of those who died in the long Iran–Iraq war. The Ayotollah Khomeini (left) pronounced a death sentence on Salman Rushdie, an author whom he thought dishonored Islam with his novel. Even though Khomeini died in June 1989, the death sentence remained in force. These women (below) supported the Ayotollah's action. Their posters say "sentenced to death."

In October 1979, the Shah of Iran sought medical help in the United States. A month later, an Iranian mob stormed the American embassy in Tehran and seized more than 50 Americans. When the U. S. refused to return the Shah to Iran, the Americans were kept hostage for over a year. One of the hostages (above) is shown to a crowd of Iranian supporters by Islamic revolutionaries.

Establishment of a Theocracy

During the next few months Iran's Shi'a leaders established a **theocracy.** First they set up revolutionary tribunals (courts) to conduct secret trials and executions of former officials, military officers, SAVAK agents, and associates of the shah. They introduced a new Islamic constitution that gave priority to Muslim law and institutions. A 12-member Council of Guardians that was led by the Ayatollah was put in charge of the government to assure that all legislation complied with Shi'a principles.

Within a year, opponents of the theocracy were weeded out, including many individuals and factions who had helped to overthrow the shah. Those no longer acceptable were Communists, socialists, secular nationalists, members of Kurdish political organizations, and even moderate Islamic republicans like Abdul Hasan Bani–Sadr, the first president of the Islamic Republic. In 1981 Bani–Sadr, once one of Khomeini's closest advisers in exile, broke with Khomeini and fled to France.

Impact of the Iran–Iraq War

Attempts to introduce economic reforms were undercut by Iraq's attack on Iran in 1980 and the subsequent Gulf War that lasted until 1988. The fighting resulted in nearly a million casualties and the near bankruptcy of the country from the allocation of its oil revenues to the war effort. Another result was the beginnings of open opposition to the policies of the theocracy.

By summer 1988 Iran peace proposal, and negotiations for a cease-fire halted the fighting. But the cease-fire in the Gulf War did not end political repression in Iran. Reports from Amnesty International and the UN indicated the political situation in Iran was as repressive as it was during the shah's regime. It will take some years to see how Khomeini's death in 1989 may affect the direction of Iran's policies.

Check Your Understanding

1. What were the effects of colonialism on Iran during the nineteenth century?
2. Why was there resistance to the modernizing efforts of the founder of the Pahlavi dynasty?
3. Why did opposition increase under his son's rule?
4. *Thinking Critically:* How did the White Revolution differ from the Islamic Revolution? What similarities exist between the White and Islamic Revolutions?

CHAPTER REVIEW

■ Chapter Summary

Section 1. Up to the nineteenth century, most people of the Middle East tended to identify themselves with religious rather than with national groups. In the nineteenth century European influence fostered the growth of nationalism, which was at first limited to a desire for decentralization under the Ottoman Empire. But continued repressive measures by the Ottoman rulers before and during World War I created a desire for independence, which Great Britain fostered wherever it furthered British interests. Expecting after World War I the independence promised by Great Britain, Arab nationalists were disappointed when the League of Nations assigned the Ottoman Empire's Arab provinces as mandates to Great Britain and France.

Section 2. The Levant, the area formerly known as the Ottoman province of Syria, was separated into two French mandates of Syria and Lebanon and two British mandates, one for Palestine and Trans–Jordan and one for Iraq. The French treated their mandate territories much like colonies until France was forced to give them their independence in 1946 after World War II. Problems of instability have plagued Syria's government from the start. Issues that have troubled Syria at various times are its role within the Arab community, its relations with other Arab states, struggles of religious groups for power, and hatred of Israel. The Ba'ath Party has been in power since 1963, becoming the dominant power in 1973.

Lebanon differs from most other Arab countries in the Middle East in that its Arab population was divided almost evenly between Maronite Christians and Muslims. This division has troubled Lebanon and increased tensions in the country as Muslims call for a change in the traditional division of power and representation in parliament to reflect the growing Muslim majority. Unable to achieve unity in the selection of a president in 1988, Lebanon divided into two competing governments—one Christian and one Muslim, each controlling part of Lebanon.

Section 3. Great Britain's mandates of Iraq and Trans–Jordan, now called Jordan, were given greater autonomy than Syria and Lebanon. Iraq became independent in 1923, forming a constitutional monarchy that lasted until 1958 when an army-led coup turned it into a military republic. Iraq has been troubled by Kurdish demands for autonomy and by its war with Iran over control of the Persian Gulf, which began in 1980 and ended with a cease-fire in 1988. Trans–Jordan became a constitutional monarchy with full independence in 1946, later changing its name to the Hashemite Kingdom of Jordan. After its occupation and annexation of the West Bank of the Jordan River in 1950, Jordan struggled with problems of uniting Palestinians of the West Bank with people of the east bank and with the refugees who fled to Jordanian territory from Israel. The Israelis captured the West Bank in 1967 and since have rejected requests for negotiation over its return to Jordan or its establishment as a separate Palestinian state. In 1988 Jordan's King Hussein renounced all claims to the West Bank, but the Arab–Israeli conflict and the refugee problems that stem from it continue to trouble Jordan, as well as the rest of the Arab world.

Section 4. Most states of the Arabian Peninsula are small principalities and sheikhdoms. The largest and richest state is Saudi Arabia. The poorest is considered to be the People's

Democratic Republic of Yemen, or South Yemen. The other states in the peninsula are the Yemen Arab Republic, Kuwait, Bahrain, Qatar, Oman, and the United Arab Emirates. Many have benefited from the vast oil resources of the peninsula. The states profiting most from these resources are Saudi Arabia, Kuwait, and the United Arab Emirates. Saudi Arabia in particular has used its wealth to support other Arab nations in the conflict with Israel and to earn for itself a position of leadership in the Arab world.

Section 5. Iran, formerly known as Persia, is an important non-Arab state in the Middle East. It became a constitutional monarchy in 1906. In 1923 Reza Khan rose to power as prime minister. In 1925 he took the title of shah and the family name Pahlavi and established a dynasty that ruled Iran until the Islamic Revolution of 1979. Reza Shah and Mohammed Reza Shah made many economic and political reforms that modernized Iran. But little of the wealth from the country's oil revenues filtered down to the people. Most of it went to building the country's military forces and defenses or into the shah's personal treasury. As discontent mounted, Mohammed Reza Shah's regime became more oppressive. Muslim fundamentalists, who resented and resisted all efforts toward modernization, led the revolution that toppled the shah's regime. With the revolution in 1979, Muslim Shi'a fundamentalists under the leadership of Ayatollah Khomeini took control of Iran, establishing a theocracy that has since become as repressive as the former shah's regime. The Iran–Iraq Gulf War has resulted in a million casualties and near bankruptcy for Iran.

■ **Vocabulary Review**

Define: sphere of influence, martial law, sect, propaganda, ideology, entrepreneur, shah, theocracy

■ **Places to Locate**

Locate: Levant, Syria, Lebanon, Iraq, Jordan, Iran, Kuwait, Yemen Arab Republic, People's Democratic Republic of Yemen, Saudi Arabia, Qatar, Oman, Bahrain, United Arab Emirates, Shatt-al-Arab

■ **People to Know**

Identify: Hussein Ibn Ali, Amir Faisal, King Hussein, Hafiz al-Assad, King Abdullah, Ahmed Hassan al-Bakr, Saddam

Hussein, Yasir Arafat, Ibn Saud, Reza Shah Pahlavi, Mohammed Reza Shah Pahlavi, Ayatollah Ruhollah Khomeini

■ Thinking Critically

1. Explain how imperialism and authoritarianism changed the thrust of nationalism from a desire for autonomy only to a desire for independence.
2. In what ways are the causes of instability in Syria and Lebanon similar? In what ways are they different?
3. What has caused Iraq's shifting relationship with the superpowers and the rest of the Arab world?
4. On what issues are most Arab states likely to agree? On which issues are they likely to disagree?
5. Why do many world leaders feel that the Middle East is the world's most serious trouble spot?

■ Extending and Applying Your Knowledge

1. Find out how life has changed for women in one or more of the countries of the Middle East that you have studied in this chapter. Write a report that provides a description of life for women before and after 1950 or some other date that you choose. A helpful book is *Women and Family in the Middle East: New Voices of Change* by Elizabeth W. Fernea, published in 1985 by the University of Texas Press.
2. Explore further the present-day conflicts between Shi'a and Sunni Muslims in the Middle East. In your research be sure to consult the *Readers' Guide to Periodical Literature* and other reference books for up-to-date information. Make a chart that lists and/or illustrates the major differences and similarities.

APPENDIX

BIBLIOGRAPHY

Reference Works

Brawer, Moshe. *Atlas of the Middle East.* Macmillan, 1988. Maps of individual countries accompanied by descriptions of geography, population, history, and politics.

Jones, Catherine E. *Middle East Materials for Teachers, Students, and Non-Specialists.* Middle East Studies Association, 1988. Listing of helpful print and audiovisual materials.

Ziring, Lawrence. *The Middle East Political Dictionary.* ABC–CLIO Information Services, 1984. Brief informative articles on people and politics within each country.

General Overview   *(Chapter 1)*

Andersen, Roy R., Robert F. Seibert, and Jon D. Wagner. *Politics and Change in the Middle East: Sources of Conflict and Accommodation (2nd ed.).* Prentice–Hall, 1987. Discussion of contemporary problems with a brief historical background.

Bates, Daniel G., and Amal Rassam. *Peoples and Cultures of the Middle East.* Prentice–Hall, 1983. Anthropological survey.

Drysdale, Alasdair, and Gerald H. Blake. *The Middle East and North Africa: A Political Geography.* Oxford, 1985. Comprehensive geopolitical analysis.

Fernea, Elizabeth W. *Women and Family in the Middle East: New Voices of Change.* University of Texas Press, 1985. Essays, stories, and poems focusing on women and the family.

Issawi, Charles. *An Economic History of the Middle East and North Africa.* Columbia University Press, 1982. Survey of economic trends and developments since 1800.

Keller, Werner. *The Bible as History,* 2nd edition. Bantam. Classic study in an updated version.

Peretz, Don. *The Middle East Today (5th ed.).* Praeger–Greenwood, 1988. Background history and discussion of contemporary problems, with chapters on individual countries.

The Ancient Middle East   *(Chapter 2)*

Aldred, Cyril. *Egyptian Art.* Oxford, 1980. Overview of ancient Egyptian art and history.

Grant, Michael. *The History of Ancient Israel.* Scribners, 1984. History of Israelites from earliest permanent settlements to about A.D. 70.

Johnson, Paul. *The Civilization of Ancient Egypt.* Atheneum, 1978. Survey with illustrations and maps.

Lesko, B. *The Remarkable Women of Ancient Egypt.* Scribe Publishers. The roles of women in ancient Egypt.

Macaulay, David. *Pyramid.* Houghton Mifflin. Details the planning and building of the burial places of the pharaohs.

McEvedy, Collin. *Penguin Atlas of Ancient History.* Penguin, 1967. Paperback atlas covering prehistoric era to A.D. 363.

Whitehouse, Ruth. *The First Cities.* Phaidon, 1977. Archaeological study of early cities in strategic river valleys.

Islam and the Muslim Empires   *(Chapters 3 and 4)*

Andrae, Tor. *Mohammed, the Man and His Faith.* Harper Torchbooks, 1960. Account of the Prophet's personal life and views.

Kritzeck, James, ed. *Anthology of Islamic Literature.* Holt, 1963. Paperback survey of classical literature.

Lewis, Bernard. *The Arabs in History.* Harper Torchbooks, 1966. Account of the rise and decline of the Arab empires.

Maalouf, Amin. *The Crusades Through Arab Eyes.* al–Saqi Books, 1984. Account of the Crusades from a Muslim viewpoint.

Pickthall, Mohammed Marmaduke. *The Meaning of the Glorious Koran.* Allen, 1939. Translation of Koran with commentary, in paperback.

Rogers, Michael. *The Spread of Islam.* Phaidon. Islamic history and art.

Von Grunebaum, G. E. *Medieval Islam (2nd ed.).* University of Chicago Press, 1953. Study of the golden age of Islam.

The Ottoman Empire and Modern Turkey   *(Chapters 5 and 6)*

Davis, Fanny. *The Ottoman Lady: A Social History from 1718 to 1918.* Role of women and their influence in late Ottoman times.

Eliot, Charles. *Turkey in Europe.* Barnes & Noble, 1965. British diplomat's account of nineteenth-century Ottoman Empire.

Harris, George S. *Turkey: Coping with Crisis.* Westview, 1985. Historical background and recent political trends.

Kinross, Patrick (Lord Balfour). *Atatürk: A Biography of Mustafa Kemal, Father of Modern Turkey.* Morrow, 1966. Biography from a sympathetic viewpoint.

Lewis, Bernard. *Istanbul and the Civilization of the Ottoman Empire.* University of Oklahoma Press, 1963. The empire at its zenith.

——————— *The Emergence of Modern Turkey (2nd ed.).* Oxford, 1968. Comprehensive study.

Makal, Malmut. *A Village in Anatolia.* Ballentine, 1954. Experiences of a modern teacher in a traditional village.

Rustow, Dankart A. *Turkey: America's Forgotten Ally.* Council on Foreign Relations, 1987. Survey of recent developments.

Modern Egypt   *(Chapter 7)*

Atiya, Nayra. *Five Egyptian Women Tell Their Stories.* Syracuse University Press, 1984. First-hand accounts of family and neighborhood life in Cairo.

282

Ayrout, Henry H. *The Egyptian Peasant*. Beacon, 1968. A reissue of a classic account of peasant life by a priest who lived in rural Egypt most of his life.

Critchfield, Richard. *Shahhati: An Egyptian*. Syracuse University Press, 1978. Narrative account of an Egyptian peasant from an anthropological perspective.

Herold, J. C. *Bonaparte in Egypt*. Harper, 1963. Napoleon's impact on the country.

Lacouture, Jean and Simonne. *Egypt in Transition*. Criterion, 1958. Account of the 1952 revolution.

Lane, E. W. *Manners and Customs of the Modern Egyptians*. East–West Publications, 1978. Survey of rural and city life in the nineteenth century.

Nasser, Gamal Abdel. *Egypt's Liberation*. Public Affairs Press, 1955. Nasser's account of the revolution.

——————————————— *The Philosophy of the Revolution*. Société Orientale de Publicité (no date). Nasser's explanation of his revolutionary thinking.

Sadat, Jehan. *A Woman of Egypt*. Simon and Schuster. Anwar Sadat's widow gives insights to Egyptian culture in this autobiography.

Waterbury, John. *The Egypt of Nasser and Sadat: The Political Economy of Two Regimes*. Princeton University Press, 1983. Case study of Egypt's economic problems and how each man dealt with them.

Modern Israel *(Chapter 8)*

Avnery, Uri. *My Friend, the Enemy*. Zed Books, 1986. Account by an Israeli of his contacts with the PLO and other Palestinians.

Cohen, Israel. *The Zionist Movement*. Zionist Organization of America, 1946. A survey.

Elon, Amos. *The Israelis: Founders and Sons*. Penguin Books, 1987. Account of modern Israel through the story of two generations.

Oz, Amos. *In the Land of Israel*. Harcourt Brace Jovanovich, 1983. Vignettes of life in modern Israel.

Peretz, Don. *The Government and Politics of Israel (2nd ed.)*. Westview Press, 1983. Background history and account of contemporary Israeli politics.

Sacher, Howard M. *A History of Israel from the Aftermath of the Yom Kippur War*. Oxford, 1987. Survey of modern Israel.

Shipler, David. *Arab and Jew: Wounded Spirits in a Promised Land*. Penguin. Cultural and social aspects of the Arab–Israeli conflict.

Tiger, Lionel, and Joseph Shepher. *Women in the Kibbutz*. Harcourt Brace Jovanovich, 1975. Analyzes common misconceptions about the kibbutz.

Other Countries of the Middle East *(Chapter 9)*

Abdulghani, Jasim M. *Iraq and Iran: The Years of Crisis*. Johns Hopkins University Press, 1984. Focus on Iraq.

Ajami, Fouad. *The Vanishing Imam: Musa al Sadr and the Shi'a of Lebanon*. Cornell University Press, 1986. Political biography of an important Lebanese religious figure.

Antonius, George. *The Arab Awakening.* International Book Center. Story of Arab nationalism.

Gubser, Peter. *Jordan: Crossroads of Middle Eastern Events.* Westview Press, 1983. Discussion of Jordan's ethnic, religious, and social diversity.

Holden, David, and Richard Johns. *The House of Saud: The Rise and Rule of the Most Powerful Dynasty in the Arab World.* Sedgwick & Jackson, 1981. A critical account.

Keddie, Nikki R. *Roots of Revolution: An Interpretive History of Modern Iran.* Yale University Press, 1981. Origins of the 1979 Revolution.

GLOSSARY

This Glossary contains definitions for the social studies terms used in this volume about the Middle East. These terms are printed in bold type the first time they appear in the text. The page number following each definition is the page on which the word is first used. Often words have more than one meaning. The definitions given below are the ones that will be most helpful to you in reading this book.

alliance   association among nations based upon mutual purpose, interest, or advantage (143)

arabesque   style of geometric or floral pattern common in Islamic art (92)

Arab socialism   series of programs in economic planning, education, and welfare adopted after 1956 by Gamel Abdel Nasser that were designed to make Egypt a society in which all citizens prospered equally (182)

authoritarianism   system of rule demanding absolute obedience to authority (152)

autocratic   having unlimited power and authority (138)

autonomy   self-government or self-rule (21)

balance of power   principle of preserving peace among nations through equal distribution of power (135)

bedouin   Arab nomadic desert dweller (23)

bloc   group united for a common purpose or action (182)

blockade   to close off; to prevent passage in or out   (126)

buffer state   region or territory located between unfriendly powers that acts as a deterrent to war (50)

bureaucracy   system of government administration by bureaus or departments (39)

caliph   religious and political leader; literally "successor to the Prophet" (72)

calligraphy   elaborate script used in Islamic art (92)

capitulation   treaty of agreement between parties, from the Latin *capitula* (116)

censorship   policy of stopping publication and distribution of literature, art, or any creative material found objectionable by the government or other authorities (139)

civilization   level of society characterized by a high degree of technical and intellectual achievements (1)

coalition   union between parties with a common interest or goal that is convenient and often temporary (154)

colonialism   policy in which weak nations are conquered and made into colonies in an effort to build and enrich an empire (168)

compromise   settlement of differences through the making of concessions (137)

conservative   person who prefers the existing social and political order (140)

constitution   document that sets forth the guiding principles and basic laws of a constitutional government (138)

constitutional government   government guided in its basic operation by either a written or an unwritten constitution (138)

constitutional monarchy   government based on a constitution and having a monarch with limited powers (177)

corvée   work, usually unpaid, that is required of a vassal by the feudal lord (171)

coup   seizure of power through force (138)

cultural diffusion   spread of cultural characteristics from one group to another (45)

cuneiform   style of writing with wedge-shaped characters that was used in Sumeria (35)

democracy   system of government in which citizens govern directly or through elected representatives (131)

developing nation   political unit with a low standard of living and little industrial development (10)

Diaspora   period of dispersal in Jewish history between the destruction of Jerusalem and the establishment of Israel (49)

dictatorship   government by a ruler with absolute power (139)

diwan   caliphate bureaucratic department (85)

dynasty   line of families that transfers its right to rule by inheritance (39)

economy   system of producing, distributing, and consuming goods and services (35)

empire   a state and the conquered lands that it rules (36)

entrepreneur   person who starts up and operates his or her own business (248)

faction   dissenting minority within a group (163)

fellaheen   Egyptian peasant (178)

feudalism   social and political system in which upper-class landowners gave lower classes protection and land in exchange for labor or military service (99)

foreign policy   guidelines followed by a nation in its relations with other nations (126)

free enterprise   economic system in which individuals choose and operate businesses and sell goods and services with a minimum of government involvement (158)

fundamentalist   person who's committed to strict observance of religious law (195)

genocide   systematic murder of an entire ethnic or national group (141)

ghazi   roving adventurers of Asia Minor; originally "warrior of faith" (109)

ghetto   section of a city where Jews were forced to live apart from the general population (204)

gross national product   sum total of all the goods and services produced in a country within a specific period of time, usually a year (157)

guerrilla   style of fighting characterized by surprise attack and hit-and-run tactics (212)

haram   section of a house reserved for women members of a Muslim household and their servants (118)

hegira   journey of the prophet Mohammed from Mecca to Medina (64)

Hellenism   Greek ideas, style, or culture (54)

Holocaust   period of systematic killing of Jews by Nazis during World War II (211)

ideology   set of rigid or inflexible political beliefs (246)

imam   person regarded by Shi'a as a successor to the prophet Mohammed; Muslim religious functionary (78)

imperialism   policy by which a nation extends its control over other lands to gain an economic or political advantage (182)

industrialization   development of a manufacturing-based economy (8)

janissary   soldier in an elite corp of Turkish troops (119)

kibbutz   collective farm or settlement in Israel (209)

Kristallnacht   date marking the beginning of the Holocaust— November 9, 1938; literally "night of broken glass" (211)

land tenure   system of landholding (15)

liberal   supporter of moderate political change and social and economic reform (139)

mandate   territory administered by a League of Nations grant after World War I (210)

martial law   control of an area by military rule (154)

mercenary   paid professional soldier (174)

military junta   group of officers who band together to gain control of a government (153)

millet   self-governing religious group in the Ottoman Empire (116)

minaret   tower on a mosque from which Islamic worshipers are summoned to prayer (69)

modernization   process of replacing traditional ideas and systems with more recent ones (20)

monopoly   control of a service or product and its price by a single source (39)

monotheism   belief in a single deity (26)

mosque   Muslim place of worship (68)

muezzin   crier who summons worshipers to prayer in Islam (69)

mufti   Muslim judge or interpreter of Sharia (97)

nationalism   feeling of devotion to and pride in one's country (22)

nationalize   to bring privately owned resources or industries under government control and ownership (183)

neutral   not supporting or assisting either side in a war or dispute (186)

nonaligned nation   state that remains neutral or apart from another nation or bloc of nations (183)

oral tradition   cultural heritage (stories, folktales, poetry, songs) passed from one generation to the next by word of mouth (92)

parliament   legislative body that creates the laws of a state (139)

partition   to divide into parts (179)

pasha   Muslim title, usually of a governor or other high-ranking official (119)

per capita income   the average income of all the people in a nation (157)

pharaoh   monarch of ancient Egypt believed to be the earthly representative of a god (39)

pogrom   massacre of Jews and destruction of Jewish-owned businesses by anti-Semitic mobs and government troops in the 1880's in Russia and later in Poland (204)

polytheism   worship of and belief in more than one deity (39)

populism   political philosophy advocating a more even distribution of wealth and power to benefit the people (147)

prime minister   head of the cabinet in a parliamentary democracy (152)

propaganda   news and information designed to persuade people to adopt a particular point of view (246)

protectorate   self-governing area whose economic and political policies are guided by another government (175)

qadi   Muslim judge (97)

radical   having a quality of being extreme (138)

refugee   person who flees to seek safe haven (213)

republic   government in which citizens elect representatives to govern them (146)

satellite   country subordinate to the national policy of a stronger power (183)

satrapy   territory in ancient Persia (51)

sect   group of people united by common beliefs and customs (26)

secularism   belief that a country should not be governed by religion or religious authorities (147)

self-determination   right of a people in an area to determine their own political status (177)

shah   title assumed by the monarch of Iran (269)

sheikh   leader of an Arab family, village, or tribe (23)

Shi'a   branch of Islam (76)

sovereignty   supremacy of authority or rule (117)

sphere of influence   region in which another nation claims the privilege to exercise economic and political control (243)

statism   state-controlled economy; one of Atatürk's six principles (147)

status quo   existing condition or state or affairs (137)

strategic location   site of a nation or area having political, geographic, or economic importance (1)

sultan   ruler, usually of an Islamic country (98)

Sunni   largest branch of Islam (76)

superpower term often used since the 1950's in reference to the United States and the Soviet Union (185)

theocracy control of government by priests in the name of a god (78)

Third World developing nations, usually nonaligned with either of the superpowers (183)

trade union group of workers in the same trade organized to promote their interests (152)

tribe group of families united by ancestry, language, tradition, and beliefs (21)

tribute payment by a conquered region to a conqueror in exchange for protection or peace (50)

ulema body of Muslim scholars (97)

vizier chief official under Abbasid rule in the Ottoman Empire, sometimes called a wazir (119)

wazir head of the caliphate bureaucracy (85)

Westernization movement by a non-Western nation toward ideas and practices of Western nations (131)

Yahweh Hebrew name for god (49)

Zionism movement to re-establish and settle Jews in a Jewish national homeland in Palestine, or Zion (204)

ACKNOWLEDGMENTS

Text Credits

The Egyptian Book of the Dead, p. 346, translated by E.A. Wallis Budge, Copyright © 1967 by Dover Publications, Inc., 1967. Reprinted by permission of Dover Publications, Inc. From *Istanbul and the Civilization of the Ottoman Empire*, by Bernard Lewis. Copyright © 1963 by the University of Oklahoma Press. Reprinted by permission of the University of Oklahoma Press. Lewis, *op. cit.*, pp. 174–175. *Turkey*, by Geoffrey Lewis. Copyright © 1960 by Praeger Publishers, a division of Greenwood Press, Inc., p. 90. *Ibid.*, pp. 90–92. *Turkey: An Economic Appraisal* by Max W. Thornburg, Graham Spry, George Soule. Copyright © 1949 by the Twentieth Century Fund, p. 23. Reprinted by permission of the Twentieth Century Fund. *The Philosophy of the Revolution* by Gamal Abdel Nasser (Cairo, Egypt: Société Orientale de Publicité, no date given), pp. 14–15. *Ibid.*, p. 22. *The Zionist Movement* by Israel Cohen (New York: Zionist Organization of America, 1946), p. 78. *Nationalism and Imperialism in the Hither East* by Hans Kohn (London: Routledge & Kegan Paul, Ltd., 1932; New York: Howard Fertig, Inc., 1969). Cohen, *op. cit.*, p. 117. Copyright © 1968 by the New York Times Company. Reprinted by permission.

Art Credits

Book designed by George McLean.
Cover concept and design by Hannus Design Associates.
Cover photograph: Guido Alberto Rossi/The Image Bank
Maps: Precision Graphics.
Title Page and Chapter Opener art: Leslie Evans.
Calligraphy, page 24, by Basim Musallem.
Drawing, page 84, by John Gretzer.

Photographs 7 *(top left)* Mehmet Biber, *(top right)* FAO/Pat Morin, *(Center and bottom)* ARAMCO; **14** *(top and bottom left)*, ARAMCO, *(bottom right)* WHO/Paul Almasy; **19** *(top left)* WHO/Paul Almasy, *(top right) United Nations, (center)* Embassy of the State of Kuwait, *(bottom)* Wide World Photos; **25** *(top left)* United Nations, *(top right)* A. DeWildenberg/Sygma, *(center)* Paul Conklin, *(bottom)* ARAMCO; **33** *(top)* The University Museum, University of Pennsylvania, *(bottom)* The British Museum; **37** *(left)* The Oriental Institute, University of Chicago, *(right)* Nelson Gallery–Atlins Museum (Nelson Fund), Kansas City, Missouri; **41** *(top)* The Metropolitan Museum of Art, Egyptian Expedition, Rogers Fund, 1930, *(bottom)* The British Museum; **47** *(left)* The Archaeological Institute of America, *(right)* The Oriental Institute, University of Chicago; **51** *(right)* The Oriental Institute, University of Chicago, *(left)* American Numismatic Society, New York; **53** Alinari/Art Resource; **54** Thames & Hudson, Ltd, London; **55** Lebanon Tourist and Information Office; **63** *(top and bottom)* Ara Güler, Topkapi Saray Museum, Istanbul, *(center)* Spencer Collection, New York Public Library, Astor, Lenox and Tilden Foundations; **69** Susan May Tell/Picture Group; **71** *(top)* Abbas/Magnum, *(bottom left, right)* WHO; **76** H. Armstrong Roberts; **79** *(left)* Jacques Jangoux, *(right)* Consulate General of Indonesia; **89** *(top)* Roland and Sabrina Michaud/Woodfin Camp and Associates, *(center left)* Bibliothèque Nationale, *(center right)* The British Museum, *(bottom)* The Metropolitan Museum of Art, Bequest of Cora Timkin Burnett, 1957; **94** *(top)* Royal Air Force official photograph, Crown Copyright Reserved, *(center)* Alinari/Art Resource, *(bottom left)* UNESCO/Cart, *(bottom right)* Pan American World Airways; **95** *(top left)* Clarendon Press, *(top right)* The Metropolitan Museum of Art, Museum Excavations, 1939, *(bottom left)* The Metropolitan Museum of Art, Rogers Fund, 1951, *(bottom right)* Museum of Fine Arts, Boston, Gift of John Goelet; **100** BBC Hulton Picture Library; **101** Bibliotèque Nationale; **109** BBC Hulton Picture Library; **113** Sovfoto; **115** Turkish Government Tourism and Information Of-

INDEX

This index includes references not only to the text of the book but also to charts, maps, and pictures. These may be identified as follows: *c* refers to a chart; *g* refers to a graph; *m* refers to a map; *p* refers to a picture.

A

Abbasid Empire, overtake of Umayyad Caliphate, 80; Bagdad as capital, 83, 84, *p*84; government of, 83, 85; golden age of Islam, 83, 87–96; trade of, 85–87; economy of, 85–87; medicine during, 87–88; scientific advances of, 87–90; art of, 91–92, *p*95; architecture of, 91, *p*94; literature of, 92–93, 96; decline of, 98–100, 108
Abdul Hamid II, 138–139, 140
Abdullah Ibn Hussein, *p*246, 255–256
Abraham, 65
Abu al–Abbas, 79–80
Abu Bakr, *p*63, 67, 68, 72, 75
Abu Dhabi, *m*266, 267; oil in, 11
Abu Simbel, *p*193
Aden, *m*103, 264, *m*266
Aegean Sea, 9, *m*115, *m*156
Afghanistan, *m*4–5
African–Arabian Shield, 3
Agaolu, Adalet, 158
Agricultural Reform Decree (Egypt), 190
agriculture, *p*7, 8–11, *p*180, *p*234; land–tenure system, 15; in ancient Middle East, 30–31; in Egypt, 170–171, *p*178, 190–191, *p*191; in Israel, 207, 255, *p*226, 227, *p*230
Ahmed Arabi, 175, *p*176
Ahmose I, 42
Ahura–Mazda, 52
Aisha, 66, 75, 91–92, 96
Ajman, 267
Akhenaton, 42
Akka, 102
Akkad, 36
Albania, *m*4–5, 110
alchemy, study of, 88
Aleppo, *m*3, 110, *m*115
Alexander II (czar), 137
Alexander the Great, 18, 43, 50, 52, *p*53, *m*53; and the Kurds, 22
Alexandria, *m*3, *m*12, 18, *m*53, *m*73, *m*103, 170, 172, *m*195; founding of, 54; and Muslims, 72

Al Fatah, 259
Alf Layla wa Layla, *See A Thousand and One Nights*
al–Fustat, 74
Alhambra, *p*76
Alhazen, 90
Ali, Ummayad caliph, 75, 98
Ali Pasha, 138
Allah, 61; idea of, 23, 25
Allenby Bridge *See* King Hussein Bridge
Alphabet, *p*24, 43, 46
al–Razi, 87–88
Amenhotep IV, 42
American University of Beirut, 240
Amman, *m*218, *m*219, 257
Amnesty International, 270, 274
Amon–Re, 39
Anatolia, 109, 114, *m*115, 125, 145, 172; and Armenian nationalist movement, 141
Anatolian Plateau, *m*4–5, 30, 131
Ancient Egypt, family life in, 39; religion in, 39, 40, 42; women in, 39, 42; government of, 39, 42–43; art of, *p*41; education in, 43–44; class system of, 43–44; Israelites as slaves in, 47. *See also* Egypt
Anglo–Persian Oil Company, 11, 269
Ankara, *m*3, 110, *m*115, *p*150, *m*156; as capital of Turkey, 146
Anti–Lebanon ranges, 3
Antioch, *m*53; Mongols in 10; founding of, 54; and Mumlak rule, 102
anti–Semitism, 204
arabesque, 92, *p*95
Arab Gulf *See* Persian Gulf
The Arabian Nights, 93, 96
Arabian Peninsula, *m*36, *m*53, *m*73, *m*115, 125; geography of, 2–6, *m*4–5; oil in, 11; states of, 260–267, *m*262
Arabian Sea, *m*3, *m*4–5, 9, *m*53, *m*73, *m*103, *m*195, *m*266
Arabic, and ethnic identification, 21; influence of Bedouins on, 23, *p*25; alphabet, *p*24; and the Koran, 68; language, 21, 23, 24, 68, 74, 86
Arab–Israeli conflict, 1, 201, *p*234; Turkish reactions to, 161; and UN involvement, 201, 211, 212–213, 214; and Balfour Declaration, 210–211; and Arab refugees, 213–214; Six–Day War, 185,

214–215; Yom Kippur War,
185–186, 215–216
Arab League, 179, 183, 195; and
Lebanon, 250; members of, 259
Arab nationalism, and Zionism, 206;
and Balfour Declaration, 210; be-
fore World War I, 240–241; and
break from Turks, 241–242; and
League of Nations, 243; in Syria,
246
Arab refugees, after 1948 conflict,
213–214. *See also* Palestinian ref-
ugees
Arab Republic of Egypt *See* Egypt
Arabs, *p*100; early history of, 21; and
religious tolerance, 75, 77; in Israel,
232–234. *See also* Saracens
Arad, *p*47
Arafat, Yasir, *p*71, *p*248, 257, 259
Aral Sea, *m*36, *m*53, *m*73, *m*103
Arameans, 46
architecture, *p*234; ziggurat, 35; of
Roman Empire, 55, *p*55; Islamic,
69, *p*76, *p*79; of Abbasid Empire,
91, *p*94; of Ottoman Empire, 112,
113, *p*113. *See also* Housing
Arif, General Abdel Rahman, 253
Aristotle, 88
arithmetic *See* Mathematics
Armenia, 21, *m*115, *m*144, *m*156;
genocide, 141
art and artifacts, of Sumer, *p*33; of
Ancient Egypt, *p*41; of Persia, *p*51;
of Muslims, *p*63; of Abbasid Em-
pire, *p*89, 91–92, *p*95
Ashkenzi *See* Judaism, Ashkenazi
Asia Minor, in Ottoman Empire,
110–111
Assad, Hafiz al–, 247–249, *p*248
Assassins, 78
Assyria, people of, 43; conquer of Is-
rael, 48
Assyrian Empire, *m*36, 50
astronomy, study of, 35, 51, 90
Aswan High Dam, 8, 175, 190, 192,
*p*193
Atatürk, Kemal, 146, 147, 148, 149,
*p*150, 158; and the Koran, 68
Athbara River, *m*195
Austria–Hungary, 143–144
Averroes, 88
Avicennes, 88
Ayn Jalut, 102

B

Ba'ath Party, in Syria, 246, 247; in
Iraq, 252, 254
Babylon, *m*36, 37–38; Jews exiled to,
48
Babylonian Empire, *m*36, 37–38,
50–51. *See also* Chaldean Empire

Babylonian Exile, 48
Baghdad, *p*102, *m*103, 110, *m*115;
population, *m*3; as capital of Abba-
sid Empire, 83, 84, *p*84; and golden
age of Islam, 87–96; Mongol inva-
sion of, 100, 101–102, *p*101
Bahrain, 2, *m*3, *m*4–5, 266, *m*266,
267; oil in, 11; per capita income,
*c*16; population, *c*17
Bakr, General Ahmed Hassen al–,
253
balance of power, 135
Balfour, Arthur, 209
Balfour Declaration, 208, 209–210
Balkan Peninsula, 110, *m*115
Bani–Sadr, Abdul Hasan, 273
Baring, Sir Evelyn, 175
Bar Kochba, Simeon, 49
bartering, 45
Basel Program, 206
Basra, *p*7, 8, *m*12, *m*73, 74
Bayar, Celal, 151, 152, 153
Baybars, 102
Bayezid I, 110
bazaars, 18
Bedouins, language and religion of,
23; influence on culture of Middle
East, 23, *p*25
Begin, Menachem, 186, *p*187,
216–217, 223
Beidha, excavation of, 34
Beirut, *m*103, *m*218, *m*219, 245
Ben–Gurion, David, 207, 208, *p*213,
*p*216, 222
Bethlehem, 212
Bible, 62, 65
Black Sea, *m*3, *m*4–5, 9, *m*12, *m*36,
*m*53, *m*73, *m*103, *m*115, 145, *m*156,
*m*195
Blue Mosque, *p*94
Blue Nile River, *m*195
Book of the Dead, 40, *p*41
Bosnia, 138, 144; annexed by Aus-
tria, 140
Bosporus, 137, *m*156
Britain, oil interests of, 11, 14; sup-
ported Turkey against Russia, 135;
and Crimean War, 136; in World
War I, 144; and Suez Canal, 172,
*p*173, 174; occupation of Egypt,
175–177; mandates of, 201, 208,
209–211, 212, 243, 252, 259; support of Hussein Ibn Ali, 241–242;
interest in Persia, 268–269
British East India Company, 264
Bulgaria, *m*4–5, 110, *m*115, 137,
138, *m*156; declares independence,
140
Buyids, invade Iraq, 98
Byzantine Empire, *m*73, *m*103; government of, 56; wars with Sassanian Empire, 60; and Seljuk Turks,
99

C

Cadiz, 46
Cairo, m3, m12, 113, m115, 172–173, m195, m218, m219; as Fatimid capital, 98; and Mamluk rule, 102, 104; as capital of Egypt, 167
calendar, Egyptian, 44; Muslim, 70
caliph, 72
caliphate, Abbasid concept of, 84–85
calligraphy, 92, p95
Canbyses, 51
camels, 10–11
Camp David Accords, 186–187, p187, 216–217
Canaanites, 48
capitulations, 116–117
caravan routes, 60, m103
carpets, 92
Carter, Jimmy, 186, p187, 216–217
Carthage, 46, m53
Caspian Sea, m3, m4–5, 9, m12, m36, m53, m73, m103, m115
Catherine the Great, 126, 267
Caucasus Mountains, m4–5
ceramics, of Abbasid Empire, 92
Chaldean Empire, 50–51. See also Babylonian Empire
chemistry, study of, 88
Chief Mufti, 133
China, m4–5, m73, 161; and Umayyad caliphate, 77
Christian Arabs, 26
Christianity, and Roman Empire, 55; spread of, 55–56; and Islam, 62, 64, 66; Muslim tolerance of, 75, 77; and the Crusades, 99–100, p100; in Ottoman Empire, 114
Church of the Holy Sepulchre, p237
cities and city–states, 18–20, p19, 31, 33, 35–36; modernization of, 20; Greek, 52
class system, of Ancient Egypt, 43–44; of Ummayad caliphate, 77
climate, m3, 6, p7, 8
coinage See money
Committee of Union and Progress (CUP), 140
Communist Party (Syria), 246
Constantine, 56
Constantinople, 18, m53, m73, m103, m115; attacked by Umayyads, 77; as capital of Ottoman Empire, 111; name changed, 111. See also Istanbul
Copts, 26, 74; in Ottoman Empire, 114
Cordoba, 80, p94
Corrective Revolution (Egypt), 194
Corvee, 171
cotton, 10, 171, 174
Council of Guardians (Iran), 273
courts, Islamic, 97

D

Crete, 140
Crimean War, 136–137
Cromer, Lord See Baring, Sir Evelyn
The Crown of Histories, 114
Crusades, 99–100, p100; massacre of Jews, 202
cuneiform, 35
currency See money
Cyprus, 162–163, p162, m218, m219
Cyrus the Great, 48, 51

D

Damascus, m3, 18, m73, 83, m103, 110, m115, m218, m219; and Muslims, 72; as Muslim capital, 76; in Umayyad caliphate, 79–80
D'Arcy, William Knox, 11
Dardanelles, 126, 137, 145, m156
Darius I, 51, p51, p53
Dasht–i–Kavir, m4–5, 6
Dasht–i–Lut, m4–5, 6
David, King of Israel, 48
Dayan, Moshe, 222
Dead Sea, m218, m219
Degania, 209, m226
De Gaulle, Charles, 245
De Lesseps, Ferdinand, 172, 184
Demavend, 3, m4–5
Demirel, Suleyman, 154, p155
democracy, in Israel, 221–224
Democratic Party, (Turkey), 151–152
deserts, 6, p7
Devshirme, 118
Dhahran, m12, m266
Diaspora, 49, 202
Diocletian, 56
Disengagement Agreements, 248
Disraeli, Benjamin, 172, 204
Ditch, Battle of the, 66
Divan, 119
Diwans, 85
Djibouti, 259
Dome of the Rock, p233, p237
Dreyfus Affair, 205
Dubai, 267

E

Eastern Question, 135
Eastern Roman Empire See Byzantine Empire
East Ghor Canal Project, 8
East Jordan, 256
economics and economy, g16; oil and the, 11, 14–15; of ancient Sumer, 35; of Abbasid Empire, 85–87; of Turkey, 148–149, 157; of Egypt, 175, 191, 194; of Israel, 225–231, g228, g229
education, in ancient Egypt, 43–44; during Abbasid Empire, 87–88, p89; in Ottoman Empire, 118, 121–122; in Turkey, 132, 133,

147–148, 158, 160; in Egypt, 170, 172–173, 175, 196–197; in Israel, 234

Egypt, m3, m12, m36, m53, m73, m115, m195, m218, m219; geography of, 2, m4–5, 6; population of, 2, 179; agriculture in, 10, 170–171, p178, 190–191, p191; industry in, 8, 170–171, 191, 194; oil in, 11; in Umayyad caliphate, 79; Muslims in, 74, 75; as part of Ottoman Empire, 125; Cairo as capital, 167; influence of France in, 168; western domination in, 168–174; under Mohammed Ali, 169–172; legal system of, 170; medicine in, 170; education in, 170, 172–173, 196–197; living conditions of, 170–171, 178–179; military of, 171–172; under Ismail, 172–174; Suez Canal, 172, p173, 174, 184; economy of, 175, 191, 194; women in, 175, 196–197; British occupation of, 175–177; in World War I, 177; Treaty of Alliance, 177; under Faruq, 178; under Nasser, 179, 180–185, p180, 190, 194; defeat in Palestine, 179–180; revolutions in, 180–181, 194; under Neguib, 180–181, p180; government of, 182–189; U.S. aid to, 182, 183; in UAR, 182–183, 246–247; Soviet aid to, 183, 190; relations with Israel, 185–186, 188–189, 213; under Sadat, 185–188, p187, 194–196; under Mubarek, 188–189, p189, 196; and Six-Day War, 214–215; and Camp David Accords, p187, 216–217; as member of Arab League, 259. See also Ancient Egypt

Egyptian Delegation, 177
Egyptian Empire, m36
Egypt–Israel Peace Treaty, 186
El Alamein, 177
Elath, m12
Elburz Mountains, 3, m4–5
Emir Jabir al-Sabah, 266
Empty Quarter, 6
Ethiopia, m4–5
Euclid, 54
Euphrates River, m3, m4–5, 8, m36, m53, m73, m103, m115
Exodus, 203
export products, 10. See also oil

F

Fahd, King of Saudi Arabia, 263
Faisal, King of Saudi Arabia, 261–263
Faisal, King of Syria, 242–243, 244
Faisal I, King of Iraq, 210, 252, p253
Faisal II, King of Iraq, 253
family life, 16–17, 27; in Ancient Egypt, 39

farming See agriculture
Faruq, King of Egypt, 178, p180
Fatimah, 75, 98
Fatimid Empire, 78, 98
Fayum Province, 191
Fazil Ahmed, 126
Federation of South Arabia, 264–265. See also People's Democratic Republic of Yemen
Fellaheen, 178–179
Fertile Crescent, 9, 31
feudalism, 99; and Mamluk rule, 104
Five Pillars of Islam, 68–71
France, and capitulation of Ottoman Empire, 116; and Crimean War, 136; in World War I, 144; influence of, in Egypt, 168; French Revolution, 204; mandates of, 243–246, 259
Francis I, King of France, 116
Frankish Kingdom, m73
Franz Ferdinand, Archduke, 144
free enterprise, in Turkey, 158
Fujaira, 267
fundamentalists See Islam, fundamentalists

G

Galabia, 194
Gallipoli, 110, m156
Gallipoli Peninsula, 145
games, p34
Gaza Strip, 186, 215, 217, 218, m218, m219, p220, 257, 259
Gemayael, Amin, p251
Genghis Khan, 101
geography, 2–6, m4–5; advances made in Abbasid Empire, 90
geometry, study of, 35
ghazis, 109
Giza, 44
Golan Heights, 186, 215, m218, m219, p222, 247, 249
government, of Ancient Egypt, 39, 42–43; Persian system of, 51–52; in Byzantine Empire, 56; in Abbasid Empire, 83, 85; of Ottoman Empire, 114–120, 124–125; of Turkey, 138–143, 151–156; in Egypt, 182–189; in Israel, 220–224
Grand Vizier, 119, p120
Great Bitter Lake, m195, m218, m219
Greece, 2, m4–5, 110, m156; city-states of, 52; Cyprus question, 162–163. See also Ottoman Empire
Greek Orthodox Church, 26
Green, David See Ben–Gurion, David
Gulf Cooperation Council, 263, 265, 267
Gulf of Aden, m4–5, m195
Gulf of Aqaba, m218, m219
Gulf of Oman, m266

Gulf of Suez, m195, m218, m219

H
Haam, Ahad, 206
Hadith, 96–97
Haganah, 212
Hagia Sophia, 113
Haifa Technical Institute, 229
Hajji, 70–71, p71
Hammurabi, 37, p37
Hanukkah, 48, 203
Hapsburgs, and the Ottoman Empire, 126
Harun al-Rashid, 93
Hashemite Kingdom of Jordan See Jordan
hat law, 148
Hatshepsut, Queen, 39, 42
Hatti Sherif of Gulhane, 134
Hebrews, 202–204; language of, 21, 46, 232. See also Israelites
Hebrew University, 229
Hegira, 64
Hejaz, 77, m266
Hellenism, 52–56, p53
Herat, m73; and Muslims, 72
Hermon ranges, 3
Herzegovina, 138, 144; annexed by Austria, 140
Herzl, Theodore, 205–206
hieroglyphics, 43
Histadrut, 208, 222, 228–229
history, study of in Abbasid Empire, 90
Hittites, Kingdom of, m36, 45, 50
Holocaust, 211
Horus, 39
House of Learning, 87
housing, 16, 19–20, p19, 34, p71; in Egypt, 178–179. See also architecture
Howe, Sir Geoffrey, p251
Hulagu, Khanate of, 101, p101, m103, 108
human rights, in Turkey, 161
Huns, 56
Hussein Ibn Ali, Sharif of Mecca, 241–242
Hussein Ibn Talal, King of Jordan, 256–257
Hussein, Saddam, 254
hydroelectric plants, 8
Hyksos, 42, 43

I
Ibn Khaldun, 90
Ibn Maymun, 88
Ibn Rushd, 88
Ibn Sina, 88
Imams, 78
income, per capita, c16
India, m4–5, m73; Islam in, 77

Indus River, m73, m103
industry, in Egypt, 8, 170–171, 191, 194; in Ottoman Empire, 127; in Israel, 227–229, 231
Infitah, 194
Inonu, Erdal, 156
Inonu, Ismet, 149, 151, 152
IPC See Iraq Petroleum Company
Iran, m266; geography of, 2, m4–5, 6; climate of, 6; agriculture of, 10; oil in, 11, m12, c13, 270; population, c17; and Kurdish nationalism, 22; Muslim sects in, 78, 271, 272; language of, 267; effects of colonialism, 267–269; Pahlavi dynasty, 269–271; in World War II, 269; and U.S. aid, 269, 271; White Revolution, 270; SAVAK, 270, 271; and Islamic revolution, 271; under Khomeini, 271, 273; and U.S. hostages, p273. See also Iran–Iraq War; Persia
Iranian Plateau, m4–5
Iran–Iraq War, 1, 254, 263, 273–274; and Turkey, 162
Iraq, m3; geography of, 2, m4–5, 6; agriculture of, 10; oil in, 11, m12, c13; population, c17; and Kurdish nationalism, 22; Muslim sects in, 78; conquered by Buyids, 98; and Arab–Israeli conflict, 213; independence of, 252; under Faisal I, 252, p253; revolt in, 252–254; since 1958, 253–254; as member of Arab League, 259. See also Iran–Iraq War
Iraq Petroleum Company (IPC), 11
iron, discovery of, 45
irrigation projects, 9
Isaac, 65
Isfahan, p94
Islam, influence of, 23, 26; spread of, 26–27, 66, 72, m73, 74–75; founding of, 61–67; and legend of Kaaba, 65; becomes militant faith, 66, 72–75; beliefs and duties of, 67–71; architecture of, 69; and tolerance of other religions, 74, 77; split in, 76, 78; golden age of, 83, 87–96; law of, 96–97; and Mongol conversions, 102; art and architecture of, 112, 113, p113, p124; fundamentalists, 195. See also Koran; Mohammed; Muslim Institution; Muslims
Islamic Revolution, (Iran), 271, p272
Ismail, 65, 172–174
Isma'ilis, 78, 98
Ismailiya, m195
Israel, m3, m12, m195, p216, m219; geography of, 2, m4–5, 201; climate of, 6; agriculture of, 10, 207, 225, p226, 227; oil in, 11; Kingdom of, 47–49; conquered by Assyria, 48;

46; Greek, 54; of Turkey, 148; of Iran, 267

law, Bedouin, 23; Code of Hammurabi, 37; Jewish, 48; Islamic, 79, 96–97; of Ottoman Empire, 122–123; of Turkey, 158; of Egypt, 170

Lausanne, Treaty of, m144

League of Arab States See Arab League

League of Mohammed, 140

League of Nations, and Balfour Declaration, 210; and Arab nationalism, 243

Lebanon, m3, m195, m218, m219; geography of, 2, m4–5; climate of, 6; agriculture of, 10; oil in, 11; settled by Semites, 45; and Arab–Israeli conflict, 213; Israeli invasion of, 217–218, 250; ethnic groups of, 244; as French mandate, 244–246; government of, 244–245; independence of, 245–246, 249; Christians in, 249; civil war in, 249–251; and the UAR, 249; as member of Arab League, 259

Lebanon ranges, 3

Levant, 244

Libya, m4–5, m195. See also Tripoli

Likud Party, (Israel), 221–224

literature, of Abbasid Empire, 92–93, 96; of Ottoman Empire, 113–114

livestock, 10–11

Lutfi Pasha, 119

Lydia, 45

M

Maccabee family, 48

Macedonian Empire, m53

Mahan, Alfred Thayer, 2

Mahmud II, 132–134

Maimonides, 88

Mamluk rule, 102, m103, 104

Mansur, 84

manuscripts, illuminated, 92, p95

Manzikert, 99, m115

Mapai, 208, 221, 222

mapmaking, during Abbasid Empire, p89, 90

Maronite Christians, 244, 249–250

Martel, Charles, 76

Masada, 49

mathematics, study of, 35, 90

Mauritania, 259

Mecca, 60, m73, m103, m115, m266; pilgrimages to, 64, 70–71, p71

Medes, 22, 50

medicine, during Abbasid Empire, 87–88; in Egypt, 170

Medina, m12, 64, 66, m73, m103, m115, m266

Mediterranean Sea, m3, m4–5, m12, m36, m53, m73, m103, m115, m156, m195, m218, m219

Megiddo, p47

Mehmed I, 111

Mehmed II, 111

Meir, Golda, 222–223, p222

Memphis, m36, 39

Menderes, Adnan, 151, 152, 153, p153

Menes, 39

Mesopotamia, rivers of, 8; early civilization in, 31, 33, 35–38; invasions of, 44–49

Mesopotamian–Persian Gulf, oil in, 11

Middle East, use of term, 2

Middle Kingdom, 39, 42

Midhat Pasha, 138

millet system, 116, 240

Mina, p71

minaret, 69, p79, 91, p94

minority groups, religion of, 26

Mohammed, 23, 26, 60; early life, 61; and the Koran, 61, 62; draws on Judaism and Christianity, 62, 64, 66; teachings of, 62; goes to Medina, 64, 66; death of, p63, 66–67, 72; house of, 91; various spellings of name, 111. See also Islam; Koran; Muslim Institution; Muslims

Mohammed Ali, 169–172

Mohammed Reza Pahlavi, 254, p270, p273; and U.S. aid, 269, 271; opposition to, 269–271; and Islamic revolution, 271

Moldavia, 125

money, 45, p51, p54

Mongols, m103; invasion of Baghdad, 100, 101–102, p101; conversions to Islam, 102

monotheism, 42, 49; and Islam, 26

Montenegro, 137

Moses, 47–48, 202

Moshav, 225, 227

mosques, p79, 91, p94

Mosul, m12

Motherland Party, (Turkey), 156

Mount Ararat, 3, m4–5

Muawiyah, 75, 79

Mubarak, Hosni, 188–189, p189, 196

Mufti of Istanbul, p120, 122–123

Muftis, 97

Muscat, m12, m103, m266; oil in, 11

Muslim Arabs, and growth of Arab nationalism, 240–243

Muslim Institution, 121–123. See also Islam; Koran; Mohammed; Muslims

Muslims, p69; defined, 21; religion and, 26–27; culture of, 26–27; art of, p63, p79; Shi'a sect, 76, 78, 98,

244, 249–250, 252, 271, 272; Sunni sect, 76, 78, 97, 248, 252; and the Crusades, 99–100, p100; Alawi sect, 244; Druse sect, 78, 244; Kurds, 21, 22, p25, 244, 242; in Iraq, 252; Wahhabi sect, 260. *See also* Islam; Koran; Mohammed; Muslim Institution

Mustafa Kamil, 176
Mustafa Kemal *See* Atatürk, Kemal

N

Nafud Desert, m4–5, 6
Namik Kemal, 138
Napoleon Bonaparte, 168, 204, 267–268; in Egypt, 43
Nasser, Gamal Abdel, 179, 180–185, p180, p182, 190, 194; influence of, in Syria, 246–247
National Democratic Party, (Egypt), 188
nationalist movements, Kurdish, 22; in Turkey, 131–134; Armenian, 141; Slavic, 143–144; and Cyprus, 162–163; Arab, 206, 210, 240–243, 246
Nationalist Party, (Egypt), 176
National Security Council, (Turkey), 154, 155–156
National Unity Committee (NUC), (Turkey), 153
National Unity Government (NUG), 223–224
NATO, Turkey as part of, 161
navigation, 90
Nazi, persecution of Jews, 211
Nebuchadnezzar II, 50–51
Negev Desert, 11, 228
Neguib, Mohammed, 180–181, p180, p182
Neutral Zone (Saudi Arabia), m266
New Kingdom, 42–43
New Turkey Party, 154
Nile Delta, 8, 9, m195
Nile River, m3, m4–5, p7, 8, m36, m73, m103, m115, 167, 172–173, m195, m218, m219
Nile Valley, 2
Ninevah, m36, 50
Noah's Ark, 3
nomads, 6, 23
North Africa, m53, m73, m115; in Ottoman Empire, 113
Nubians, 43
NUG *See* National Unity Government
Nuri Pasha es–Said, 253

O

October War, 185–186
Officers Society, 179
oil, g13, m266; importance of, to Middle East, 1, 11, 14–15; location of, 11, m12, c13, p14; foreign development of, 11, 14; in Iraq, 252; in Arabian Peninsula, 260; in Saudi Arabia, 261; in Yemen, 264; in Kuwait, 265; in Abu Dhabi, 267; in Iran, 269, 270

Old Kingdom, 39
Oman, m3, m12, m195, 266, m266, 267; geography of, 2, m4–5; oil in, 11; per capita income, c16; population, c17
optics, study of, 88, 90
oral traditions, 92
Oriental Jews *See* Judaism, Sephardim
Orkham, 109–110
Orontes River, 8
Orthodox Christians, 74
Osman, and founding of Ottoman Empire, 108, 109, p109
Ottoman Empire, 2, m115; founding of, 108; expansion of, 108, 109–114; Constantinople as capital, 111; military achievements, 111, 113, 119–120; culture of, 112, 113–114; religion of, 114, 116, 122; government of, 114–120, 124–125; women in, 118; education in, 118, 121–122; Muslim Institution, 121–123; legal system, 122–123; decline of, 123–127, 143–146; trade and industry of, 127; and Arab nationalism, 240–242. *See also* Greece; Turkey
Ottomanism, 139
Ottoman Ruling Institution, 118–120
Ozal, Turgut, 156, 157

P

Pakistan, m4–5
Pale of Settlement, 204
Palestine, m36, m53; Thutmose II invades, 42; settled by Semites, 45; Egyptian defeat in, 179–180; partitions of, 201, 211, 212–213, 214; Jewish attachment to, 202; and Zionism, 204, 205–211 Palestine Liberation Organization (PLO), 217–218, 257, 259, p262
Palestine National Council, 220
Palestine Workers' Party *See* Mapai
Palestinian Arabs, independence of, 219–220
Palestinian refugees, in Israel, 213–214; uprising of, 218; in Jordan, 256, 257, p258. *See also* Arab refugees
Palmyra, m53, 55
Pan–Turanists, 139–140
papyrus, 17
Paris Peace Conference (1920), 243
Paris, Peace of (1856), 137